Demographic Vistas ★

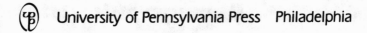

University of Pennsylvania Press   Philadelphia

David Marc

Demographic Vistas ★
Television in American Culture

Design by Tracy Baldwin

Library of Congress Cataloging in Publication Data

Marc, David.
  Demographic vistas.
  Bibliography: p.
  Includes index.
  1. Television broadcasting—United States.
2. Comedy programs—United States—History and
criticism. 3. United States—Popular culture.
I. Title.
PN1992.3.U5M26   1984   302.2'345'0973   83-12329
ISBN 0-8122-7907-7
ISBN 0-8122-1164-2 (pbk.)

Printed in the United States of America

To Mnemosyne, more beautiful than Beta Max

Contents

Contents

Please let me tell you about boredom, let me go on about the exquisite varieties of boredom I have known and attempt to describe the range of my indifference, I promise to make it absorbing—indeed the very prospect of doing so opens before me such an ocean of boredom, such a dismal, flat immensity in which to pull you in after me that I'd better not try it because it probably won't work. The failure of boredom is that it is never gripping.

Ken Jacobs, "The Day the Moon Gave Up the Ghost"

Special thanks to Sherman Paul for his tireless imaginative precision.

I am grateful to Jim Berkowitz, Daniel J. Czitrom, Ken Fox, J. Hoberman, Sam Klingensmith, Jeffrey Miller, Robert Pepper, Steve Perry, Cathy Scherer, Steve Smith, Albert Stone, Marion Weinstein, and Kathleen Welch for their help in the preparation of this book.

Preface ★

"A most confusing thing in American History," observed William Carlos Williams, "is the nearly universal lack of scale."[1] Television is very much at home in this history. Inviting nothing but superlatives ("dullest," "greatest opportunity," "most asinine," "quickest," etc.), it has generated more cash and less prestige than any other activity that could be even loosely described as having a collateral relationship with art. But the extreme reactions and predictions that are easily heard in casual and critical discussions of the medium stand in stark contrast to the processional flow of recognitions, appreciations, and evaluations that continue to characterize normal viewing. This is a book about living with television in the culture that turns it on, creates it, rewards it, despises it, forgets it, and remembers it. There is no posture that honestly separates the author from that culture.

In *Reading Television,* the British critics John Fiske and John Hartley write:

> the tools of traditional literary criticism do not quite fit the television discourse. At best they can be used in the way a metaphor works—the unknown tenor of television might be apprehended by means of the known vehicle of literary criticism.[2]

By "traditional literary criticism," I take it, the authors refer to what some now consider the rather old-fashioned practice of personally encountering texts, researching their historical contexts, and offering idiosyncratic, autobiographical readings of them. This book owes much to that method. Decisive authority is awarded to neither impression nor empirical research but rather to their endless synthesis. Metaphor is indeed used here in attempts to apprehend "the unknown tenor of television." "If reality is description," the anthropologist Stan Wilk has astutely argued, "metaphor is technology."[3] I have striven to put that technology at the reader's service. James Carey, Raymond Williams, and other leading communications and culture critics have pointed out the limitations of communications theories that ignore the aesthetic analysis of artifacts.[4] I would go further and say that if any theory of communication is to be meaningful it must admit that it proceeds from the aesthetic vision of its creator and that it aims to understand the aesthetic vision of the artifact's creator.

While I have no doubt that those with uses for communications theories will continue to seek them, I have stopped short of proposing any in this study. Like the practitioners of "traditional literary criticism," I have tried to give my first loyalty to the texts I examine and not to any theory of what makes them tick. Despite formulaic or generic similarities among these texts, under close scrutiny each reveals individual quirks—continual reminders that all television images are created by people. This is not to say that one should stray too far from the historic, economic, political, and social influences to which television images are subject; but a writer about anything ought to do no less. I have tried to respect television. In some cases I found work that earned my admiration. In other cases I found rich repositories of ideas, styles, and historical moments—artifacts worth keeping. Elsewhere I came across the insidious. I even encountered work of such utter aesthetic aridity as to stagger the imagination. Texts that held none of these qualities were generally avoided because they were so boring.

It is not unusual to find books on television written by sociologists, psychologists, cliometricians, psycholinguists, physicists, and the specialists of many other widely diverse disciplines. Therefore, the reader should be alerted to some of the methods not employed and controversies not addressed in this book:

I have not created or made extensive use of quantitative surveys that purport to describe the reactions of millions of TV viewers by the examination of "representative" hundreds. Even if I were convinced that this widely used method did not hold threats to the dignity of the individual, I could still find reason to question its verity. I am the case study. Who is representing you?

I have not found—or sought—an axiomatic method with which to describe television programs or the watching of them. While I confess an attraction to the neatnesses of functionally descriptive transformational grammars, I feel that the critical dialogue lacking in American culture, at least insofar as television is concerned, is the vigorous exchange of idiosyncratic viewings of programs and other televised phenomena. Gilbert Seldes initiated such a dialogue as a lonely voice in the 1950s, recognizing its crucial function in a democratic culture. In recent years, it has begun to grow with the work of Horace Newcomb, Michael Arlen, James Wolcott, Marc Eliot, Jeff Greenfield, and a handful of others. None of these writers, it is worth noting, is committed to any codified theory of video perception. Performance, visual composition, writing, makeup, and the other arts and crafts that go into the production of television time are likely to perpetually confound efforts to rationalize them into replicable formulas. This is true even where it is the intention of the artist or artisan to find such a formula.

This book seeks neither to justify television's existence nor to eradicate it from the face of culture. That issue is a popular red herring of technicolor hue. Television has its viewers, and, given painful twentieth-century history, the fantasy of playing culture czar is more embarrassing than appealing. At the same time, I have purposely declined the mask of "value-free" investigator; we are already suffering from far too much freedom from values.

Instead, I have searched for germinating centers in my own television experience and consciousness. I have done this on the assumption that a reader might find points of identity with which to share and evaluate these recuperations. A Whitmanian

faith in the ability of the individual consciousness to mingle
with a collective cultural consciousness is therefore crucial to
this study.[5]

In terms of bibliography, the landmark reference works
that have been published in recent years, including those by
Tim Brooks and Earle Marsh, Alex McNeil, Vincent Terrace, and
others, have been of invaluable help. Their extensive catalogs
of programs, casts, schedules, ratings, and authors have provided a record of bibliographic detail that is indispensable for
xiv critical writing about American commercial television shows.
Though these archival volumes cannot easily be read from first
page to last, they invite a kind of thumbing-through that in some
ways imitates flipping around the dial.

Videotape recording devices played a less important role
in the preparation of the book. Though I was allowed access to
such equipment through the generous auspices of the University of Iowa American Studies Program, I preferred to follow
series as they were telecast on the air. By allowing the viewer
the opportunity to pull programs off the daily schedules automatically, freeze them in time, and view them repeatedly at will,
these recording devices successfully challenge network/station
programming control, thus altering the character of viewing.
Because my greater concern in this study is television's life in
American culture and not the shows out of context, I generally
followed the schedules of the stations that were available to me
wherever I happened to be living at a given time. These locations included both cable and noncable markets and were usually determined by circumstances not directly related to the
study. When available, cable did prove useful; the intense commitment to syndicated reruns of independent superstations such
as WTBS (Atlanta), WGN (Chicago), WOR (New York), and the
Christian Broadcasting Network (Virginia Beach, Virginia) provided the bulk of primary material that needed to be reviewed.

Discussions of comedians, comic forms, and comedy dominate the study. I am convinced that American television has
defined itself as a comic medium. Most of what it does best is
funny; almost every citizen may patronize it. It was my intention
in chapter 1 to set the tenor of the study and to move in this
direction. Attempting to leave behind the quagmire of debates

over whether television is the end of Western civilization and/ or a scientific theory of mass behavior, I hastened to the stage, an ancient medium. Blessed with an unimpeachable pedigree (its critics include Aristotle; its artists, Shakespeare), theater has exerted tremendous formal influence over both cinema and television. In the case of the movies, they were (at least until quite recently) shown primarily in theater buildings and even shared the stage with live acts during their early years. Television, the home miniature, not only must narrate each feature it offers but also is obliged to create continuities between these offerings. It was therefore my aim to define modes of theatricality on television so as to provide critical language with which to talk about it. The taxonomy I found includes three main types: the presentational (theatrical illusion managed by an interlocutory figure); the representational (imitation of the proscenium effect); and the documentary (reality offered as such). Chapter 1 concludes that these three modes of illusion are not monolithic obstacles to the imagination of either the television-maker or the viewer; rather, they are so easily seen through as to provide a bottomless pit of satirical transformations.

xv

Chapters 2–4 take license from these assumptions. They are studies of a comic *auteur* (Paul Henning), a comic genre (the crimeshow), and a comic personality (Jackie Gleason). In each case I encountered the subject floating free in space and attempted to retrieve as many of its relationships to history/ television/culture as possible. The Henning and Gleason chapters are largely attempts at biography. One rural and western, the other urban and eastern, each used the medium in a peculiar way to present a personal vision of—and to—America. Each also brought a tradition with him that gives the lie to the assumption that American television just somehow popped out of mass society's thin air. A self-consciously good old boy from Independence, Missouri, Henning traveled a well-worn path into show business and popular culture. A bona fide waif of New York proletarian tenements, Gleason American-Dreamed his way to millionairedom on the strength of endless jokes at the expense of what he might have been had he failed. In each case it is significant that the complex machinery of the production and distribution system could be put so thoroughly in the service of personal expression. The successful use of these expressions to sell cornflakes and automobiles enriches their mystique by tying them to specific historical periods. As any Madison Avenue executive is likely to tell you, neither Henning nor Gleason would be a safe bet for the prime-time advertising dollar in 1984, though both were able to air their work during the most expensive advertising hours of the fifties and sixties.

Both comic visions find happiness in America more than a touch bittersweet. The Clampetts, whose sense of blood community has been sacrificed for money and Lifestyle, sit around **xvi** their Beverly Hills estate with little sense of purpose, the objects of their neighbors' derision. The Kramdens, the last white family in the eternal 1930s of Williamsburg, Brooklyn, wait, without either telephone or television, for Ralph's ship to come in at last. In between these sketches of the behind-the-scenes auteur and the public star personality, I have placed chapter 3, a history of the crimeshow. My aim here is to describe this genre's dominant narrative model and the styles and trends that have given it character. Unlike the sitcom and the comedy-variety show, the TV crimeshow does not announce itself as comic but earns that description in its effect. I attempt to demonstrate this through reconsiderations of several concepts, auteurs, and stars that shaped it and of the relationship between historical circumstances and narrative transformations. McCarthyism (1950s), the Generation Gap (1960s), and Lifestylism (post-1960s) are the three historical watersheds that receive attention in this respect. Happy endings are provided for all.

"Who can recreate the experience of going to the pictures in the radiant dawn of popular mass culture?" asks Robert Sklar in *Movie-made America.*[6] In the fifth and final chapter, I ask a similar question about television, a phenomenon that might better be placed at the high noon of "popular mass culture." To answer it, I leave prime time for the ragged edges of what the industry calls "marginal hours" in search of an avant-garde that might portend an opening of the field for television comedy— and, one might hope, for American television in general. This leads me to the late-night weekend satire shows that have made television—its programs, stars, auteurs, and even its scheduling practices—the self-reflexive target of their material. The *Saturday Night Live* of the late seventies and *SCTV Comedy Network* make use of the canon and history that American television has created since World War II. Like Fielding's jabs at the novel, Swift's absurd travel literature, and Pope's attacks on contemporary British society in the eighteenth century, *SCTV* and the original *SNL* confront the tragedy of mass culture by finding sense in its humor. Television has become adult enough to have a childhood that is capable of embarrassing it. This loss of innocence is likely to push it toward more self-conscious efforts at self-improvement. I set the limits of the book's intentions at this point, refusing to speculate on what character these efforts might assume or how likely they are to be successful. Whatever develops will in any event be hooked up to the cable, effectively preserving the first forty or so years of three-network hegemony as an important etiological period.

xvii

Having concentrated on prime-time and late-night comedy, I have obviously left much out; this study in no way pretends to account for all, most, or even much of what appears on American television. The made-for-TV movie, and its extended cousin, the miniseries, both of which take up so much prime-time network air and investment, are not discussed. The prime-time soap opera, the most important new serial genre to emerge in the last decade, is completely ignored, as are daytime soap operas and gameshows, public broadcasting, and independent video. The vast quantity of texts produced for television (what Martin Esslin calls "the drama explosion") makes any attempt to review American television comprehensively in a single volume futile. Even within the relatively circumscript bounds I have set for this study, many readers are apt to find important omissions. "Where is *M*A*S*H*?" and "How about Rodney Dangerfield as performance artist?" are among the many reasonable questions that could be asked. I remember that the first reaction of the folklorist Harry Oster to the manuscript of this book was, "But what about *Gilligan's Island*?" As I have already admitted, my method in writing this book was something less than mechanically systematic. To borrow a phrase from Allen Ginsberg, I have walked which way my beard has pointed. No slights were intended. Apologies are offered to neglected fans, performers, technicians, and producers.

Then too there is the problem of time. The relentless pace of life and death among television shows and styles threatens any book on the subject with the specter of anachronism. This book was written for the most part before May 1982. Minor revisions continued to be made until May 1983. This may help solve such puzzles as why there is no discussion of *St. Elsewhere* in chapter 3 and why *Late Night with David Letterman* is missing from chapter 5.

The notion of culture, a concept that continually spawns and confounds interdisciplinary studies, has not been dealt with extensively in any theoretical way. I have taken it for granted that television and television programs have become a part of the "complex whole" described by Edward Burnett Tylor in his famous definition of the term.[7] As a teacher, I have walked into classrooms, mentioned obscure television programs that aired for only a season or two a dozen years ago, and found that not only are most of the class members (gathered from all over the United States) familiar with these shows but many are quick to express opinions about them. If this is not an example of "shared culture," I cannot imagine what is.

Like most Americans, I was already an avid TV watcher of some years when I learned to read. The banality of the Dick-and-Jane texts used by the New York City Board of Education to accomplish that task was not lost on a child who had already seen World War II narrated by Walter Cronkite on Prudential's *Twentieth Century.* Having spent many Saturday mornings in a Brooklyn apartment envying Joey Newton because he had both a TV show and a horse named *Fury,* I was an early believer in the day-to-day strength of the box's fantasy power. My first notions of irony came from the disembodied narrator of *Rocky and Bullwinkle.* This discussion of television, like any by a viewer, is autobiographical.

Providence, Rhode Island
April 1983.

Beginning to Begin Again ★ 1

Never was there, perhaps, more hollowness at heart than at present, and here in the United States. Genuine belief seems to have left us. The underlying principles of the States are not honestly believed in (for all this hectic glow and these melodramatic screamings), nor is humanity itself believed in. What penetrating eye does not everywhere see through this mask?

Walt Whitman, *Democratic Vistas* (1871)

An unholy marriage of sociology and art—the shotgun is pointed at art—American television is a perplexing montage. The programs are conceived as stimuli for the masses, but it is left to the viewer to establish a text in a personal, even private, way. Whatever is exposed to television is under attack. Ideals are confounded by the depressing spectacle of astonishing technical acumen aimed at gross simplification. Belief is disappointed; the soul is not visible on the screen. Traditional political ideologies have been unable to respond coherently. The Left finds conspiracy snarling behind the pervasive promotion of consumer outlook even as it envies the industrial medium's ability to organize millions at the flick of a switch. On the Right, there is no less conflict. Television has become an integral factor in the processes of modern capitalism. Entrepreneurial success is largely based on effective use of it. As a consequence, however, what José Ortega y Gasset called "the bigotry of Culture" has itself become the victim of discrimination; the prerog-· atives of cultivated taste have become buried in an avalanche of processed styles. The achiever is awed by the material accomplishment of the national communications system but hates to waste time on the nonsense it delivers. The dreamer welcomes the continuous, coast-to-coast, willing suspension of disbelief but is let down by the obsessive neatness of the narrative. The lover knows that all truths wait in all things.

In one of the few famous speeches given on the subject of television, Federal Communications Commission chairman Newton N. Minow shocked the 1961 Convention of the National Association of Broadcasters by summarily categorizing its membership's handiwork as "a vast wasteland."[1] The general acceptance of Minow's metaphor is outstripped only by the appeal of television itself. Americans look askance at television, but look at it nonetheless. Owners of thousand-dollar sets think nothing of calling them "idiot boxes." The home stereo system, regardless of what plays on it, is, by comparison, holy. While millions of dollars change hands daily on the assumption that 98 percent of American homes are equipped with sets and that these sets play an average of over six and a half hours each day,[2] a well-pronounced distaste for TV has become a prerequisite to claims of intellectual and even ethical legitimacy. Social scientists, perhaps less concerned with these matters than others, have rushed to fill the critical gap. Denying the mysteries of teller, tale, and told, they have reduced the significance of this American storytelling medium to the study of the effect of stimuli on masses, producing volumes of data that in turn justify each season's network schedules. A disillusioned advertising executive, his fortune safely socked away, has even written a book entitled *Four Arguments for the Elimination of Television*. Hans Magnus Enzensberger preempted such criticism as early as 1962 when he wrote:

> The process is irreversible. Therefore, all criticism of the mind industry which is abolitionist in its essence is inept and beside the point, since the idea of arresting and liquidating industrialization (which such criticism implies) is suicidal. There is a macabre irony to any such proposal, for it is indeed no longer a technical problem for our civilization to destroy itself.[3]

Though Jerry Mander, the abolitionist critic, dutifully lists Enzensberger's *Consciousness Industry* in his bibliography, his
zealous piety—the piety of the convert—could not be re-
strained. Masses of television viewers (Who else would read
such a book?) scooped up the copies at $7.95 each (paperback).
As Enzensberger points out, everyone works for the consciousness industry.

Despite the efforts of Erik Barnouw, Horace Newcomb, and
a few others, the chilling fact is that the most effective purveyor
of language, image, and narrative in American culture has failed   **3**
to become a subject of lively humanistic discourse. It is laughed
at, reviled, feared, and generally treated as persona non grata
by university humanities departments and the "serious" jour-
nals they patronize. Whether this is the cause or merely a symp-
tom of the precipitous decline of the influence of the humanities during recent years is difficult to say. In either case it is
unfortunate that the scholars and teachers of *The Waste Land*
have found "the vast wasteland" unworthy of their attention.
Edward Shils spoke for many literary critics when he chastised
"those who know better" but still give their attention to works
of "mass culture" for indulging in "a continuation of childish
pleasures."[4] Forgoing a defense of childish pleasures, I still
cannot imagine a more destructive attitude in terms of the
future of both humanistic inquiry and television. If the imagination is to play an epistemological role in a scientific age, it
cannot be restricted to "safe" media. Shils teased pop culture
critics for trying to be "folksy"; unfortunately, it is literature that
is in danger of becoming a precious antique.

As the transcontinental industrial plant built since the Civil
War was furiously at work meeting the new production quotas
allowed by modern advertising techniques, President Calvin
Coolidge observed that "the business of America is business."
Since that time, television has become the art of business. The
intensive specialization of skills called for by collaborative production technologies has forced most Americans to the market-
place for an exceptional range of goods and services. "Do-it-
yourself" is itself something to buy. Necessities and trifles blur
to indistinction. Everything is for sale to everybody. As James M.
Cain wrote, the "whole goddamn country lives selling hot dogs
to each other."[5] Choice, however, is greatly restricted. The per-
mutation-bound structure of mass marketing theory has formal-

ized taste into a multiple-choice question. Like the menu at McDonald's and the suits on the racks, the choices on the dial—and, thus far, the cable converter—are limited and guided. Yet even if the material in each TV show single-mindedly aims at the quality of quantity, too much happens along the way to cavalierly dispose of this body of dreams as a mere series of surface realizations of some master socioeconomic deep structure. If, as Enzensberger claims, we are stuck with television and nothing short of nuclear Armageddon will deliver us, then what choice is there but consciousness? Scripts are written. Sets, costumes, and camera angles are imagined and designed. Performances are rendered. No drama, not even melodrama, can be born of a void. Myths are recuperated, legends conjured. These acts are not yet carried out by computers, as much as network executives might prefer such a system.

When Marcel Duchamp signed a urinal "R. Mutt" and sent it to the Society of Independent Artists in 1917 for exhibition, he invited viewers to take advantage of the presentational structure of a show in order to look at what they live with. Television continually thanks us for inviting it into our homes and returns the invitation emphatically. A TV show or a commercial or any random moment of the broadcast day entreats the viewer to love it and live with it, and as even the programming executives must admit, the success or failure of the seduction, no matter how carefully and rationally ("scientifically") planned, is not predictable. Every television program that has been canceled for failing to capture an audience is the successful survivor of a battery of audience tests. But beyond the reams of Audience Research Reports stockpiled during these decades of agency billings, there is the living work of scores of TVmakers who accepted the marketable formats, found ways to satisfy both censors and the popular id, hawked the Alka-Seltzer beyond the limits of indigestion, and still managed to leave behind images that demand reimagining. The life of this work in American culture is a matter of taste, not test. It is ludicrous to crucify *Sgt. Bilko* for the sins of General Sarnoff. A fantastic, wavy, glowing procession of images hovers over the American antennascape, filling the air and millions of screens and minds with endless reruns. To accept a long-term relationship with a television program is to allow a vision to enter one's life. That vision is peopled with characters who speak a familiar idiosyncratic language, dress to purpose, worship God, fall in love, show élan and naiveté, become neurotic and psychotic, revenge themselves, and take it easy. While individual episodes—their plots and climaxes—are rarely memorable, though often remembered, cosmologies cannot fail to be rich for those viewers who have shared so many hours in their construction. The salient impact of television comes not from "special events," such as the coverage of the Kennedy assassinations or men on the moon playing golf, but from day-to-day exposure. The power of television resides in its normalcy; it is always there at the push of a button. Despite the frenzy of promotion that accompanies each new season, the debut of a series is not much of an event. It rarely creates the will to view. The comedies uniformly promise nonstop laughter. The copshows dutifully guarantee fast-paced action. The melodramas will of course be warm, human stories of contemporary life. There is little significance in any of this. Why watch? Are the sex objects compelling? Does the camera take me somewhere I like to be? Is the time slot convenient? Should I make a "special effort" to watch? It may take years to come to a show. If a show is a hit, if the Nielsen families go for it, it is likely to become a Monday-through-Friday "strip." The weekly series in stripped syndication is television's most potent oracle. Sitcoms, with their half-hour formats, may air two or even three episodes a day on local stations. Months become weeks, and years become months. Mary accelerates through hairdos and hem lengths; Phyllis and Rhoda disappear as Mary moves to her high-rise swinging-singles apartment. Simple identification and suspense yield to the subtler nuances of cohabitation. The threshold of expectation becomes fixed as daily viewing becomes an established procedure or ritual. The ultimate suspension of disbelief occurs when the drama—the realm of heightened artifice—becomes normal. The aim of television is to be normal. The industry is obsessed with the problem of norms, and this manifests itself in both process and product. Whole new logics, usually accepted under the general classification of "demographics," have been imagined to create transformational models that explain the perimeters of objectionability and attraction. A network sales executive would not dare ask hundreds of thousands of dollars for a prime-time ad on

5

f his high opinion of the show that surrounds it. The sponsor is paying for "heads." What guarantees, he demands, can be given for delivery? Personal assurances—opinions—are not enough. The network must show scientific evidence in the form of results of demographic experiments. Each pilot episode is prescreened for test audiences who then fill out multiple-choice questionnaires to describe their reactions. Data are processed by age, income, race, religion, or whatever cultural determinants the tester deems relevant. Thus the dull annual autumn dialogue of popular television criticism:

6

Why the same old junk every year? ask the smug, ironic television critics after running down their witty lists of the season's "winners and losers."

We know nothing of junk, cry the "value-free" social scientists of the industry research factories. The people have voted with their number 2 pencils and tuners. We are merely the Board of Elections in a modern cultural democracy.[6]

But no one ever asked me what I thought, puzzles the viewer in a random burst from stupefaction.

Not to worry, the chart-and-graph *virtuosi* reassure. We have taken a biopsy from the body politic, and as you would know if this was your job, if you've seen one cell—or 1,200—you've seen them all.

But is demography democracy?

Walter Benjamin warned that ignoring such unquantifiable properties as creativity, genius, eternal value, and mystery as criteria for the creation and distribution of technologically reproduced art "would lead to a processing of data in the Fascist sense."[7] Though authoritarian use of the plebiscite can be well demonstrated from Napoleonic France to Khomeini's Iran, this need not be the case with American television. TV is capable of inspiring at least as much cynicism as docility. The viewer who can transform that cynicism into critical energy can declare the war with television over and instead savor the oracular quality of the medium. As Roland Barthes, Jean-Luc Godard, and the French devotees of Jerry Lewis have realized for years, television is American dada,[8] Charles Dickens on LSD, the greatest parody of European culture since *The Dunciad*.[9] Yahoos and Houyhnhnms battle it out nightly with submachine guns. Sex objects are stored in a box. Art or not art? This is largely a lexicographical quibble for the culturally insecure. Interesting?

Only the hopelessly genteel could find such a phantasmagoria flat. Yesterday's trashy Hollywood movies have become recognized as the unheralded work of auteurs; they are screened at the ritziest "art houses" for connoisseurs of *le cinéma*. Shall we need the French once again to tell us what we have?

Television Is Funny

Comedy is the axis on which broadcasting revolves.
>> Gilbert Seldes, *The Public Arts*

Though network executives reserve public pride for the achievements of their news divisions and their dramatic specials, the fact remains that comedy—entertainment of a primarily humorous nature—has always been an essential, even dominant, ingredient of American commercial television programming. The little box, with its squared oblong screen, egregiously set in a piece of overpriced wood-grained furniture or cheap industrial plastic, has provoked a share of titters in its own right from a viewing public that casually calls it "boob tube." Television is America's jester. It has assumed the guise of an idiot while actually accruing the advantages of power and authority behind the smoke screen of its self-degradation. The Fool, of course, gets a kind word from no one: "Knee-jerk liberalism," cry the offended conservatives. "Corporate mass manipulation," scream the resentful liberals. Neo-Comstockians are aghast, righteously indignant at the orgiastic decay of morality invading their split-level homes. The avant-garde strikes a pose of smug terror before the empty, sterile images. Like the abused jester in Edgar Allan Poe's "Hop-Frog," however, the moguls of Television Row make monkeys out of their tormentors. Their deposit slips are drenched in crocodile tears; the show must go on.

In 1927, TV inventor Philo T. Farnsworth presented a dollar sign for sixty seconds in the first public demonstration of his television system.[10] The baggy-pants vaudevillians Farnsworth televised in 1935 have been joined by a host of modern cousins, including the sitcom character actor, the stand-up comedian, the sketch comic, and the gameshow host. No television genre is without what Robert Warshow called "the official euphoria which spreads over the culture like the broad smile of an idiot."[11] Police shows, family dramas, adventure series, and made-for-TV movies all rely heavily on humor to mitigate their bathos. Even The News is not immune to doggerel, as evidenced by the spread of "happy-talk" formats in TV journalism in recent years. While the industry experiments with new ways to package humor, television's most hilarious moments are often unintentional, or at least incidental. Reruns of ancient dramatic series display plot devices, dialogue, and camera techniques that are obviously dated. Styles materialize and vanish with astonishing speed. Series such as *Dragnet, The Mod Squad,* and *Ironside* surrender their credibility as "serious" police mysteries after only a few years in syndication. They self-destruct into ridiculous stereotypes and clichés, betraying their slick production values and achieving heights of comic ecstasy that dwarf their "serious" intentions. This is an intense comedy of obsolescence that grows richer with each passing television season. Starsky and Hutch render Jack Webb's Sgt. Joe Friday a messianic madman. The *Hill Street Blues* return the favor to *Starsky and Hutch.* The distinction between taking television on one's own terms and taking it the way it presents itself is of critical importance. It is the difference between passivity and activity. It is what saves TV from becoming the homogenizing, monolithic, authoritarian tool that the doomsday critics claim it is. The self-proclaimed champions of "high art" who dismiss TV shows as barren imitations of the real article simply do not know how to watch. They are like freshmen thrust into survey courses and forced to read Fielding and Sterne; they lack both the background and the tough-skinned skepticism that can make TV meaningful experience. In 1953 Dwight Macdonald was apparently not embarrassed to condemn all "mass culture" (including the new chief villain, TV) without offering any evidence that he had watched television. Not a single show is mentioned in his famous essay, "A Theory of Mass Culture."[12] Twenty-five years later it is possible to find English professors who will admit to watching *Masterpiece Theatre.* But American commercial shows? How could they possibly measure up to drama produced in Britain and tied in form and sensibility to the nineteenth-century novel? There is an important reply to this widespread English Department line: TV is culture. The more one watches, the more relationships develop among the shows and between the shows and the world. To rip the shows out of their context and compare them with the works of other media and cultural traditions is to deny their history—their American history— and misplace their identities.

The influence of other American media in the genesis of TV programming is obvious. Radio and movies immediately come to mind. In the early days of network telecast, however, viewers were treated to generous doses of "exhibition sports," such as professional wrestling and roller derby, phenomena that were new to electronic media. The outrageous antics of the performers on these shows were more in the realm of burlesque or the dance than sport. Wrestler Gorgeous George (the late George F. Wagner) was an early superstar of the genre who was capable of sending pre-space-age viewers rolling off their couches. Borrowing a page from Max Fleischer's cartoon hero Popeye, he would struggle to his corner at the point of defeat, take a few hits from an oxygen tank marked "Florida Air," and, born again, return to the center of the squared circle to defeat his perennially wide-eyed opponent. The carnival-freak-show ambience of the program was enhanced by special matches featuring midgets and women. Wrestling was TV's first original comedy, a grotesque comedy of violence. Not only did the performers have to be excellent acrobats possessing numerous circus skills in order to execute their complex ballets of flying dropkicks, atomic skullcrushers, and airplane spins, but they were also called upon to prove their mettle as character actors and stand-up comedians during the "interview" segments of the show, which can take up as much as half of a wrestling telecast. Playing various archetypal American figures, including ethnic stereotypes that date back to minstrelsy and the vaudeville stage, such characters as Killer Kowalski, Baron Fritz von Erich, and "Country Boy" Haystacks Calhoun would rant and rave, threaten their opponents' lives, and make promises to their fans, never for a moment stepping out of character. Roland Barthes has compared the technique of wrestling with that of the *commedia dell'arte*.[13]

The early tone that wrestling set in television comedy is in direct opposition, however, to the comic framework that even-

9

tually won commercial favor. As television strove to legitimize itself as a medium worthy of the attention of a middle-class sensibility (circa 1950s, U.S.A.), programming came packaged in more identifiably respectable wrappings. The "play area" or stage of the wrestling show was vague and undefined; the viewer could not automatically distinguish between stage and world. Was that wrestler leaving the arena on a stretcher truly unconscious? Was the blood on his face real? Were those women actually tearing chunks of hair out of each other's heads? The ring announcer said yes. Many viewers had their doubts. Could television lie? Was this any way to sell a Chevrolet? Previous to 1955, all four networks (including the now defunct DuMont Network) had offered coast-to-coast wrestling telecasts during the heart of prime time.[14] Though wrestling continues to be locally produced in many U.S. markets and has even reappeared nationally on superstations, it has disappeared from the network programming taxonomy. The only wrestling matches carried by the networks today are occasional telecasts of amateur wrestling on such shows as *The Wide World of Sports* and *Sportsworld*. Barthes likens the experience of watching this "respectable" sport to attending a suburban cinema; it is devoid of the spectacular distension of the professional variety.[15] The present-day descendants of professional wrestling on television are such shows as *Real People* and *That's Incredible!* These schlockumentary magazines (*TV Guide* calls them "sit-life shows")[16] perhaps fill the void left by the cancelation of the wrestling spectacle. Just as wrestling played on its superficial resemblance to the relatively respectable sport of boxing in order to establish a framework of legitimacy for outrageous spectacle, the schlockumentaries borrow their form from the respectable TV newsmagazine (notably *60 Minutes*).[17] These shows stage phony sporting events (e.g., man in tug-of-war with the Goodyear Blimp; daredevil attached to giant rubber band leaping off bridge), and freaks are gratuitously displayed (two-headed man; child savant, etc.); all is presented by a straight-faced ersatz newsman, the successor to wrestling's ersatz sports announcer.

10

Enter the Proscenium

The forms that came to dominate television comedy (and therefore television) were video approximations of theater: the situation comedy (representational) and the variety show (presentational). The illusion of theater is a structural feature of both.
It is created primarily by the implicit attendance of an audience
that laughs and applauds at appropriate moments and thus as-
sures the viewer that the telecast is originating within the safely
specified walls of the proscenium stage. Normal responses are
thus defined. The "audience" may be actual or an electronic
sound effect, but this is a small matter. The consequence is the
same; the jokes are underlined. The ambiguities of wrestling
are thus avoided.

    The situation comedy has proved to be the most durable of
all commercial television genres. Other types of programming
that have appeared to be staples of prime-time fare at various
junctures in TV history have seen their heyday and faded (the
western, the comedy-variety show, and the big-money quizshow
among them). The sitcom, however, has remained a consistent
and ubiquitous feature of prime-time network schedules since
the premiere of *Mary Kay and Johnny* on DuMont in 1947. The
TV sitcom obviously derives from its radio predecessor. Radio
hits such as *I Remember Mama, The Burns and Allen Show, The
Goldbergs,* and *Amos 'n Andy* made the transition to television
overnight. Then, as now, familiarity was a prized commodity in
the industry. In terms of preelectronic art forms, the sitcom
bears a certain physical resemblance to the British comedy of
manners, especially in terms of its parlor setting. A more direct
ancestor, as Jack Gladden has shown, may be the serialized
family comedy adventures that were popular in nineteenth-
century American newspapers.[18] Perhaps because of the nature
of its serial continuity, the sitcom had no substantial presence
in the movies.[19] Though *Andy Hardy* and *Ma and Pa Kettle* films
deal with sitcomic themes, their feature length, lack of audience
response tracks, and relatively panoramic settings make them
very different viewing experiences. Serial narratives in the movies were usually action-oriented. *Flash Gordon,* for example,
was constructed so that each episode built to a breathless, unfulfilled climax designed to bring the patrons back to the thea-

11

ter for next Saturday's resolution. The action of the sitcom is far too psychological for this. Urgent continuity rarely exists between episodes. Instead, climaxes occur within episodes (though these are not satisfying in any traditional sense). In the movie serial (or a modern television soap opera) the rescue of characters from torture, death, or even seemingly hopeless anxiety is used to call attention to serialization. The sitcom differs in that its central tensions—embarrassment and guilt—are almost always alleviated before the end of an episode. Each episode may appear to resemble a short, self-contained play; its rigid confinement to an electronic approximation of a proscenium-arch theater, complete with laughter and applause, emphasizes this link. Unlike a stage play, however, no single episode of a sitcom is likely to be of much interest; it may not even be intelligible. The attraction of an episode is the strength of its contribution to the broader cosmology of the series. The claustrophobia of the miniature proscenium, especially for an audience that has grown casual toward Cinemascope, can be relieved only by the exquisiteness of its minutiae. Trivia is the most salient form of sitcom appreciation, perhaps the richest form of appreciation of any television series. Though television is at the center of American culture—it is the stage upon which our national drama/history is enacted—its texts are generally unavailable upon demand. The audience must share reminiscences to conjure the ever-fleeting text. Giving this the format of a game, players try not so much to stump each other as to overpower each other with increasingly minute, banal bits of information that bring the emotional satisfaction of experience recovered through memory. The increased availability of all-rerun stations being brought about by cable services can only serve to intensify and broaden this form of grass-roots TV appreciation. Plot resolutions, which so often come in the form of trite didactic "morals" in the sitcom, are not very evocative. The lessons that Lucy Ricardo learned on vanity, economy, and female propriety are forgotten by both Lucy and the viewer. A description of Lucy's living room furniture (or her new living room furniture) is far more interesting. The climactic ethical pronouncements of Ward Cleaver conjure and explore the essence of *Leave It to Beaver* less successfully than a well-rendered impersonation of Eddie Haskell does. From about the time a viewer reaches puberty, sitcom plot is painfully predictable. After the tinkering of the first season or two, few new characters, settings, or situations can be expected. Why watch, if not for a visit to the sitcosmos?

The sitcom is a representational form, and its subject is American culture: It dramatizes national types, styles, customs, issues, and language. Because sitcoms are and have always been under the censorship of corporate patronage, the genre has yielded a conservative body of drama that is diachronically retarded by the precautions of mass marketing procedure. For example, *All in the Family* can appropriately be thought of as a sixties sitcom, though the show did not appear on television until 1971. CBS waited until some neat red, white, and blue ribbons could be tied around the turmoil of that extraordinarily self-conscious decade before presenting it as a comedy. When the dust had cleared and the radical ideas being proposed during that era could be represented as stylistic changes, the sixties could be absorbed into a model of acceptability, a basic necessity of mass marketing procedure. During the historical sixties, while network news programs were offering footage of student riots, civil rights demonstrations, police riots, and militant revolutionaries advocating radical changes in the American status quo, the networks were airing such sitcoms as *The Andy Griffith Show, Petticoat Junction, Here's Lucy,* and *I Dream of Jeannie.* The political issues polarizing communities and families were almost completely avoided in a genre of representational comedy that always had focused on American family and community. Hippies occasionally would appear as guest characters on sitcoms, but they were universally portrayed as harmless buffoons possessing neither worthwhile ideas nor the power to act, which might make them dangerous. After radical sentiment crested and began to recede, especially after the repeal of universal male conscription in 1970, the challenge of incorporating changes into the sitcom model finally was met. The dialogue that took place in the Bunker home was unthinkable during the American Celebration that had lingered so long on the sitcom. But if the sitcom was to retain its credibility as a chronicler and salesman of American family life, these new styles, types, customs, manners, issues, and linguistic constructions had to be added to its mimetic agenda.

13

The dynamics of this problem are perhaps better explained in marketing terms. Five age categories are generally used in demographic analysis: (1) 0–11; (2) 12–17; (3) 18–34; (4) 35–55; (5) 55 +.[20] Prime-time programmers pay little attention to groups 1 and 5; viewing is so prevalent among the very young and old that, as the joke goes on Madison Avenue, these groups will watch the test pattern. Prime-time television programs are created primarily to assemble members of groups 3 and 4 for commercials. While members of group 4 tend to have the most disposable income, group 3 spends more money. Younger adults, presumably building their households, make more purchases of expensive "hard goods" (refrigerators, microwave ovens, automobiles, etc.). This situation was profoundly exacerbated in the late sixties and early seventies by the coming of age of the "baby-boom" generation. The top-rated sitcoms of the 1969–70 season included *Mayberry R.F.D., Family Affair, Here's Lucy,* and *The Doris Day Show.* Though all four of these programs were in Nielsen's Top 10 that season, their audience was concentrated in groups 1, 4, and 5. How could the networks deliver the new primary consumer group to the ad agencies and their clients? Norman Lear provided the networks with a new model that realistically addressed itself to this problem. In *Tube of Plenty,* Erik Barnouw shows how the timidity of television narrative can be traced directly to the medium's birth during the McCarthy Era. If the sixties had accomplished nothing else, it had ended the McCarthy scare. The consensus imagery that had dominated the sitcom since the birth of TV simply could not deliver the new audience as well as the new consensus imagery Norman Lear developed for the seventies. This break in the twenty-year-old style of the genre self-consciously defined itself as "hip." The historian Daniel Czitrom has called this phenomenon "Lifestyle."[21]

In the fifties and sixties, the sitcom had offered the Depression-born post–World War II adult group a vision of peaceful, prosperous suburban life centered on the stable nuclear family. A generation that had grown up during hard times, and that had fought what Herbert T. Gillis always referred to as "The Big One," had seen its desires fulfilled on the sitcom. The economic, political, and social travail of the thirties and forties had been left behind by the brave new teleworld. Instead, there was a family: a husband and wife raising children. This family was white and had a name that bespoke Anglo-Saxon ancestry and Protestant religious affiliation. Surprisingly enough, the darnedest things happened to them. Each week a family member—usually a child—would encounter some ethical crisis or moral dilemma in the course of this relentlessly normal state of affairs. Dennis (the Menace) Mitchell hits a line drive through Mr. Wilson's kitchen window after being warned not to take batting practice in the backyard. Beaver unwittingly discovers a copy of tomorrow's history test, which Miss Landers has dropped in the school corridor. The man of her dreams finally asks Patty Duke out for an evening; should she send her twin cousin Cathy to keep her regular date with Richard? These families were all above the pressures usually associated with financial uncertainty. The father was comfortably placed in the professions—lawyer, doctor, insurance executive—or sometimes just amorphously well fixed (e.g., Ozzie Nelson). Furthermore, Dad was never in short supply of moral provisos, bromides, and panaceas to alleviate the anxiety of his little citizens-in-training. Mom, who worked for love not wages, though she was rarely shown doing any household tasks more demanding than serving dinner, managed to keep the family's spacious quarters in a state that can be best described as ready for military inspection; she could do it in formal attire to boot.

15

In these shows—*Father Knows Best, Ozzie and Harriet, The Donna Reed Show, The Trouble with Father, Make Room for Daddy,* et al.—actual humor (jokes or shticks) is always a subordinate concern to the proper solution of ethical crises. They are comedies not so much in the popular sense as in Northrop Frye's sense of the word: No one gets killed, and they end with the restoration of order and happiness.[22] What humor there is derives largely from the "cuteness" displayed by the children in their abortive attempts to deal with problems in other than correct (adult) ways. Sometimes an extra element of humor becomes the task of marginal characters from outside the nuclear family. Eddie Haskell (Ken Osmond) is among the best remembered of these domestic antiheroes. A quintessential wiseguy, Eddie's deviation from the straight and narrow—as walked by Wally Cleaver—is implicitly blamed on his parents. The fact that Eddie is uniformly punished by the scriptwriters makes his rebellion all the more heroic.

A transformation on this model is the single-parent sitcom.

Here the same moral universe remains intact. Instead of the traditional mom-and-dad, however, a widow, widower, aunt, or uncle is raising the children (divorce would not come to this subgenre until Norman Lear's *One Day at a Time* [1975]). This narrative format, pioneered in such shows as *My Little Margie* and *Bachelor Father,* makes it possible to augment the cuteness of the children's moral educations with situations involving romantic possibilities for the adult. Though Hays Office standards are rigorously adhered to, some relief is offered from the sexless picture of married life that otherwise prevailed in the genre.

16

Beneath the stylistic variances of *Father Knows Best* and *All in the Family* (and *Bachelor Father/One Day at a Time*), these shows are bound together by their unwavering commitment to didactic allegory. Lear indeed updated the conversation in the sitcom living room, but his sitcoms were actually quite conservative in terms of their form. Like the sitcoms of the fifties, Lear's shows reinforce what Dorothy Rabinowitz calls "our most fashionable pieties."[23] "Fashionable" is the key term. As Roger Rosenblatt has pointed out, the greatest difference between *Father Knows Best*'s Jim Anderson and Archie Bunker is that Jim, the father, is the source of all wisdom for the Anderson family while Archie is more likely to be the recipient of lessons from Mike, Gloria, and Edith.[24] In marketing terms, the representation of the higher spending power is consistently heroic.

Though didacticism may be a structural feature of the sitcom (and all storytelling), a strain of situation comedy has developed that is less emphatically moralistic and more concerned with being funny. *I Love Lucy* is one such sitcom; it is the prototype of the "zany" variety. Here, father still knows best, but his task is not so much to preach sermons to the children as to restrain his wife from doing "crazy" things that threaten middle-class order. Lucy is in no way the imperturbable wife and mother embodied in her contemporary, Margaret Anderson. She overspends her budget, acts on impulse, and does not hesitate to drop Little Ricky with Mrs. Trumble at the slightest hint that her dream of something more than a hausfrau existence might be satisfied by an audition for a show at the Tropicana. Lucy refuses to allow bourgeois role destiny to stifle her organic desires, no matter how often she is repressed. Her attempts to escape from what Ricky and society define for her as "her place in the home" turn her into a buffoon, and this is the center of the show. By the end of each episode she has been whipped back into middle-class-housewife shape. Her weekly lapse into "childish" behavior, however, makes her into a freak whose comic talents are far more compelling than the dismal authoritarian morality that controls her.[25]

Though Lucy was copied in such shows as *I Married Joan* and *Pete and Gladys,* the imitators could not easily come by the comic talents of Lucille Ball. To compensate for Lucy's personal magic, they frequently turned to the supernatural. In shows such as *Bewitched, I Dream of Jeannie, Mr. Ed,* and *My Favorite Martian,* an otherwise realistic (or at least scientifically feasible) vision of middle-class life is invaded not by a mere madcap but by a character (woman, animal, or alien) possessed of supernatural powers. Magic is both the cause of and the antidote to the much-feared curse of zaniness. The relatively naturalistic Lucy often becomes the victim of her own harebrained scheming and has to own up to Ricky in humiliation before the final credits. On the other hand, Samantha Stevens, a witch, can set things right with a twitch of her nose—with husband Darren often none the wiser. In each case the wife possesses energies and desires that tempt her to rebel against the constraints of middle-class-housewife status. The husbands, both the immigrant striver Ricky Ricardo and the Madison Avenue executive Darren Stevens, are determined to keep their contractual slaves/ lovers locked safely away at home. Though a bandleader himself, Ricky simply forbids Lucy from pursuing a show business career. Darren is an even crueler sexist. He constantly expects Samantha to entertain his business contacts at home but forbids her to use her magical powers. Though she can prepare an elegant banquet with a spell (usually one heroic couplet) and a twitch of her nose, he forces her to slave over a hot stove all day for no other reason than to satisfy his incorrigibly puritanical "principles."

The domestic sitcom has strayed from its compelling middle-class center upon occasion. Though the conventions of tele-culture define the middle class as a vast amalgamation of all those Americans who neither depend on welfare payments nor have live-in servants, there have been self-consciously proletarian sitcoms, including such early shows as *The Life of Riley* and *The Honeymooners.* As the titles suggest, there is little of Clifford Odets in them, though the Kramdens' stark two-room flat is notable. Interestingly enough, the working-class sitcom was virtually absent from the networks during most of the sixties. It was Lear who revived the idea with *All in the Family*. The black sitcom has a similar history. It appeared in TV's pioneer days (e.g., *Amos 'n Andy, Beulah*), only to disappear from view during the sixties and then make a comeback under Lear's tutelage. In acknowledgment of the protests of civil rights organizations against the lily-whiteness of the sitcosmos, NBC premiered its *Julia* series in 1968. This was a single-parent situation starring Diahann Carroll as a widowed, professional, middle-class mom; the tokenism of the series was as obvious as its resemblance to *The Doris Day Show,* which made its debut that same season. Lear and his Tandem Productions restyled and resurrected the black sitcom in *Sanford and Son,* which premiered in 1972. Other black sitcoms, such as *The Jeffersons* and *Good Times,* followed.

Faced with the problem of seeming fresh and different without upsetting expectations of the familiar formula, sitcom-makers have attempted to bring the form to various settings. In addition to the ubiquitous contemporary middle-class living room, sitcoms have taken place in military barracks, prehistoric caves, tenement flats, mansions, extraterrestrial space, junkyards, offices, police stations, and high school and college classrooms; in New York, Los Angeles, Minneapolis, Mayberry, Bedrock, Indianapolis, Moscow, Milwaukee, a Nazi prison camp, and Anytown, U.S.A. The military sitcom has been a strong subgenre. *Sgt. Bilko, McHale's Navy, F Troop, Gomer Pyle, U.S.M.C., I Dream of Jeannie, Hogan's Heroes, C.P.O. Sharkey, M*A*S*H,* and *Private Benjamin* (to name just a few) have extended the military setting through war and peace, present and past, and every branch of the U.S. armed services, save the Coast Guard. Deviation from "normal" (that is, nuclear family) life also occurs in a subgenre of the sitcom that focuses on single career girls. Early examples include *Our Miss Brooks* and *Private Secretary* (also known as *The Ann Sothern Show*). Like the blue-collar and black sitcoms, the career-girl sitcom faded from the homescreen during the halcyon days of the middle-class domesticom, only to resurface in the late sixties. *That Girl* (1966) was at the crest of the revival. Marlo Thomas starred as Ann Marie, a young woman who leaves her parents' suburban New York home to move to

Manhattan and pursue a career as an actress. Ann's ties to her family, however, were emphasized. Both her father and mother were series regulars who kept a close watch on their daughter's fortunes in Sin City. Her thoroughly innocuous steady boyfriend stood between Ann and promiscuity. It was *The Mary Tyler Moore Show* and the MTM Enterprises spin-offs that finally presented a picture of women out in the world on their own. The career-woman sitcom became a staple of the seventies. The heroine, freed at last from her role as chief cook and bottle washer, as well as from the moral authority of a husband or father, entered the pantheon of telemythology.[26]

19

For all the stylistic variations on a theme that have characterized sitcom history, the comic success of a show ultimately has depended on the talents of its actors and their collaborative success as a troupe. As performers as diverse as Don Rickles and Jimmy Stewart have learned, the sitcom simply does not work as a one-star vehicle; the laughs—and usually the ratings—have gone to the well-formed ensemble. Andy Griffith's "stardom" fades from memory if isolated from Don Knotts's woefully neurotic Deputy Barney Fife, Howard McNear's apoplectic Floyd the Barber, and the other citizens of Mayberry. Compare the brilliant kabuki-like choreography of the original *Honeymooners* to the awkward, misplayed revival in the sixties; Audrey Meadows and Joyce Randolph were never quite replaced. Though Lucille Ball was able to stay atop the ratings throughout her sitcom career, she would never again attain the comic heights she had achieved with Desi Arnaz, Vivian Vance, and William Frawley. Lucy's artistic demise was due not only to the inferior comic technique of her later efforts (*The Lucy Show* and *Here's Lucy*), which can be explained in show business terms as "inferior timing," but more importantly to the absence of the mythological syntheses of *I Love Lucy:* male and female (Ricky/Fred vs. Lucy/Ethel); native-born and immigrant (Lucy/Ethel/Fred vs. Ricky); old and young (the Ricardos vs. the Mertzes); and organic and genteel (Lucy vs. the middle-class world she lived in). These paradigms tightened the interstices of the field of American comedy. The later shows invested all comic tensions in the conflicts between Lucy and the hyperbolically genteel Gale Gordon; they pale in comparison.

Perhaps the reason that the sitcom has been looked down

by critics as a hopelessly "low" or "masscult" form is that a search for "the best which has been thought and said" is a wild-goose chase as far as the genre is concerned. R. P. Blackmur, though certainly no TV fan, commented germanely that the critic "will impose the excellence of something he understands upon something he does not understand. Then all the richness of actual performance is gone. It is worth taking precautions to prevent that loss, or at any rate to keep us aware of the risk."[27] Television is not yet a library with shelves; it is a flow of dreams, many remembered, many submerged. How can we create a bibliography of dreams? Blackmur also wrote that "the critic's job is to put us into maximum relation to the burden of our momentum."[28] As a culture, television is the engine of our momentum. It has heaped thousands upon thousands of images upon the national imagination:

Gleason rearing back a fist and threatening to send Alice to the moon.

Phil Silvers's bullet-mouthed Sgt. Bilko conning his platoon out of its paychecks.

Jack Benny and Rochester guiding an IRS man across the crocodile-infested moat to the vault.

Dobie Gillis standing in front of "The Thinker" and pining for Tuesday Weld.

Carroll O'Connor giving Meathead and modern philanthropic liberalism the raspberries.

Jerry Van Dyke settling down in the driver's seat of a Model T Ford for a heart-to-heart talk with *My Mother, the Car*.

Whitman, in *Democratic Vistas*, called for a new home-grown American literary art whose subject would be "the averge, the bodily, the concrete, the democratic, the popular."[29] The sitcom is an ironic twentieth-century fulfillment of this dream. The "average" has been computed and dramatized as archetype; the consumer world has been made "concrete"; the "bodily" is fetishized as the unabashed object of envy and voyeurism; all of this is nothing if not "popular." The procession of images that was Whitman's own art, and which he hoped would become the nation's, is lacking in the sitcom in but one respect: its technique is not democratic but demographic. The producers, directors, writers, camera operators, set designers, and other artists of the medium are not, as Whitman had hoped, "breathing into it a new breath of "life."[30] Instead, for the sake of industrial science, they have contractually agreed to create the hallucinations of what Allen Ginsberg called "the narcotic ... haze of capitalism."[31] The drug indeed is on the air and in the air. Fortunately, the integrity of the individual resides in the autonomy of the imagination, and therefore it is not doomed by this system. The television set plays on and on in the mental hospital; the patient can sit in his chair, spaced-out and hopeless, or get up and push at the doors of consciousness. This is the happy ending for the sitcom.

21

In Front of the Curtain

"The virtue of all-in wrestling," wrote Roland Barthes in 1957, "is that it is the spectacle of excess."[32] I have tried to show that the sitcom, on the other hand, is a spectacle of subtleties, an incremental construction of substitute universes laid upon the foundation of a linear, didactic teletheater. Even the occasional insertion of the *mirabile* or supernatural is underlined by the genre's broader commitment to naturalistic imitation. Presentational comedy, which shared the prime-time limelight with the sitcom during the early years of TV, vacillates between these poles. The comedy-variety show has been the great showcase for presentational teleforms: stand-up comedy, impersonation, and the blackout sketch. This genre is similar to wrestling in that it too strives for the spectacle of excess. Its preelectronic ancestors can be found on the vaudeville and burlesque stages: the distensions of the seltzer bottle and the banana peel; the fantastic transformations of mimicry; the titillations of the physical, psychological, and cultural disorders that abound in frankly self-conscious art forms. But the comedy-variety show does not go to the ultimate excesses of wrestling. Like the sitcom, it is framed by the proscenium arch and accepts the badge of artifice.

While the representational drama of the sitcom and its cousins, the action/adventure series and the made-for-TV movie has flourished to the point that these genres consume almost all of the "most-watched" hours, the comedy-variety show has been in steady decline since the 1950s, when it was a dominant genre of prime-time television. Since the self-imposed cancelation of *The Carol Burnett Show* in 1978, the few presentational variety hours that have appeared in prime-time have been hosted by singers (Barbara Mandrell, Marie Osmond), and comedy has been relegated to a rather pathetic secondary concern on these programs. The demise of the genre has deprived prime time of some of television's most promising possibilities. Stand-up comedy, as developed in the American nightclub, is one of the most intense and compelling of modern performance arts. Eschewing the protection of narrative superstructure and continuity, the stand-up comedian nakedly faces the audience. He truly works in the first person, making no distinction between persona and self. When successful, the monologist offers an awesome display of charismatic power: the lone individual controlling the imaginative and physical responses of millions. By the same token, nowhere is failure more pathetic or painful. The rhythm of the stand-up monologue demands the punctuation of the audience's response; when it is missing, the spectacle of impotence is shattering. The stand-up comedian laying an egg is one of the few phenomena on television or in mass entertainment in general where the visible pressure to produce the desired effect emerges through even the slickest production values. That pressure is unrelenting. Like the wrestler who must continue to play his role during "interviews" outside the ring, the television stand-up comic is expected to remain in character at all times. After doing "five minutes," he must join Johnny and his guests as "himself," a clown, a wit, a funnyman. The ability to do this often provides satisfying performance art. Failure cracks apart the smooth veneer of TV "normalcy."

Television as a medium is particularly well suited to the presentation of stand-up comedy. The comedian is easily framed on the small screen. Perspective can be spontaneously shifted by the director from the full body portrait, which gives the comic the authority of a public speaker, to close-ups that are advantageous to mimicry and face-making. The intermediary teletheater is devoid of drunken hecklers and clattering dishes, making it a propitious showcase for the carefully rehearsed, well-timed routine (though admittedly, for some stylists, this loss of spontaneous give-and-take is regrettable). The structure of the show business industry, however, has inhibited stand-up comedy as a television art. Comedians, even the handful who employ writing staffs, must beware the plague of overexposure. A powerful nightclub monologue can become worthless in Las Vegas and Atlantic City after even a single television appearance. Furthermore, the fetishization of "dirty words" on television puts severe limits on stand-up text. It is perhaps principally for these reasons that the stand-up comedian has been largely squeezed out of prime time into what the industry terms "marginal hours." On daytime television, for example, stand-up performers abound as players on gameshows and as guests on *Merv* and *Mike*. Gameshows such as *The Hollywood Squares* and *Battlestars* have even been tailored as stand-up vehicles. The real stronghold for presentational comedy on television, however, has become the late-night spot.

23

In May of 1950, NBC premiered *Broadway Open House* in a late-night time period (i.e., 11:30, eastern time), and ever since, this segment of the NBC schedule has been reserved for presentational comedy. It has even become a relatively safe zone for artistic freedom (or at least TV's equivalent of "blue" material). Alex McNeil describes *Broadway Open House* as "a heavy-handed mixture of vaudeville routines, songs, dances and sight gags."[33] The cohosts were vaudeville veterans Jerry Lester and Morey Amsterdam, and much of the humor derived from their interplay with the Dolly Parton of early TV, "a buxom blonde named Jennie Lewis, better known as Dagmar, who played it dumb."[34] By the midfifties, the program had evolved a more sedate format: a 105-minute, Monday-through-Friday, "desk-and-sofa" talk show known as *The Tonight Show*. It was hosted by *bon mot* comedians such as Steve Allen, Ernie Kovacs, and Jack Paar. The opening monologue became an institution, television's only daily comic paratext to The News. In 1981 Johnny Carson continues to deliver the only regularly scheduled comedy monologue on national television, but Johnny's ever-expanding vacation schedule has made even that an iffy proposition; the show has dwindled to a mere one hour due to Johnny's seemingly unquenchable thirst for recreation. The *Tonight Show* sofa, once filled with guests, including two or three comics a show, is relatively empty these days.

Weekly late-night comedy shows, such as *Saturday Night Live* and *SCTV,* have taken up some of the stand-up slack, but the great work of these shows has been to grandly resuscitate TV blackout. The blackout sketch, or short skit, was pioneered as a distinctive teleform in the early days of TV. Before two-hour television movies ate up such a large chunk of network prime time, the viewer did not have to wait for the wee hours of the weekend to see sketch comedy. Milton Berle, Jimmy Durante, Jackie Gleason, Sid Caesar, Ernie Kovacs, Martha Raye, and Ed Wynn were just a few of the comedians who hosted their own weekly comedy hours. These stars were the pampered children of Television Row. Jackie Gleason was able to get CBS to build him a Hudson River mansion during the fifties; later, when he got Sunbelt Fever, CBS chairman William Paley granted him a complete new production facility in Miami Beach. Milton Berle, "Mr. Television," was signed to a thirty-one-year contract by NBC in 1951. The role of Uncle Miltie in the early proliferation of the medium itself is, of course, legendary. His subsequent fall from Nielsen grace parallels the decline of the genre. From 1948 to 1956, the Berle show was a Tuesday night ritual. The first official ratings season was 1950–51, and A. C. Nielsen ranked Berle's *Texaco Star Theater* as the Number One attraction on television.[35] General Sarnoff's multimillion-dollar investment seemed to be paying off as the show consistently finished among the Top 5 for the next three seasons. However, in 1954–55, it slipped to Number Thirteen, and in 1955–56 it dropped out of the Top 20 altogether.[36] It is too easy to dismiss the Berle phenomenon as merely a case of the public's fickle favor. Not a single comedy-variety hour made the Top 10 in 1955–56.[37] Few variety shows hosted by comedians would finish in the Top 10 ever again. At the end of the 1955–56 season, the unthinkable happened—Berle was yanked off the air. After a two-year layoff, NBC tried him again, this time in a reduced half-hour format; the new show was not renewed for a second season. By 1960, stuck with an expensive long-term contract, Sarnoff was using Milton Berle as the host of *Jackpot Bowling.* Finally, with over fifteen years remaining on his contract, Berle and NBC came to an agreement, and the once indomitable star was let go. Last-place ABC promptly signed him for a comedy-variety comeback, but *The Milton Berle Show* could not survive six months in 1966.

The early rush to sign the stars for eternity ended as the networks entered the age of entropy.

The reasons for the failure of Berle and his "hellzapoppin'" burlesque style of presentation are not obvious. What can be said with some assurance is that this failure took place amid increasing demand for a "product" as opposed to a "show" in the growing television industry. As the prime-time stakes rocketed upward, sponsors, agencies, and networks became less tolerant of the inevitable ups and downs of a star-centered presentational comedy. The sitcom and other forms of representational drama offer the long-term rigidities of shooting scripts, which make "quality control" easier to impose. Positive demographic responses to dramatic "concepts" are dependable barometers. Performance comedy is only as good as an individual performance; the human element looms too large. Furthermore, the dreaded extremes of presentational comedy can be avoided. Kinescopes of *The Texaco Star Theater* reveal Berle in transvestite sketches whose gratuitous lewdness rivals wrestling at its most intense. The passionate vulgarity of these sketches could not have been wholly predictable from their scripts. Instead, it derives directly from Berle's confrontation with the camera—his performance. Censorship of such material presents complex editing problems, which are easily preempted in representational drama by script changes. It is my own feeling that the high-tech mystique of television itself—the sterile promise of the machine—is what kept the show from crossing the border from "family fun" to pornography in the early days of television. Gilbert Seldes described Berle's comedy as "good clean dirt."[38] Seldes called the early Berle a "stag entertainer," offering this observation: "The basic material of the stag entertainer, whether he dresses in women's clothes, pretends to be homosexual, or develops some other specialty, is still the off-color story, and the basic style is always the public one of maximum projection."[39] Perhaps the blinding gloss of the "modern miracle" of television was becoming subdued during television's second decade. Time, boredom, and the further technicization of the American household were making the future banal enough to generate a critical response. Were the full implications of burlesque beaming into the home becoming a bit too clear for Berle's family audience? Brooks and Marsh have indeed attrib-

25

uted the undoing of Uncle Miltie to increasing "sophistication" among the viewing public: "By 1956 the steam had run out for 'Mr. Television.' TV was by then becoming dominated by dramatic-anthology shows, Westerns, and private eyes, and the sight of a grinning comic jumping around in crazy costumes [i.e., women's clothing] no longer had the appeal it did in 1948."[40] When NBC gave Berle his second chance in 1958, the show was considerably toned down:

26

> Two years after his departure from the Tuesday line-up, Berle returned to prime time with a half-hour variety series for NBC. He was a more restrained performer this time— no slapstick or outrageous costumes—attempting to function more as a host than the central focus of the show.[41]

The consequence was clear: Berlesque, like wrestling, had been blackballed from television's increasingly genteel prime-time circle. The late fifties, of course, was the heyday of *Playhouse 90, The U.S. Steel Hour,* and *The Armstrong Circle Theater,* the "Golden Age" of respectable drama. TV then, as now and always, was on the verge of becoming sophisticated. The NBC late-night spot had passed from the wacky vaudevillian Jerry Lester to the neurotically urbane Jack Paar. Berle was certainly neurotic; he simply could not be urbane.

A survey cited by Sterling and Kitross shows the number of "Evening Network Television" hours given to comedy-variety shows declining from a high of 21.5 hours in 1951 to 5 hours in 1973.[42] The censorship problems I have mentioned have checkered the history of the genre. The case of the Smothers Brothers provides an example. Tom and Dick won their network wings with an innocuous sitcom in the 1965–66 season. When CBS gave them their own comedy-variety show, *The Smothers Brothers Comedy Hour,* the network suddenly found itself with a severe Standards and Practices crisis. As Brooks and Marsh have written, the show "poked fun at virtually all the hallowed institutions of American society—motherhood, church, politics, government, etc."[43] Controversial guests, such as folk singer Pete Seeger and Dr. Benjamin Spock (after his conviction for aiding draft evaders), were invited to appear on the show. Many segments were severely censored or deleted. An embarrassed CBS canceled the series on a technicality: A tape was delivered past the usual deadline. That tape contained a sequence in which Joan Baez dedicated a song to her husband, David Harris, who was serving a sentence in federal prison for draft evasion.[44] In 1981 the Smothers Brothers were back on the air, the stars of a short-lived representational drama series, *Fitz and Bones.*

Nat King Cole was a singer, not a comedian, but the peculiar case of his ill-fated variety series makes a stark point about the qualitative distinctions between presentation and representation on network television. Black actors and actresses were not complete strangers to television in the 1950s. Ethel Waters had played the title role in *Beulah* (ABC, 1950–53), and Tim Moore, Spencer Williams, Ernestine Wade, and the rest of the cast of *Amos 'n Andy* (CBS, 1951–53) were of course black (the radio cast had been white). Amanda Randolph played the part of Louise (the maid) on *The Danny Thomas Show* from 1953 to 1964. But when Nat King Cole was given his own variety show in 1956, not a single sponsor could be found. NBC affiliates in the North as well as the South declined to carry the program.[45] Even the appearances on the show of such mainstream white stars of the day as Tony Bennett, Frankie Laine, and Peggy Lee could not dissuade affiliates from their boycott. To its credit, NBC continued to air *The Nat King Cole Show* as a sustaining program for more than a year, juggling its time slot twice in an attempt to find a place for it. But a black entertainer stripped of the representational mask would not be successful in prime time until *The Flip Wilson Show* (NBC, 1970–74).

The comedy-variety genre never completely died off in prime time. A handful of hits such as *The Carol Burnett Show, The Flip Wilson Show,* and George Schlatter's innovative *Rowan and Martin's Laugh-In* managed to keep it alive. But pop singers, including Sonny and Cher, Tom Jones, Englebert Humperdinck, Tony Orlando and Dawn, the Captain and Tenille, and Donnie and Marie, took over the lion's share of the dwindling hours given to vaudeville-style presentation in the sixties and seventies. A later full-fledged attempt to revive the comedy-variety hour was *The Richard Pryor Show,* which premiered on the NBC fall schedule in 1977. It was destroyed by the old comedy-variety devil—censorship—after only five airings.

27

Generally speaking, the comedian has had to step back from in front of the curtain, cross the proscenium arch, and don the mask of a representational character to find a place in prime-time television. The networks have thus provided themselves with a modicum of protection from the unreliability of individual personalities. Presentational comedy—performance art—may simply be too dangerous a gamble for the high stakes of today's market.

Interestingly, the disappearance from TV of the clown who faces the audience without a story line has occurred more or less simultaneously with rising interest in and appreciation of performance art in avant-garde circles. In "Performance as News: Notes on an Intermedia Guerrilla Group," Cheryl Bernstein writes:

> In performance art, the artist is more exposed than ever before. The literal identification of artistic risk with the act of risking one's body or one's civil rights has become familiar in the work of such artists as Chris Burden, Rudolf Schwarzkogler, Tony Schafranzi and Jean Toche.[46]

Burden, for example, invites an audience into a performance space where spectators sit atop wooden ladders. He then floods the room with water and drops a live electrical wire into the giant puddle. The closest thing television offers to a spectacle of this kind is Don Rickles, who evokes audience terror by throwing the live wire of his insult humor into the swamp of American racial and ethnic fears. Rickles, for the most part, has been prohibited from performing his intense theater of humiliation in prime time. Twice NBC has attempted to contain him in sitcom proscenia, but these frames have constricted his effect and turned his insults into dull banter. In recent years he has been unleashed upon a live studio audience only during his infrequent appearances as a guest host on *The Tonight Show*. The erratic quality of Rickles's performances on *Tonight* offers a clue to the networks' reluctance to invest heavily in the presentational comedy form.

Bernstein points to The News as the great source of modern performance art on television. She deconstructs "The Kidnapping of Patty Hearst" by the Symbionese Liberation Army as a performance work. The SLA was a troupe that was formed to create a multimedia work—the kidnapping—principally for television. The mass distribution of food in poor neighborhoods in the San Francisco Bay area (one of the SLA's demands), as well as the shoot-outs and police chases that occurred, were all part of a modern theatrical art that can take place only on television. Perhaps the proliferation of The News on television can be tied to the decline of presentational comedy; the two have seemed to occur in direct proportion to each other. The sit-life schlockumentary is the point at which the two genres meet. Furthermore, the bombardment of the home-screen with direct presentations from every corner of the earth has created a kind of vaudeville show of history. The tensions of the nuclear Sword of Damocles create a more compelling package than even Ed Sullivan could have hoped to assemble. The nations of the world have become a troupe of baggy-pants clowns on TV. They are trotted out dozens of times each day in a low sketch comedy of hostility, violence, and affectation. The main show, of course, is the network evening news. Climb the World Trade Center. Fly an airplane through the Arc de Triomphe. Plant a bomb in a department store in the name of justice. Invade a preindustrial nation with tanks in the name of peace. Can Ted Mack compare with this?

29

The Theater Collapses

Random House, a subsidiary of RCA, publishes a dictionary that defines the verb "entertain" as follows:

1. to hold the attention of agreeably; divert; amuse
2. to treat as a guest; show hospitality to
3. to admit into or hold in the mind; consider
4. *Archaic.* to maintain or keep up
5. *obs.* to give admittance or reception to; receive
6. *v.i.* to exercise hospitality; entertain company
Late Middle English: *entertene,* to hold mutually[47]

The television industry is at the forefront of a vast entertainment complex that oversees the process of coordinating consumption and culture. "Entertainment" has been established as a buzz word for narratives and other imaginative presentations that make money. It is used as a rhetorical ploy to specialize popular arts and isolate them from aesthetic and political scrutiny; such scrutiny is reserved for "art." An important implication of the definition of "entertain" is the intimate social relationship it implies between the entertainer and the entertained. In 1956 Gunther Anders wrote that "the television viewer, although living in an alienated world, is made to believe that he is on a footing of the greatest intimacy with everything and everybody."[48] The technological means to produce this illusion have since been greatly enhanced. Anders describes this illusion as "chumminess." Television offers itself to the viewer as a hospitable friend: Welcome to *The Wonderful World of Disney.* Good evening, folks. We'll be right back. See you next week. Y'all come back now. As technology synthesizes more and more previously human functions, there is a proliferation of anthropomorphic metaphor: Automatic Teller Machines ask us how much money we need. Computers send us bills. Channel 7 is predicting snow. The car won't start. It is in this context that television entertains. There is an odd sensation of titillation in all this service. Whitman and other nineteenth-century optimists foresaw an elevation of the common man to a proud master in the technoworld. Machines would take care of life's dirty work; this created the prospect of slavery without guilt. Television enthusiastically smiles and shuffles for the viewer's favor. Even bad television programs contribute to the illusion (i.e., "We are not amused"). In Faulkner's *Absalom, Absalom!,* Sutpen comes down out of the classless *Gemeinschaft* of frontier Appalachia and discovers his low station in *Kultur* when the slave butler of a Piedmont plantation refuses him entry at the front door of the mansion and sends him around back for a handout. Determined never to suffer such an indignity again, he does not return to Appalachia but works single-mindedly until he can buy a gang of his own slaves. These slaves build him a mansion and he becomes a colonel. It was of course cost efficient to buy female slaves and impregnate them personally. One of his mulatto sons finally shoots him. Similarly, the tele-American emerges from the innocence of childhood into his or her first apartment. Success in life is measured largely by the quantity of machines in the quarters. Are all the household chores mechanized? Do you have HBO? Work is minimized. Leisure is maximized. There is more time to watch television— that is, to live like a king.

Backstage of this public drama, quite a different set of relationships is at work. In a demography, the marketing apparatus becomes synonymous with the state itself. As the quality of goods takes a backseat to the quantity of services, the most valued good of all—the measure of truth—becomes information on the consuming preferences of the hundreds of millions of consumer-kings. Every ticket to the cinema, every book, every tube of toothpaste purchased is a vote. The shelves of the supermarkets are stocked with referenda. Watching television is an act of citizenship, participation in culture. The networks entertain the viewer; in return, the viewer entertains thousands of notions on what to buy (that is, how to live). The democrat Whitman wrote that "the average man of a land at last is only important."[49] The demographer Nielsen cannot agree more:

> While the average household viewed over 49 hours of television [per week] in the fall of 1980, certain types viewed considerably more hours. Households with 3 or more people and those with non-adults watched over 60 hours a week. Cable subscribing households viewed about 7 hours a week more than non-cable households.[50]

Paul Klein, chief programmer at NBC for many years, characterized his programming philosophy as based on what he called the Least Objectionable Program (LOP) Theory.[51] This theory, expounded by Klein in the seventies, downplays the importance of viewer loyalty to specific programs. Instead, it asserts that television watching is more often dependent on a formal decision. The viewer does not turn on the set so much to view this or that program as to fulfill a desire "to watch television." R. D. Percy and Company, an audience research firm, has come to a conclusion that supports Klein's thesis. David Chagall, summarizing Percy's two-year experiment with 200 Seattle television families, wrote: "Most of us simply snap on the set rather than select a show. The first five minutes are spent *prospecting* channels, looking for gripping images."[52] Faced with the impulse (compulsion?) to view, the viewer then turns to the secondary consideration of choosing a program. In evolved cable markets this can mean dozens of possibilities. The low social prestige of TV watching, even among heavy viewers, coupled with the remarkably narrow range of what is usually available, inhibits the viewer from expressing enthusiasm for any given show. The viewer or viewers (TV, it must not be forgotten, is one of the chief social activities of the culture) must therefore "LOP" about, looking for the least bad, least embarrassing, or least objectionable program. While I am ill prepared to speculate on the demographic truth of this picture of the "average man," two things are worth noting: Anyone who watches television has surely experienced this; and NBC fell into last place in the ratings under Klein's stewardship.

I cite Klein (and Nielsen) to demonstrate the character of demographic thought, the ideological template that ultimately produces most television programs and always is employed to authorize or censor their exhibition on the distribution system. The optimistic democratic view of man as a self-perfecting individual, limited only by superimposed circumstance, is turned on its head. Man is defined as a prisoner of limitations seeking the path of least resistance. This is an industrial nightmare, the gray dream of Fritz Lang's *Metropolis* reshot in glossy technicolor. Workers return from their multicollared tasks, drained of all taste and personality. They seek nothing more than merciful release from the day's production pressures; they want only to "escape." "Escapism" is a much used but puzzling term. Its ambiguities illustrate the overall bankruptcy of the criticism of television that uses it as a flag. The television industry is only too happy to accept "escapism" as the definition of its work; it constitutes a carte blanche release from responsibility for what is presented. Escapist critics seem to believe that the value of art should be measured only by rigorously naturalistic standards. Television programs are viewed as worthless or destructive because they divert consciousness from "reality" to fantasy. However, all art, even social realism, does this. Brecht was certainly mindful of this fact when he found it necessary to attach intrusionary Marxist sermons to the fringes of social realist stage plays. Is metaphor possible at all without "escapism"? Presumably, the mechanism of metaphor is to call a thing some-

32

thing it is not in order to demonstrate emphatically what it is. When the network voice of control says, "NBC is proud as a peacock," it is forcing the perceiver of this message to "escape" from all realistic data about the corporate institution NBC into a fantastic image of a bird displaying its colorful feathers in a grand and striking manner. This is done on the assumption that the perceiver will be able to sort the shared features of the two entities from the irrelevant features and "return" to a clearer picture of the corporation. Representational television programs work in much the same way. If there are no recognizable features of family life in *The Waltons,* if there are no shared features of Lifestyle in *Three's Company,* if there are no credible features of urban paranoia in *Baretta,* then watching these shows would truly be "escapism." But if those features are there—and I believe they are—the viewer is engaging in an act that does not differ qualitatively from reading a Zola novel (though the latter may be more successful in creating a "clearer picture" of society). The escapist argument makes a better point in relation to the structure of narrative in the television series. In the world of the series all problems are not only solvable but usually solved. To accept this as "realistic" is indeed an escape from the planet Earth. But how many viewers accept a TV series as realistic in this sense? John Cawelti has convincingly demonstrated that the success of popular formula narrative is not based on fooling a dull audience.[53] Interestingly, it is the soap opera— the one genre of series television that is committed to an anticlimactic, existential narrative structure—that has created the most compelling illusion of realism for the viewing audience.[54] The survival and triumph of an action series hero are neither convincing nor surprising but merely a convention of the medium. Like the theater audience that attends *The Tragedy of Hamlet,* the TV audience knows what the outcome will be before the curtain goes up. The seduction is not "What?" but "How?"

    Thus far, I have limited my discussion to rather traditional ways of looking at television. However, television—as both a medium and an industry—has made a commitment to relentless technological innovation. The act of viewing cannot remain static in the face of this. The cable converter has already made the twelve-channel VHF tuner obsolete. From a comfortable

33

vantage point anywhere in the room, the viewer can scan dozens of channels with a fingertip. From the decadent splendor of a divan, the viewer is less committed to the inertia of program choice. It is possible to watch half a dozen shows more or less simultaneously, fixing on an image for the duration of its allure, dismissing it as its force disintegrates, and returning to the scan mode. Unscheduled programming emerges as the viewer assumes control of montage. It is also clear that program choice is expanding. The grass-roots public-access movement is still in its infancy, but the network *mise-en-scène* has been at least somewhat augmented by new corporate cousins such as the superstations and the premium services. Cheap home recording and editing equipment may turn the television receiver into a bottomless pit of "footage" for any artist who dares.

Michael Smith, the Chicago-born New York grantee/comedian, is perhaps pointing the way in this respect. Whether dancing with *Donnie and Marie* in front of a giant videoscreen at the Whitney or performing rap songs at the Institute for Contemporary Art in Boston, Smith offers an unabashed display of embarrassments and highlights in the day of a life with television. Mike (Smith's master persona) is the star of his own videotapes (i.e., TV shows). In "It Starts at Home," Mike gets cable and learns the true meaning of public access. In "Secret Horror," reception is plagued by ghosts. The passive viewer—that well-known zombie who has been blamed for every American problem from the Vietnam War to Japanese technological hegemony—becomes do-it-yourself artist in Smith. If "interpretation is the revenge of the intellect upon art,"[55] parody is the special revenge of the TV viewer.

Whatever the so called blue-sky technologies bring, there can be no doubt that the enormous body of video text generated during the decades of the Network Era will make itself felt in whatever follows. The shows and commercials and systems of signs and gestures that the networks have presented for the last thirty-five years constitute the television we know how to watch. There won't be a future without a past.

In *Popular Culture and High Culture*, Herbert Gans takes the position that all human beings have aesthetic urges and are receptive to symbolic expressions of their wishes and fears.[56] As simple and obvious as Gans's assertion seems, it is the wild card in the otherwise stacked deck of demographic culture. Buhle and Czitrom have written:

> We believe that the population at large shares a definite history in modern popular culture and is, on some levels, increasingly aware of that history. We do not think that the masses of television viewers, radio listeners, movie-goers, and magazine readers are numbed and insensible, incapable of understanding their fate or historical condition until a group of "advanced revolutionaries" explains it to them.[57]

Evidence of this shared, definite history, in the form of self-reflexive parody, is already finding its way to the air. The television babies are beginning to make television shows. In the signatory montage that introduces *SCTV* each week, there is a shot of a large apartment house with dozens of televisions flying out the windows and crashing to the ground. As the viewer learns, this does not mean the end of TV in Mander's sense but signifies the end of television as it has been officially experienced. *SCTV* is television beginning to begin again. The traditional theatrical notions of representation and presentation that have guided the development of programming genres are ground to fine dust in the crucible of a satire that draws its inspiration directly from the experience of watching television. *SCTV* was the first commercial network television program that absolutely demanded of its viewers a knowledge of a tradition, a self-conscious awareness of cultural history. In such a context, viewing at last becomes an active process. Without a well-developed knowledge of and sensitivity to the taxonomic framework and individual texts of the first thirty-five years of TV, *SCTV* is meaningless—and probably not even funny. In 1953 Dwight Macdonald described "Mass Culture" as "a parasitic, a cancerous growth on High Culture."[58] By this, I take it, he meant that mass-consumed cultural items such as television programs "steal" the forms of "High Culture," reduce their complexity, and substitute infantile or worthless content. The relationship of mass culture to high culture, Macdonald tells us, "is not that of the leaf and branch but rather that of the caterpillar and leaf."[59] *SCTV* bears no such relationship to any so-called high culture. It is a work that emerges out of the culture of television itself, a fully realized work where history and art synthesize the conditions for a new consciousness of both. Other media—theater, film, radio, music—do not bend the show to televised renderings of their own forms but instead are forced to become television. The viewer is not pandered to with the apologetic over-defining of linear development that denies much of television its potential force. Presentation and representation merge into a seamless whole. The ersatz proscenium theater used by the networks to create marketing genres is smashed; the true montage beaming into the television home refuses to cover itself with superficial framing devices. The pseudo-Marxist supposition that *SCTV* is still guilty of selling the products is boring—the show is not.

The breakthrough of *SCTV,* as well as the force of such shows as *Burns and Allen, Ernie Kovacs, Jack Benny, The Honeymooners,* and the *Saturday Night Live* of 1977–79, will be discussed in greater detail in later chapters. I mention *SCTV* now because it is among the first tangible responses born of a critical stance of TV viewing that is more widespread than a reading of the TV critics would indicate. TV was born a bastard art of mass marketing theory and recognizable forms of popular culture. Thirty-five years later, a generation finds this dubious pedigree its identity and heritage. The poverty of TV drama in all traditional senses is not as important as the richness of the montage in the cubist sense. For the TV-lifer, a rerun of *Leave It to Beaver* or *I Love Lucy* or *The Twilight Zone* offers the sensation of traveling through time in one's own life and cultural history. The recognizable, formulaic narrative releases the viewer from what become the superficial concerns of suspense and character development. The greater imaginative adventures of movement through time, space, and culture take precedence over the flimsy mimesis that seems to be the intention of the scripts. The whole fast-food smorgasbord of American culture is laid out for consumption. This is not merely kitsch. Clement Greenberg wrote that "the precondition of *kitsch* (a German term for 'Mass Culture') is the availability close at hand of a fully matured cultural tradition, whose discoveries, acquisitions, and perfected self-conscious *kitsch* can take advantage of for its own ends."[60] In fact, this process is reversed in television appreciation. The referent culture has become the mass or kitsch culture. Instead of masscult ripping off highcult, we have art being

fashioned from the junkpile. The banal hysteria of the super-
market is capable of elegant clarity in Andy Warhol's "Campbell's Soup Can." Experience is reformed and recontextualized,
reclaimed from chaos. Television offers no few opportunities in
this regard.

The networks and ad agencies care little about these partic-
ulars of culture and criticism. The networks promise to deliver
heads in front of sets and no more. But, as will happen in any
hierarchical or "downstream" system, there is a personal stance
that will at least allow the subject of institutional power to
maintain personal dignity. In the television demography this
stance gains its sustenance from the act of recontextualization.
If there is no exit from the demographic theater, each viewer
will have to pull down the rafters from within. What will remote
control "SOUND: OFF" buttons mean to the future of American
retailing? What images are filling the imaginations of people as
they "listen" to television on the TV bands of transistor radios
while walking the streets of the cities wearing headphones?
Why are silent TV screens playing at social gatherings? When
will the average household using TV (HUT) be equipped with
split-screen, multichannel capability? What is interesting about
a gameshow? The suspense of who will win, or the spectacle of
people brought frothing to the point of hysteria at the prospect
of a new microwave oven? What is interesting about a copshow?
The "catharsis" of witnessing the punishment of the criminal
for his misdeeds, or the attitude of the cop toward evil? What is
interesting about a sitcom? The funniness of the jokes, or the
underlining of the jokes on the laugh track? The plausibility of
the plot, or the portrayal of a particular style of living as "normal"? What is interesting about Suzanne Somers and Erik Es-
trada? Their acting, or their bodies? Television is made to sell
products but is used for quite different purposes by lonely,
alienated people, families, marijuana smokers, born-again
Christians, alcoholics, Hasidic Jews, destitute people, millionaires, jocks, shut-ins, illiterates, hang-gliding enthusiasts, intel-
lectuals, and all of the members of the vast heterogenous
procession that continues to be American culture in spite of all
demographic odds. If demography is an attack on the individual, then the resilience of the human spirit must welcome the
test.

"To be a voter with the rest is not so much," Whitman

37

warned in his *Democratic Vistas* of 1871.[61] The shopper/citizen of the demography ought to know this only too well. Whitman recognized that no political system could ever summarily grant its citizens freedom. Government is a system of power; freedom is a function of personality. "What have we here [in America]," he asked, "if not, towering above all talk and argument, the plentifully-supplied, last-needed proof of democracy, in its personalities?"[62] Television is the Rorschach test of the American personality. I hope the social psychologists will not find our responses lacking.

38

The Situation Comedy of ★ 2
Paul Henning: Modernity
and the American Folk
Myth in *The Beverly*
Hillbillies

Any man thet'll hang onto an old farm jes' 'cause he sort o'
promised his dead mother he'd never sell it, ain't got no
business to live in this bustlin', go-ahead, money-makin',
devil-take-the-hindermost day of ours—thet's all I've got to
say.

    Josiah Blake, in James A. Herne, *Shore Acres* (1892)

While relatively much critical attention has been given to
the "sophisticated" sitcoms of Norman Lear and Grant Tinker,
little has been said about what was probably the most popular
sitcom—if not the most popular show—in television history,
Paul Henning's *Beverly Hillbillies* (CBS, 1962–71). Even among
those critics who do not treat television itself as a pariah, most
have treated Henning as one. No less an explicator of popular
American phenomenon than Russel Nye wrote of Henning's comedies, "They deal in neither sex, nor issues, nor problems, but
only in laughter."[1] This of course is not true, nor could it be.
Comedy, like tragedy, cannot take place without a context, with-

out a relationship to what people believe about themselves and the world. The theater of Beckett, Ionesco, and Pirandello has shown us at least that much. A situation comedy cannot provoke laughter in the same way the tickling of the bottom of the foot does. The TV maker dreams a world and builds it with scripts and actors and cameras and political constrictions and audience market tests and network transmission lines. The success of *The Beverly Hillbillies* (and every other series that Henning was ever associated with) cannot be dismissed as coincidental, nor can the failure of dozens of sitcoms each season. Kenneth Burke has observed that drama gets its material from the historical conversation of a given culture.[2] Televised drama is no exception.

The immense popularity of *The Beverly Hillbillies* and Henning's other creations is worth noting even within the context of mass-produced culture. During the *Hillbillies'* nine-year production life, it not only occupied a weekly prime-time spot on CBS (almost always in the Nielsen Top 20 and often Number One) but was stripped nationally on the network's weekday morning schedule as well. A glance at the Nielsen pantheon reveals that as late as 1982 nine individual episodes of the series remained among the fifty most watched hours in television history, with ratings comparable to those of *Super Bowls.*[3] Rivaled only by the family western, *Bonanza* (NBC, 1959–73), the Henning sitcom was perhaps the most popular weekly series of the 1960s. The program enjoys lively rerun syndication even today. It is distributed by the Viacom Company to stations throughout the United States and other non-Communist countries.

As is the case with most TV shows, very few of the tens of millions who watched *The Beverly Hillbillies* were aware of the fact that a distinct personality had conceived, written, and produced it. Anonymity of authorship has been a distinctive feature of commercial television; the emergence of an auteur superstar, such as Norman Lear, has been a rare exception to the rule. Geoffrey Hartman has identified this as a general tendency in modern art:

The humanists of the sixteenth and seventeenth centuries created the institutions of criticism as we know it; the re-

covery and analysis of works of art. . . . We are now nearing
the end of Renaissance humanism. . . . The notion of unique
works of art, certified by the personal, or located in their
place of origin . . . fades into nostalgia.[4]

Shows indeed come beaming into the living room like visions
from some powerful force so mighty that its name cannot even
be imagined. The indecipherable roll of credits that spins across
the screen at the end of each program serves only to further
obscure the mystery. Beneath the slick, mechanical, faceless
veneer of network broadcast, however, the sweaty hands of the
individual are still to be found at work.

41

Born in 1911 in Independence, Missouri, Paul Henning was
a veteran of twenty-five years of sitcommaking when he launched
what would prove to be his greatest hit. He was the industrious
son of midwestern middle-class parents. A boy soda jerk, his
customers included Harry Truman. As a student at the Kansas
City School of Law during the Depression, he supported himself
as a jack-of-all-trades at a local radio station, working as a sound
effects man, disc jockey, singer, and scriptwriter for station KMBC
during the mid-thirties. In 1937 he took his law degree, but that
same year his unsolicited manuscript was accepted for production by *The Fibber McGee and Molly Show*. This gained Henning
a regular position on the writing staff of the popular Chicago-
based radio sitcom and ended his aspirations for a legal career.
Within a year the young writer was off to Hollywood to try his
hand at free-lancing. He eventually won a staff job with *The
Rudy Vallee Show*, where he worked with a number of seasoned
show business pros, including Abe Burrows. By the late 1940s,
Henning had become a successful staff writer for the top-rated
Burns and Allen Show, then airing on NBC Radio. When CBS
chairman William Paley lured George and Gracie over to his
infant television network for the 1948 season, he got Paul Henning in the bargain.[5] Here the radio writer learned the nuts and
bolts of sitcom production in the new medium. Though *Burns
and Allen* was essentially a showcase for the virtuoso talents of
its stars, Henning occasionally managed to make his interest in
his Missouri background felt, especially in one cluster of episodes, during which Ronnie Burns became friendly with a "hillbilly" classmate at UCLA, eventually dating his sister from "back

home." At this time, Henning also collaborated with fellow *Burns and Allen* writer Stanley Shapiro to create the hillbilly persona of "Charlie Weaver" for the late comedian Cliff Arquette.[6]

Henning's hillbilly creations are of course recognizable figures from American popular tradition. The ethical as well as the physical superiority of the backwoodsman to his city slicker cousin has been a popular theme in America since immigrants began leaving European civilization to live in the wilderness of the New World. In fact, this theme found its way to the stage in the very first comedy written and produced in the United States, Royall Tyler's *The Contrast* (1789). The belief that a life lived close to the land creates a superior moral sensibility—and that this sensibility dissipates in urban experience—is part of a pastoral tradition that can be traced back at least as far as Virgil's *Eclogues*. The treatment of rustic characters in the comic mode has an even longer tradition, dating back to the Atellan farces of ancient Greece. Since the dawn of the industrial age, many writers, including Rousseau, Chateaubriand, and Coleridge, lamenting the urbanization of Europe, looked to America as an opportunity to regain the spiritual benefits of life in a natural setting. The cyclical movement of time in Arcadia was celebrated by these and other commentators as preferable to the delusion of endlessly spiraling "progress" fostered by city life. In his early American play, Tyler sets up the trade-off in stark terms. The city slickers Dimple and Jessamy have gained nothing from their urban (European) experiences but a superficial air of sophistication. Though at first glance the country bumpkin Jonathan seems to be naive or even dim-witted, he possesses a sense of fairness and decency that more than compensates for his inarticulate style. For Tyler, virtue is indigenous; it grows in the American soil. When the charlatan Dimple chides the heroic country gentleman Manly about his never having been to Europe, Manly proudly replies that he "was never ten leagues from the [American] continent."[7] The greatest virtues of the frontiersmen are their independence and self-sufficiency; the city slickers, by contrast, are parasitical schemers with little more than pretentious affectations to offer.

Tyler's geocultural paradigm became an archetypal American myth. As the frontier moved west from Tyler's inland Massachusetts, this myth followed and developed. It was a common theme among humorists of the Old Southwest, Henning's region. When a city slicker armed with his fancy guns tries to make a fool of the frontiersman in Mark Twain's "Dandy Frightening the Squatter," one punch in the nose sends him careening into the Mississippi. In Thomas Bangs Thorpe's "Big Bear of Arkansas," the hillbilly tale-teller exclaims:

> Some of them thar [in New Orleans] called me *green*—well perhaps I am, said I, *but I arn't so at home;* and I ain't off my trail much. The heads of them perlite chaps themselves wern't much the hardest; for according to my notion, they were real *know-nothings,* green as a pumpkin vine—couldn't in farming, I'll bet, raise a crop of turnips.[8]

43

There is a strain of Old Southwest backwoods brutality that is largely absent from Henning's comedies; however, like Twain, Thorpe, Augustus Baldwin Longstreet, and other humorists of the region, he is unabashed and hyperbolic in his idealization of backwoods folk.

Henning's break as a television auteur came in the mid-fifties. He created, produced, and wrote *The Bob Cummings Show* (NBC, 1955; CBS, 1955–57; NBC, 1957–59; ABC, 1959–61; known in syndication as *Love That Bob*). Though he did not address himself directly to the country/city paradigm in his first sitcom, Henning did manage to establish a number of his insistent concerns. The show starred Bob Cummings as a Hollywood playboy who shares a house with his widowed sister and her teenage son. Bob Collins is a swinging fashion photographer, constantly on the make for the models and starlets who fill his studio. His style is often cramped, however, by his sister Margaret, who is determined to give her son Chuck (Dwayne Hickman) a wholesome, "old-fashioned" home life. Chuck embodies a Henning dilemma. Drawn to the slick glamour of his Uncle Bob's Southern California life, he is continually reminded of the moral superiority of his mother's "traditional" values, values she has carried with her from the Midwest. Bob, a product of the same midwestern home, seems frustrated but ultimately acquiesces to Middle American righteousness. In this early work, Henning also created the character of the lovelorn dilettante Pamela Livingston for actress Nancy Kulp. She would reprise the role as Jane Hathaway in Henning's next project, *The Beverly Hillbillies*.

After flirting with hillbilly characters and themes from time to time throughout his career, Henning finally got the opportunity to explore and exploit the concept fully in his new show. "I've wanted to write something about these lovable people ever since [childhood]," he said of the *Hillbillies* in the press release that accompanied its premiere on the fall 1962 CBS schedule.[9] According to Henning, the key to success of a sitcom lies in the creation of likable characters: "You can hate someone in a movie and enjoy it, but you don't want to see him again— or ever. In television, you need characters you'll like and want to see every week for years."[10] He felt sure he had found such a character in a backwoods frontiersman whose virtue would dazzle amidst the decay of modern Southern California life. Henning recalls building his concept into a series "by working out the character of Jed Clampett, patriarch of the hillbilly clan."[11]

The narrative thrust of Henning's tale is succinctly outlined in the lyrics of the bluegrass song that accompanies the signatory montage opening each episode:

Come and listen to my story 'bout a man named Jed,
A poor mountaineer, barely kept his family fed,
Then one day he was shootin' at some food,
When up through the ground come 'a bub-a-lin' crude,
—oil that is; black gold, Texas tea.

Well first thing you know old Jed's a millionaire,
The kinfolk said, "Jed, move away from there!"
They said, "Californie is the place you ought to be!"
So they loaded up the truck and they moved to Beverly,
—Hills that is; swimming pools, movie stars.

[Words and music by Paul Henning. Copyright Hen-Ten
Corporation, 1962; used with permission of Carolintone
Music Company, Inc.]

This etiological exordium was recorded by Lester Flatt and Earl Scruggs and released to Country and Western radio stations as "The Ballad of Jed Clampett." It soon found its way to the top of the C&W charts. Walt Disney had demonstrated the effectiveness of songs and other cultural artifacts in promoting films and TV shows (e.g., "The Ballad of Davy Crockett" and the

Official Davy Crockett Coonskin Cap), and the popularity of this song probably can be credited with helping to establish an immediate and loyal viewing audience. The song contains within it a number of familiar strains of American folklore and, in some ways, is suggestive of Henning's own Missouri-rags-to-California-riches story. In the grandest tradition of American dreaming, we have the story of a poor-but-honest rugged agrarian individual who acquires spectacular wealth. In Jed Clampett's story, however, unlike such earlier American success stories as Owen Wister's Virginian or Chicago's Al Capone, the trials of hard work have been deleted from causality. Jed simply lets go a round of buckshot, misses his prey, and we witness the marvelous oozing forth from the American soil of the much-prized fossil fuel. We can only speculate whether Henning viewed his own Hollywood fortune as a similar miracle. In any case, in creating the Clampett legend he follows Mark Twain's dictum, "You can't throw too much style into a miracle. It costs trouble, and work, and sometimes money; but it pays off in the end."[12] And pay off it did; *The Beverly Hillbillies* was an instant hit, reaching Nielsen's Top 10 in a matter of weeks.

Though the value of oil in the outside "modern" world is unknown to the preindustrial Ozark mountaineer (Jed fears the black sludge will only ruin his land for farming), corporate geologists who have been scouting the area get wind of the discovery, and a deal is quickly consummated with a multinational conglomerate, leaving Jed and his family with $25 million. We see, too, another trek westward by a backwoods family in the epic of American emigration. Here again there is a transformation on the familiar model. The Clampetts reach the golden shores of California not as penniless Okies looking for stoop labor but with their millions already on deposit at the bank and a mansion waiting for them. Yet, despite this invitation to catapult to the heights of the boom-time sixties, Jed is a reluctant emigrant.

"A man would have to be a fool to give up all this," Jed says of his log cabin home, despite its lack of electricity and indoor plumbing. "All this," he knows—and the viewer will learn—is a spiritual and not just a physical place. It is Jed's status-conscious Cousin Pearl, a town lady and a piano teacher, who convinces Jed to leave his beloved hills. She does this with three inducements, which form the narrative center of the more than

200 episodes that will follow. She argues that Jed must move the family to California because only in that promised land can his daughter Elly May find a suitable husband and her own son Jethro a proper career; furthermore (least important to the humble Jed), only in such a place can a man of his newfound means live a fitting Lifestyle among the "right" people. Like the duty-bound Lincoln departing his beloved Illinois for the burdens and responsibilities of Washington, D.C., Jed wistfully agrees to follow Pearl's counsel.[13] Jed's Granny, who helped to raise him and has kept his home since the death of his wife, is less easily convinced. Like Steinbeck's Grampa Joad, she must be taken forcibly in her rocking chair and placed in the family's flatbed truck.

Over the next decade, all of Cousin Pearl's promises remain unfulfilled. Elly May never marries. Jethro never settles on a career. Granny never loses her desire to return to the hills. Neither Jed nor the other members of the family are able to establish genuine ties to the "modern" world they enter. The urban utopia proves sterile. An impressive bank account is all they will ever share with their neighbors.

"Jed was to be a tall man of simple, homespun honesty and dignity—the kind of Ozark mountaineer I knew as a boy," Henning recalled. "I had Buddy Ebsen in mind from the beginning. I knew he'd been a dancer, with all kinds of grace and presence, who really knew how to carry himself."[14] Ebsen, who had played second banana roles ranging from Shirley Temple's dancing partner in *Captain January* (1933) to Davy Crockett's sidekick in the 1950s Disney film series, did not disappoint Henning in the starring role. Jed indeed is selfless, honest, fair, and upright, a yeoman beyond the fantasies of Jefferson. Even vast and sudden wealth does not reorder his righteous priorities. Often seen sitting out in front of his thirty-two-room mansion whittling, or attending to menial chores around the grounds, Jed (like Tyler's Jonathan) is more importantly a moral interlocutor than a dramatic protagonist. In him, Henning establishes a vortex of identification. Jed's unshakable moral logic and solid horse sense are constantly contrasted with the various alternatives embodied in the identities of the other characters.

Pearl's son Jethro, played by Max Baer, Jr. (son of the one-time heavyweight boxing champion) leaves his mother's home in Bug Tussle to go to California with his rich uncle. He is the only truly enthusiastic emigrant. In the early episodes Henning, at his burlesque best, had the brawny Baer double in the drag role of Jethro's twin sister, Jethreen. The plot line had to be dropped, however, when Bea Benaderet, the actress who played the shy Jethreen's mother, was spun off into another Henning show. As a young man entering adulthood, Jethro is chiefly concerned with his education and career. He is enrolled in the fifth grade at the Potts School, an exclusive Beverly Hills day school. The genteel principal and faculty are aghast at the very idea of a twenty-year-old hayseed in jeans and a rope belt even entering the school building. They are coerced into enrolling him, however, through the efforts of Milburn Drysdale, the Clampetts' banker, who holds the school's mortgage. There is nothing in Beverly Hills considered so grotesque that it cannot be overlooked in the name of the almighty dollar. Eventually Jethro "graduates" the sixth grade and attempts to pursue careers as a brain surgeon, "double-naught" spy, charismatic leader of a hippie cult, and astronaut. (The Bodines, both mother Pearl and son Jethro, show a streak of status consciousness which is absent from the Clampett character. This may reflect the fact that they are "from town," as opposed to the backwoods Clampetts.) Jethro's aborted career attempts constitute one of Henning's major narrative themes. While Jethro occasionally expresses romantic feelings, he proves hopelessly naive and unsuccessful as a lover, ultimately preferring Granny's cooking to any of the money-hungry city women he meets. Like Al Capp's Li'l Abner, whom he resembles in figure and dress, Jethro's exaggerated physical prowess in no way extends to his love life. Of all the hillbillies, he is decidedly the most sympathetic to the modern, technology-based culture of Southern California. He is the only hillbilly who can drive a car and the only one susceptible to the media fads that seem to dominate Henning's Beverly Hills. Perhaps most to the point in terms of Jethro's role is that despite his "superior education" and "broader awareness," or perhaps because of it, he commits acts of stupidity so gross as to be obvious not only to the viewer but to the other family members as well. Uncle Jed, though uneducated, is a paragon of common sense and is most often Jethro's foil in matters of simple intelligence. At the same time, though he is a strapping young mountain man, Jethro must live in constant fear of his female cousin Elly May who repeatedly "whups" him

47

in wrestling matches. In this too there is the suggestion of Li'l Abner. As a would-be "modern" youth, Jethro often mocks Granny for clinging to the customs of the hills. He has nothing but derision for her home remedies and poultices, yet they invariably prove more effective than his "scientific" approaches. Jethro is, in many ways, a striking burlesque of American middle-class values. He is young, strong, handsome, wealthy, a defender of the "modern" point of view, not to mention white, male, and heterosexually inclined, and yet he is, in effect, a total zero, a *nebbish* of the most pathetic order. Jethro suffers the humiliations of displacement more severely than any of the Clampetts. He has been seduced by urban life, but he cannot become a part of it.

The beautiful Elly May (Donna Douglas), a paragon of sweetness and virtue, is more interested in her "critters" than in any of the suitors procured for her through the efforts of Jed, Granny, or the family's banker/next-door neighbor Mr. Drysdale. At one point Jed buys a bankrupt movie studio in the simple hope of discovering at least one contract player who will interest his daughter. Elly, however, is unimpressed by Dash Riprock, Biff Steel, or any of the studio's stable of vapid male ingenues, preferring the company of Cousin Bessy, her pet chimpanzee. Displaying none of the domestic virtues embodied in Granny (Elly is particularly notorious in the kitchen), her Diana-like qualities are regarded affectionately but worrisomely by Jed, who expresses anxiety over her maidenhood. She is not unhappy in her new surroundings, however, as she is able to establish a menagerie of "critters" to love and care for on the mansion grounds. If anything, she is enamored of the exotic forms of wildlife she encounters at the Los Angeles pet shops and zoos. The cages that imprison these animals are the only things that incite her anger; she buys and brings home all the "critters" she can. Elly's character remains virtually undeveloped beyond these simple givens throughout the series. She is rarely the center of dramatic attention. Henning tended to use her primarily as an ornament, offering long D. W. Griffith-like portrait shots of her face and dressing her in tight flannel shirts and tighter jeans. For variety, he occasionally outfitted her in swimsuits and even formal evening wear.

Granny, as the chief antagonist to modern culture, is perhaps the most compelling of the hillbillies. Master chef, house-keeper extraordinaire of the sprawling mansion, natural/organic doctor, and stubborn partisan of the Confederacy, Irene Ryan's Granny is an important element of Henning's sitcosmology. Her role personifies the continuing tensions between the idealized mother-culture community of the hills and the technologically governed *Gesellschaft* of Beverly Hills. As a displaced priestess of the old culture living in exile among nonbelievers, Granny is not swayed from her faith. She expresses her alienation from the technoworld in no uncertain terms. At one point she arrives **49** at Drysdale's Commerce Bank with her century-old wheelbar-row, demanding her cut of the Clampett millions in gold, ready to push it across the Rockies in time for the Annual Spring Possum Festival, which, much to her outraged amazement, is uncelebrated in Beverly Hills.

It is principally through the efforts of Granny that the old culture remains intact behind the superficial facade of the man-sion. Her cuisine—various dishes making use of possum, hawk, gopher, and the like—is considered beyond compare by the family as well as visiting home folks. The culturally narrow moderns react with revulsion to these unfamiliar dishes and rarely stay for dinner. Granny remakes the mansion into a suit-able habitat for the familiar culture. The leisure-class billiards room becomes the "fancy eatin' room." Curtains are hung over the entrance to the living room, making it into a traditional parlor, suitable for "courtin' and sparkin'." A root cellar is dug out on the patio. At one point an exact replica of the family's log cabin is built right on the mansion grounds; Granny promptly moves in. But perhaps the most profound transformation is the naturalization of the Olympic-sized swimming pool that sits behind the house into the "cee-ment pond." Here the estate merges with nature, such as it is in Beverly Hills. The "cee-ment pond" becomes an ersatz ecosystem, surrounded by the ever-growing menagerie of critters brought home by Elly May. Barn-yard chickens cluck around the edges as Elly teaches her cats to swim. An ostrich stares confusedly at Henning's camera.

Yet Granny is unsatisfied by her relatively circumscript vec-tor of cultural hegemony. In the *Gemeinschaft* of the hills, she was respected and depended upon; she was a doctor, midwife, matchmaker, moonshiner, and meteorologist. Beverly Hills has respect for neither age nor functional prowess; she is regarded as little more than a crank. Unimpressed by store-bought detergents, she insists on making lye soap in the backyard. Her neighbors find the smell distasteful and call the police. When she practices her proven "doctoring" talents even in the privacy of her own home, she is threatened with legal action by the local chapter of the AMA. The city dwellers cannot accept her methods because they do not conform to industrial-leisure-class standards. As Thorstein Veblen points out, hard work and self-reliance become emblems of shame in a society whose values are pecuniary.[15] Granny is a conspicuous nonconsumer, and this provokes the hostility of neighbors in what Waldo Frank referred to as "our comfort worshipping Republic."[16] She is proud and self-confident enough to remain unshaken, though she is resentful that her proven, practical talents are not appreciated. In the age of specialization her diverse capabilities distort her into a lunatic. And yet, in the face of it all, Granny repeatedly triumphs. If Cecil, her weather beetle, indicates that it's going to rain and a television meteorologist predicts zero percent chance of precipitation, the viewer can expect showers within the half hour.

Granny's stubbornness and quick temper (she goes for her shotgun at the slightest provocation) remove her, however, from the heroic realm. Henning's persona is clearly the less radical Jed. More intelligent than Jethro, more aware of the ways of the world than Elly May, more tolerant and adaptable than Granny, and stronger, more fair-minded and compassionate than any of the city people, Jed becomes the sole heroic possibility, with the soft underbelly of his naiveté as his more frustrating than tragic flaw. Henning makes it easy to become distanced and amused by Jed's never-ending innocence of modern appurtenances, language, customs—and corruption. However, we respect him all the more as the superficiality of these things becomes obvious in the light of his rigorous adherence to a spotless code of crudely stated though elegantly conceived ethics. This is precisely the ploy used by Royall Tyler in his eighteenth-century Jonathan character. Jed—and not the assimilation-minded Jethro—remains the family leader in the new land. Unlike Jethro, who makes a greenhorn fool of himself, Jed does not pretend to understand the styles of the new culture, but his dedication to the "code of the hills," a universal and eternal guide to living, allows him to distinguish good from evil and to protect his family's integrity.

Outside the Clampett family, Henning creates an ethical landscape of modern society that is a decidedly bleak wasteland. The Clampetts, whose money frees them from daily worry and allows them the luxury of their naiveté, wrestle with what Henning treats as the relatively esoteric problems of stubbornness, pride, or vanity. These problems are resolved easily enough with simple moral homilies delivered by Jed in the traditional sitcom style of a Jim Anderson, a Danny Williams, or perhaps more precisely, a Sheriff Andy Taylor or a Grandpappy Amos McCoy. The city folk, on the other hand, seem far past redemption.

Milburn Drysdale (Raymond Bailey), a greedy banker from beyond the novels of Dreiser, is Jed's next-door neighbor and financial chargé d'affaires. While Drysdale is fond of touting the virtuous, hardworking ways of the Clampetts in his public rhetoric, he is actually shocked and horrified by their ethically ruled, as opposed to money-ruled, thinking. He often faints dead away at Jed's generous suggestions of charity and fairness, as when Jed insists on paying for his nephew's equipment and training when Jethro faces military induction (Vietnam Period). As the series progresses over the years, Drysdale's greediness grows in both intensity and pettiness. Henning overplays the caricature until it reaches a point of burlesqued hyperbole in the latter episodes.

If Mr. Drysdale's capacity for emotion is limited to financial matters, mere money seems beneath the contempt of his wife Margarette (Harriet MacGibbon). Their marriage is singularly loveless. Even the miraculous appearance of Sonny Drysdale ("a perennial college student and playboy,"[17] portrayed by veteran television comedian Louis Nye) does nothing to mitigate the coldness of the only marriage regularly portrayed in the series; we learn he is Mrs. Drysdale's child by a previous husband. Though an émigré herself (from the blue-blooded townhouses of Beacon Hill), Mrs. Drysdale is horrified and disgusted by the "primitive riffraff" who have invaded her exclusive neighborhood. A "true aristocrat," she cares nothing for the Clampett millions lying in her family's bank and objects to the

51

hillbillies on frankly class grounds. By contrast, her nouveau riche husband (who is president of the bank by virtue of their marriage) is a fawning sycophant to the Clampetts. Unlike her contemporary sitcom millionairess counterpart, Lovey Howell of *Gilligan's Island* (CBS, 1964–67), who is also forced by circumstances to live among her inferiors, Mrs. Drysdale is in no way sweet or sensitive beneath her frippery. Pretentious, obnoxious, and antidemocratic, she rarely gains our sympathies, even when suffering self-perceived humiliations at the hands of her uncouth neighbors. In one cluster of episodes, we see the absurdity of her snobbery and class pretension with particular clarity. With the chairperson of her antiquarian society about to pay a visit from New England, Mrs. Drysdale fears that the Clampetts' very presence in the neighborhood will result in her being thrown out of the organization. She unsuccessfully tries every trick she can think of to get them out of town. Madam Chairman (played by Henning veteran Rosemary De Camp) arrives but is far from horrified by the Clampetts. Instead, she is thrilled to discover in them the simple virtues that made America great, not to mention the gold mine of Colonial Period artifacts in daily use at the Clampett estate.

The distinctive mark of culture on character is not limited by Henning to his human characters. The Clampett dog, Duke, seems to be a lazy, good-for-nothing old hound; the camera often finds him asleep beneath a bench in the noonday sun. Yet, when called upon by his master, Duke proves himself an able watchdog and hunter. Claude, Mrs. Drysdale's stylishly coiffed French poodle, on the other hand, pays weekly visits to a psychiatrist and regularly consumes tranquilizers. Both of these addictions are his mistress's as well. When Mrs. Drysdale imports a suitable mate for Claude from the old country (France, of course), the concubine secretly escapes and spends the evening with Duke, this resulting in a litter of mongrels that sends the unsuspecting Mrs. Drysdale into a swoon.

And yet the neurotic obsessions of the Drysdales are merely emblematic of the endless procession of con persons, goldbricks, gold diggers, and otherwise morally debauched city people who cross the Clampett threshhold, palms wide.

The only nonhillbilly character worth an ethical slug nickel is the witty and urbane, if terminally dilletantish, Vassar-educated Jane Hathaway. Nancy Kulp is brilliant in the role of Mr. Drysdale's self-consciously flat-chested secretary. As in *Love That Bob,* she is Henning's personification of *Kultur.* (Her subsequent effort in Lear and Yorkin's *Sanford and Son* is a pale reprise.) Though sexually frustrated, Miss Hathaway displays more libidinous energy than any of Henning's other characters. Jethro is the continuing object of her desire, though he never manages to pick up on her more than obvious cues. Of the city folk, she is clearly the moral paragon, berating Mr. Drysdale for his greediness, even at the risk of her job, and clearly opposing Mrs. Drysdale's blind snobbery, often with lofty speeches on the theoretical virtues of democratic attitudes. Despite her hard work and conscientiousness, she is underpaid and overworked by Banker Drysdale. More than once he fires her. Of course she is ultimately indispensable to the operation of the bank, and Drysdale gets her back to her desk by tearfully exploiting her unflagging loyalty. Miss Hathaway's quest for sexual gratification is painfully pathetic. She is consistently judged by her homely appearance and despised for her "culture" and education—except by the Clampetts. They often do not understand what she is talking about when she breaks into Elizabethan soliloquies on any of a thousand topics, but they do understand Miss Jane as a "nice" person and are happy to treat her as one of their own. While Jed is the head of the Clampett household because of his moral authority, Jane Hathaway is the least powerful modern as a result of her ethical concerns.

The Beverly Hillbillies clearly represents a departure from the formula that dominated the sitcom throughout the 1950s. Sitcoms, especially nuclear-family sitcoms, had most often portrayed idyllic hierarchical families living in homogeneous community settings. A member of the family—usually a child—succumbs to some hedonistic temptation or a "too easy" solution to some pressing problem. This morally lax attitude or act precipitates a crisis of guilt and alienation, which is then solved by the delivery of a moral pronouncement by the father, mother, or sometimes even another child. Such top-rated sitcoms as *The Trouble with Father* (CBS, 1950–55), *Make Room for Daddy* (a.k.a. *The Danny Thomas Show;* ABC, 1953–56; CBS 1957–64), *Leave It to Beaver* (CBS, 1957–63), and *The Donna Reed Show*

(ABC, 1958–64), among others, clearly come out of this mold. *Father Knows Best* (CBS, 1954–55; NBC, 1956–58; CBS, 1958–64) is perhaps the sterling exemplar. This tradition, popular since the Andy Hardy movies and radio days, went into decline in the midsixties though a few favorites, notably *The Andy Griffith Show* (CBS, 1960–68), managed to hang on well into the Beatles/Vietnam Period. *The Beverly Hillbillies* differs from these shows in that the individual crisis of a family member is not the weekly center of narrative concern. Perhaps Henning's break with formula is best illustrated by a comparison with *The Real McCoys* (ABC, 1957–64), a show that appears to share a number of its thematic concerns. Like the Clampetts, the McCoys are poor dirt farmers (in this case from the hills of West Virginia) who come west to make a new start. They settle not on the Southern California Gold Coast but rather on a modest family farm in the Steinbeckian regions of the San Joaquin Valley. Like most of the series made by Danny Thomas Productions, *The Real McCoys* never transcends a rigorous obligation to a light-hearted species of social realism. The McCoys remain at least somewhat at the mercy of the cyclical ups and downs of entrepreneurial family farming. As in the Henning series, the narrative focuses on the problems of the emigrant family in adapting to the "modern" cultural climate of California, the perennial bellwether of the future. Its humor, however, is always a secondary concern to the resolution of shame and guilt tensions that arise for the McCoys in their cultural dislocation. The girls at school make fun of the teenager Hassie for her unstylish clothing. Little Luke gets into a fight at school over an arrogant remark about West Virginia. Pepino, the McCoys' Mexican-American hired hand (who, incidentally, addresses Grandpa McCoy as "Señor Grampa") makes his home in the family barn, an outsider among outsiders. The viewer is invited to empathize with the pathetic and luxuriate in the cathartic triumph of values over pettiness.

This is not the case in *The Beverly Hillbillies*. As millionaires, the Clampetts are not subject to the pressures to adapt and conform that are incumbent upon the McCoys. The feelings of Henning's characters are never really vulnerable to the pathetic sting. Instead, we are invited to turn our attention to their outlooks, beliefs, and methods of coping with the world and evaluate these in terms of our own—and official—wisdom. Free of Dickensian emotional identification, *The Beverly Hillbillies* invites the viewer into the epic arena of testing cultural assumptions. Moral didacticism and humor may indeed be inherent structural elements of the sitcom form. Henning simply reverses the old family sitcom priorities and makes humor the prominent object of the weekly episode, reducing the moral element to a single continuing cultural struggle between the country folk (healthy, good) and the city people (neurotic, bad). The Clampetts will not be corrupted; the Drysdales will not be purified. Establishing these as givens, Henning proceeds to slapstick farce.

55

Grandpappy Amos McCoy (Walter Brennan) is Granny's geriatric counterpart as defender of the old faith and is every bit as stubborn and prideful as she is. But he is forced by the family's modest circumstances to make painful compromises of his beliefs. Granny is insulated from compromise by virtue of her wealth and can continue to live purely by her creed. Amos McCoy often feels the pain of rejection and displacement directly. His farming methods—and indeed his very ideals of family life—are constantly undermined by the California host culture. On the other hand, Granny is not so much insulted by, say, Mrs. Drysdale's rejection of her as she is outraged by such unprovoked hostility from a neighbor. Mrs. Drysdale, a bad neighbor, offends her cultural sensibility, and she simply writes her off as "downright o'nery." Amos McCoy cannot afford such an attitude toward his neighbor George MacMichaels; they belong to the same grain cooperative.

Jethro, like Big Luke McCoy, is a young man seeking to become successful in life, yet the consequences of failure are never real possibilities for him. When Jethro decides to become a film director, for example, he simply puts on a beret and shows up for work at his uncle's studio. When he expresses a desire to go into the business world, Mr. Drysdale immediately appoints him Vice-President of the Commerce Bank in Charge of Clampett Money. Jethro can afford to play Hamlet with his life; Luke McCoy's problems are far more banal.

Even the idealized beauty of Elly May, when contrasted with the plain-Janeishness of Hassie McCoy, demonstrates Henning's rejection of sympathetic identification as a dramatic device. In

The Real McCoys, identification derives from the weekly trials of the various characters. In *The Beverly Hillbillies,* the plot is restricted to farce. Jessica Milner Davis has pointed out that the etymological root of the term "farce" is the Latin verb *farcire,* "to stuff." Henning conjures a single paradigm, country-folk innocence/city-slicker decadence, and "stuffs" it with slapstick humor. Identification occurs not so much with one character or another as it does with one cultural point of view or the other. The antagonists are cultures. A pitched battle is fought in each **56** episode between the homespun, right-minded values of the Clampetts, which represent a traditional, folkish, "real American" culture, and a cutthroat, money-ruled technocracy, represented by the city people. Though as consumers we may find ourselves coveting the slick and easy value-free luxuries of "modern" Beverly Hills, in our hearts we cannot help but root for Henning's fair and friendly preindustrial culture. Disarming the critical capacity of the viewer with his relentless mockery of modernity, Henning glorifies this folkish vision of a golden preindustrial American past. That such a past ever existed in America or elsewhere is a dubious proposition at best. It is easy to believe in such a past, however, as a relief from the bleak prospects of life in a mechanical world. If we find ourselves on a treadmill running after money, why not blame the machine itself for our corruption? Erik Barnouw writes:

> To [the critics'] consternation the series [*The Beverly Hill-billies*] won admirers among sophisticates, who saw it rather as a lampoon on a money-oriented society represented by Beverly Hills. The unchanging ways of the Clampett clan seemed a kind of uncorruptibility.[18]

Henning presents us with characters who are charged cultural entities. The children of society are corrupt; the children of the land are noble. The Clampetts are a noble possibility conjured from America's cultural unconscious. Paradoxically, it is the Clampett money, the very symbol of corruption, that protects them from the dissipating influences of the metropolis. It is impossible to take this model seriously if one doesn't have the $25 million. Clampett virtue is, alas, paradise lost for most of us. Henning's vision is not dynamic but merely whimsical and nostalgic. He has created a nihilistic caricature of modern life, not a satire. We are mocked but not instructed. This is terrifying and funny, but mostly funny.

Given these limitations, the Clampetts' rejection of modern conveniences is still a wild slap at modern decadence. Not only are the hillbillies satisfied by the simple comfort, cleanliness, and cuisine of Granny's preindustrial home (they reject all attempts to supply them with servants), but they cannot even understand the concept underlying many of the modern appurtenances that lie, unused, at their fingertips. Henning often makes this point with abandoned absurdity. For example, the Clampetts are unable to establish a cause-and-effect relationship between the ringing of the mansion's electric doorbell and the arrival of guests:

"There's that strange music again, Uncle Jed," says Jethro.

"What is that, boy?" Jed asks his "educated" nephew.

"I don't know, but I'll tell you one thing: There's always somebody a'comin' to the door five minutes after we hear it," Jethro replies.

Eventually the frustrated visitor pounds on the door with the ornamental knocker. The concept of "ornamental" in such a context is of course culturally alien to the functionally minded Clampetts.

The transfiguration of the billiards table into the "fancy eatin' table" logically follows. It is another Veblenesque dig. Confronted with the racks of seemingly useless pool cues on the wall, the Clampetts naturally seek to deduce their function. They are used as "handy pot passers." The head of a rhinoceros mounted on the wall is assumed to be the head of a strange game animal: a "bill-ee-ard."

In a similar vein, Granny rejects store-bought products not so much as emblems of laziness and spiritual decay but more emphatically for their inferiority to her homemade products. As viewers, we are teased that the products we strive so hard to afford aren't as good as those we might make ourselves. Henning's barbs at consumerism are of course interrupted by commercials, and this is the value-free ballet of television. Yet the viewer identifies with Granny's point of view because of its obvious moral superiority. The consumer is guilty; the producer is rich. Unlike the McCoys or most Americans, the Clam-

57

petts can proudly live their mother-culture lives in the ghetto they establish on the mansion grounds. They refuse to be assimilated.

Henning continued to treat and exploit these themes in the two series he spun off from *The Beverly Hillbillies: Petticoat Junction* (CBS, 1963–70) and *Green Acres* (CBS, 1965–71), especially the latter.

58   *Petticoat Junction* is in many ways a flaccid retreat to the "realistic" solving of ethical family dilemmas of the 1950s sitcom, as outlined above. Henning conceived the series principally as a vehicle for Bea Benaderet, an actress who had played Henning roles for years, first as Blanche Morton on *The Burns and Allen Show* and later as Cousin Pearl on the *Hillbillies*. *Petticoat Junction* was not a spin-off in the strictest sense of the term; the identity of the key character was completely changed. After a few years, with Cousin Pearl gone and forgotten, Henning was able to initiate crossover episodes between the two shows. Fond of Benaderet's matriarchal qualities, Henning originally had her test for the role of Granny. Though she did not get that role, he was effusive in his praise of her:

> I'd known Bea and her great talents for twenty years, and I had her in mind for the part of Cousin Pearl. But I told her to go ahead and test for Granny—which she did, along with Irene Ryan and others. Then Bea took one look at the way Irene did the part and said to me, "There's your Granny." Of course she was right—and Bea became Cousin Pearl at the beginning of the series. A year later I tailored the starring role of Kate Bradley on *Petticoat Junction* for Bea. She was modeled on my boyhood memories of a friendly little woman who operated a rural hotel in Eldon, Missouri. Here again, it was a case of creating likable, memorable characters and telling their problems in a humorous way.[19]

Kate Bradley is the widowed proprietress of a tiny backwoods hotel lying on the single-track branch railroad between Hooterville and Pixley. Three daughters meant, of course, endless crises of manners, mores, and morals, and, as can always be expected in the Henning world, the old ways were indeed the best ways. Having moved his setting out of the modern city,

Henning restricted the possibilities of city/country contrast in this show. The unfortunate result was that the country folk became nauseatingly cute. Only a few elements of Henning's badinage managed to surface in *Petticoat Junction*. Uncle Joe (Edgar Buchanan) is a kind of Social Security–aged Jethro—still searching for a career but without a millionaire uncle to fall back on. His undoing is his incorrigible laziness, a perception of him shared by the other characters and the viewer. Though a failed would-be bourgeois and, in fact, something of a financial burden to the struggling Bradleys, he is indulged, loved, and cared for by the more industrious members of his family and the Hooterville *Gemeinschaft*. Perhaps more to the point is the character of Homer Bedloe (Charles Lane), the corporate railroad efficiency expert who is bent on closing down the branch line that keeps the Shady Rest Hotel in business. Structurally, he performs the same function as Drysdale in the *Hillbillies*. However, the immediate threat he represents to an important institution of the "hills" culture makes him a more onerous villain. The vulnerability of the Bradleys, as compared to the invincibility of the millionaire Clampetts, reinforces his evil image. Bedloe is more than merely greedy. His villainy is on the level of the corporate businessmen who take the Joads' farm in *The Grapes of Wrath*. Armed with "scientific" charts and graphs that condemn the tiny rail line to oblivion in red ink, he cares nothing for the damage its closing would cause the Hootervillians; he can see no farther than the bottom line. Yet the branch is repeatedly saved by the Chairman of the Board of the railroad who, like Henning, despite appearances to the contrary, is just a sentimental hillbilly boy at heart. The greatest contribution of *Petticoat Junction,* however, was not its weak, predictable story line but its establishment of the geographical cosmos of Hooterville that Henning would use to greater advantage in *Green Acres.*

With *Green Acres,* Henning achieves his wildest and freest vision of American society and values—and his greatest artistic success. By setting *Petticoat Junction* in the backwoods, Henning sacrificed the watershed of his humor: the daily confrontation of American ancient and modern. He recaptured it in *Green Acres* by bringing a pair of hyperbolic moderns right into the heart of the hills culture. The show is essentially a mirror reversal of *The Beverly Hillbillies*. Oliver Wendell Douglas (Eddie Albert) is a wealthy New York attorney who decides to give up his lucrative practice and Park Avenue penthouse and "drop out" (1965) of the rat race to fulfill his boyhood dream of working an American family farm. His wife Lisa, a former Hungarian countess played with Stanislavskian passion by Eva Gabor, is not anxious to forsake Metropolis for Hooterville. The opening signatory montage intercuts shots of Hooterville and Manhattan as the principals sing:

60

OLIVER: Green Acres is the place to be,
             Farm livin' is the life for me,
             Land stretching out so far and wide,
             Keep Manhattan, just give me that countryside.
LISA: New York is where I'd rather stay,
             I get allergic smelling hay,
             I just adore a penthouse view,
             Darling I love you, but give me Park Avenue.
OLIVER: The chores!
LISA: The stores!
OLIVER: Fresh Air!
LISA: Times Square!
OLIVER: You are my wife. . . .
LISA: Goodbye, city life. . . .
ENSEMBLE: Green Acres, we are there.
[Words and music by Vic Mizzy; © 1965 Fwy Music Company; assigned 1983 to Orion Music Publishing, Inc.* Administered by Fricourt Music Company (ASCAP)]

The dapper Douglases arrive in their Lincoln Continental convertible at a ramshackle old farm, which has been sold to them by Mr. Haney (Pat Buttram). The Henning knave figure is familiar. On the scale of a rural drummer, Haney is every bit as much a cutthroat capitalist as Drysdale and Bedloe. He mercilessly bleeds Oliver, the naive city slicker (naiveté has come full circle), selling him every manner of device and machine necessary for "modern American agriculture." None of them works. Oliver can see no conflict between his romantic visions of run-

*Lyrics to "THEME FROM GREEN ACRES." Printed by permission of Orion Music Publishing, Inc. All Rights Reserved.

ning a "traditional American yeoman's farm" and, at the same time, using all the "latest methods" to do it. "Isn't that," demands the idealistic attorney, "what made America great?" He continually seeks "scientific" advice from the county agent, Hank Kimball. Alvy Moore, in the role of the modern bureaucrat Kimball, provides some of Henning's most hilarious comic moments in classical "double-talk" scenes that follow the tradition of Al Kelly and Professor Irwin Corey. Undaunted, Oliver is resolved to farm by the book—and teach the doubting locals a lesson or two about modern American agriscience. However, the alarming truth of which everyone but urbane Oliver is aware is that cause-and-effect, as preached by such as Newton, Descartes, and Luther Burbank, is simply not the operative principle of the Hooterville universe. Lisa, no empiricist, instinctively comprehends this and, despite her reluctance to become a farm wife, fits in well with the local culture. Perhaps her roots in a traditional, preindustrial European feudal system make this at least somewhat logical. Neither Lisa nor any of the locals has any trouble accepting the fact that at Green Acres one pushes down the toaster to turn on the lights or opens the refrigerator door to light the oven. Fred Ziffel's pig, Arnold, is an avid television watcher and is working on a book. New Yorker Oliver simply stands by and watches in open-mouthed disbelief.

61

Oliver's faith in reason and scientific order is as messianic as Granny's faith in her notion of the universe. At Sam Drucker's General Store (this becomes the center of the Henning universe; it is patronized by the residents of *Petticoat Junction* and even the visiting Clampetts from time to time), the former barrister can often be seen expounding on these beliefs. Echoing the public-speaking style of Jane Hathaway, he makes romantic speeches about the virtues of American family farming, shamelessly posing for the camera as a heroic country gentleman. A fife and drum strike up "Yankee Doodle Dandy" on the sound track. "Uh-oh," Fred Ziffel says to the good old boys around the cracker barrel. "There goes that music again. Mr. Douglas is about to make one of his speeches. I've got some chores to do."

The farmers shrug and return to their work, getting by with their traditional methods as they always have. Oliver meanwhile must live off his New York bank account.

The Douglases attempt to create a "modern" cultural ghetto

inside their dilapidated old farmhouse, just as the Clampetts create a "traditional" ghetto inside their fabulous mansion. Oliver and Lisa are not nearly so successful. They order a telephone, but the local phone company has only enough cable to reach the top of the telephone pole outside their house. They climb the pole when the phone rings, most often too late to get the call. They bring their "miracle age" appliances from New York, but these prove a bit too much for the farmhouse's electrical system. Their king-size designer bed takes up virtually the entire bedroom so that they must climb over it to cross the room.

In *Green Acres,* Henning subjects the audience itself to cultural dislocation. As citizens of the technoworld, viewers cannot help but identify with Oliver and his faith in rational order, but Henning pulls the rug out from beneath our empirical feet. The laws of scientific thinking may hold true where they are subscribed to as cultural assumptions—in places such as New York and Los Angeles (except for the Clampett mansion)—but then other orders also obtain where they are believed in. "Reality" is merely a function of culture.

Henning used the same dramatic formula for *Green Acres* that he created for the *Hillbillies.* Russel Nye incorrectly describes this as "the one joke series."[20] In fact, Henning's shows are filled with thousands of jokes. They could more appropriately be called "one dramatic conflict series." In *Green Acres,* Henning gives us the same dramatic conflict as the basis for humor that he gave us in the *Hillbillies:* modern culture versus folk culture. In both cases, the object of lampoon is modernity.

Both *The Beverly Hillbillies* and *Green Acres* were still in Nielsen's Top 20 in 1970. However, they became casualties of the sweeping changes in television programming—and cultural programming in general—that occurred as Vietnam-Era polarization began to stabilize into Me-Decade hip. Refinements in demographic audience analysis techniques pushed the advertising agencies and networks toward a courtship of "hip" and "relevant" programming that would institutionalize the styles of the emerging group of 18–34-year-olds. After twenty years of measuring success in terms of absolute headcount, the term "quality audience" was first heard bouncing between the concrete walls of Madison and Sixth avenues. Henning had not completely avoided the tumult of the sixties. Beatniks, hippies, and counterculture types of all kinds had visited the Clampett mansion at one time or another, but these were obvious burlesques and, furthermore, Henning had always managed to avoid the direct treatment of immediate political issues. The Clampetts were "above" politics. They were neither liberal nor conservative in any of the modern political senses. Individual virtue and evil were epic, apolitical qualities. The Henning sitcom was the opposite of what the new wisdom called for.

CBS, the industry's sitcom pacemaker since its inception, wiped its slate clean of these "rural comedies" at the end of the 1970–71 season in favor of a more "realistic" portrayal of domestic urban/suburban American life[21]—hence the rise to prominence of Norman Lear and Grant Tinker. The political debate of Archie and Mike replaced the absurd conversation of Jed and Jethro. The "believable" dilemmas of career woman Mary Richards displaced the surrealistic dilemma of Oliver Wendell Douglas. The Polarization Era was over, and it was time to make a sitcom of it. The 1971 television season found the prime-time network schedules without new Henning work for virtually the first time in television history. More than a decade later, echoes of Henning's sitcom style could be heard in the corn-pone antics of Boss Hogg and Sheriff Roscoe P. Coltrane on *Dukes of Hazzard,* one of the most popular prime-time series of the eighties.

63

The Comedy of ★ 3
Public Safety

She's filing her nails while they're dragging the lake,
She's watching the detectives,
Ooh, he's so cute.
Elvis Costello, "Watching the Detectives" © 1977 PLAN-
        GENT VISIONS MUSIC LIMITED for the world.

The sitcom offers representation of the interior, the domestic, the banal, and the intimate. The genre comments on American society microscopically, portraying the effects of culture on
a family, extended family, vocational group, or other micro-
cosmic social unit. Culture is revealed in the opinions and styles
of the various demographic components of this grass-roots unit.
Periodic revisions of taste in dress, interior decoration, linguistic construction, personal hygiene, and so on, serve the con-
sumerist obligation of the industry. The sexes, the generations,
the races, and occasionally the classes confront each other in
long-term dialogues. A ritual quality grows out of the singular
direction of these exchanges: from the divisive clash of styles to
the solidarity of family and community. Husbands and wives
yield to the magical democratic centralism of marriage. The
young are instructed, the old reminded. A note of racial harmony speaks to a vision of the brighter day. The poor resolve
to overcome their dilemma by emulating the rich. The chaotic
incompatibilities of personal tastes and desires are exposed as
merely superficial. These disjunctions are even celebrated as

the humorous spices of life. A whirlwind resolution of conflicts reaffirms the tantalizing illusion of structural order in family, community, nation, and cosmos, which Plato made popular even before radio.

The crimeshow reaches a similarly comic conclusion but does so by means of obverse technique. Its focus is on the exterior, the exotic, and the broadly social. Dramatic conflict is not merely an inflated miniature misunderstanding but a brutal threat to civilization itself, which is deflated to manageable proportions. From a relatively panoramic *mise en scène* emerges a close-up of individuals—cops/private eyes and criminals—that reaffirms faith in the order of collective security promised by civilization in the form of the state.

Much has been written on the mythology of American crime. John Cawelti, a prolific writer on the subject, has called it our "great imaginative obsession."[1] Few who read American newspapers or fiction, or watch American film or television, could argue with this statement. American democracy has been repeatedly tested by outlaws, robber barons, gangsters, and crooked politicians; the threats of explicitly revolutionary political ideologies have been minor nuisances by comparison. The two epic arenas of American crimelore have been the Old West and the Inner City. In *The Six-Gun Mystique,* Cawelti argues that the definition and containment of crime were for more than a hundred years the central problem of the frontier nation.[2] The continuing glorification of laissez-faire competition and social Darwinist ideology since the realization of manifest destiny has fostered a heroic vision of the man of action that often engenders a benevolent indulgence of rule breaking. Al Capone, Bugsy Siegal, and Vito Corleone stand with Benjamin Franklin, Henry Ford, and the heroes of Horatio Alger's novels in the American pantheon. The nation's history is indeed richly colored by a heritage of crime, or at least legal ambiguity. In the Colonial Period, Anglo-America was largely populated by the persecuted practitioners of illegal European religions and felons transported from British jails. As Hawthorne demonstrates with distinctive clarity in "The May-Pole of Merry Mount," the newly freed victims of persecution were often anxious to establish rigid legal codes of their own to legitimize their status. Nationhood itself was achieved through revolution—a blatant act of treason against the crown. The first years of the Republic were plagued by the complexities of creating a legal system to replace the one that had been violated. The Constitution of the United States has been used to legalize chattel slavery and the carrying of guns—and to criminalize chattel slavery and the drinking of alcohol. The willingness to break the treaties that established national hegemony on the frontier was at least as strong as the inclination to sign them. The romance of the escape to the garden has been tempered by a passionate fear of the swamp.

67

Thus American legend comes to meaningful crisis at the vanishing point of individualism, nonconformity, zealous will— and crime. For every Wyatt Earp there is a Billy the Kid; for every J. Edgar Hoover there is a Pretty-Boy Floyd. A prism of belief separates the mad-dog terrorist from the valiant champion of legitimate rights. Where is heroic excitement? Out on the run with the desperadoes, or in the marshall's office? In the nightclub headquarters of the gangster, or in the interrogation room down at the stationhouse? Who are the heroes? Matt Dillon and Eliot Ness, with their low salaries and high moralities, or Jesse James and Legs Diamond, with their high styles and low-down ways? This rich ambiguity continues to concern American literature; the coexistence of Bellow's Moses Herzog and Mailer's Stephen Rojack underlines it. The movie screen has probably been the greatest scene of this battle for hearts and minds. From *Little Caesar* and *Public Enemy* to *Bonnie and Clyde* and *The Godfather,* the cinema, a historical cousin to psychoanalysis, has provided compelling glimpses of the criminal point of view and thus heightened the sense of tragedy created by climactic Hays Office punishment. Robert Warshow appropriately titled his essay on this film phenomenon, "The Gangster as Tragic Hero."[3]

Television, however, has thus far been less indulgent of crime or criminals. While the antiserial format of the American feature film provides a hospitable medium for sympathy or even adoration of the criminal, the TV series, due to its structure, is unable to explore this realm. Tragedy, according to most definitions, is impossible on a weekly series. Rigid convention protects the protagonist from death. If he has a flaw, it is far from a hamartia; in fact, it is usually decidedly comic. Point of view is conclusively restricted to the law and its representative. The occasional exceptions to this rule—from Richard Kimball to *The A-Team*—are so thoroughly designated as victims of bizarre circumstance that the viewer is hard put not to get the point. The vicissitudes of evil are rarely up for discussion. Binary distinctions between sin and psychosis are avoided; both are plotted on the continuum of evil. This is necessary to justify the decisive actions taken by the hero against his antagonist. The cop or private eye must survive to return next week, same time, same station. The criminal's guilt must therefore be established beyond doubt—often beyond sympathy—and he must be brought to the justice of prison or death before the final credits. There is no *Kojak* without Theo; there are no *Rockford Files* without Jim. On TV, the series, the law, and their champion constitute a single entity. This is equally true of Joe Friday and Frank Furillo. The death or defeat of any one of these components cancels them all from the prime-time schedule. This peculiar constraint on a traditionally noncomic subject has produced a drama so narrowly conservative in its transformational possibilities that it cannot fail to parody itself. The sitcom forthrightly offers familiar personalities involved in day-to-day events, creating a harmony of subject and object in a parlor room comedy of manners. The crimeshow is a more complex vehicle for the delivery of a similar product. It *seems* to take on the epic struggle of good and evil as its subject matter. The outcome of this struggle is never in doubt, however, and it recedes to the function of a setting for a comic character study. The identity of a given crimeshow grows not out of its comment on the universal, eternal struggle between order and chaos or good and evil but rather from the personality of the lawman as it is revealed in his handling of trivial crises (his "Lifestyle"). As Alexander Pope demonstrated in *The Rape of the Lock,* the confusion of the epic and the banal is likely to yield an absurd, parodic *tertium quid.*

Some of the compelling attractions of classical crime mystery are forfeited by the TV crimeshow. Many of the shows are not mysteries in any traditional sense. "Whodunit?" is often a nonquestion. In most shows the perpetrator is obvious enough, even if he is not revealed in the first minute (as in *Columbo*). This perpetrator will not only be captured but will indeed be a villain deserving of the punishment he receives. The protoexistentialist innovations in crime narrative made in the name of Darwin by such novelists as Thomas Hardy, Jack London, and Frank Norris do not lend themselves to weekly serialization. Not only will justice triumph on TV, but the methods of its agent will prove unimpeachable. These methods may be conventional (as in *Barnaby Jones*) or eccentric (as in *Rockford*), but it is determined that the devil will lose to the forces of light.

It can be argued that the attraction of this apparently flat formula is its ritual affirmation of the potency of law and order in an increasingly paranoid, or perhaps merely crime-conscious, society. A demographic research study by the R. D. Percy Company reveals that a number of viewers often watched only the first six and last six minutes of *Police Woman*.[4] This radical mode of televiewing would seem to indicate that these viewers have stripped the crimeshow down to two gestalt elements: the "set-up" (danger) and the "wrap-up" (amelioration of danger). The intervening forty-eight minutes (including commercials) are discarded as tedious and irrelevant. I must say, however, that I find this form of crimeshow appreciation bizarre (as must the ad agencies and sponsors who buy time on such programs). With the sequence of action so predictable, the personality (or, in marketing terms, the Lifestyle) of the protagonist—the very concern of those discarded forty-eight minutes—becomes the compelling imaginative attraction of the genre. Convention demands a crime, a series of interviews with witnesses and suspects, and an action scene culminating in an arrest or death. But like a sitcom—which suffers similarly tight conventional constraints—each crimeshow gradually constructs an idiosyncratic cosmos, which gives it a character that betrays homogeneous narrative conformity. The TV crimeshow is a sitcom in which The Law is married to Chaos. In each episode, Chaos steps out of line, but The Law whips her back into shape before the final commercial. Because crime, evil, man's inhumanity to man, social terror, atheism, rebellion, and the impending collapse of civilization are the "situations" of the crimeshow (as opposed to the education of children, spats between friends, and forgotten anniversaries), the crimefighter's attitude toward the handling of evil is a key signifier of personality. Before discussing individual examples of these personalities, it is worth

69

noting that they usually can be divided into two broad types, which I will call "hot" and "cool."

TV cops, including such diverse brethren as the law-and-order avengers of *Highway Patrol* and the community-minded knights of *CHiPs,* tend toward the messianic. Strong emphasis is given to the lifelong commitment of the cops to their perilous, self-sacrificing work. The stress of policework can be borne only by an unwavering faith in the righteousness of the law. The cop isn't in it for the money; policework is a calling. The private detective, on the other hand, is for hire. He can take a cooler, more cautious view of the dogma of the law and weigh it against his own standards of justice. Not an employee of the collective security State, the free lancer is able to examine the contradictions of institutional order and human experience with greater detachment. Commenting on the print detectives of Raymond Chandler and Mickey Spillane, Cawelti writes:

> the hard-boiled detective is a traditional man of virtue in an amoral and corrupt world. His toughness and cynicism form a protective coloration protecting the essence of his character, which is honorable and noble. In a world where the law is inefficient and susceptible to corruption, where the recognized social elite is too decadent and selfish to accomplish justice and protect the innocent, the private detective is forced to take over the basic moral functions of exposure, protection, judgment and execution.[5]

While TV private eyes have never reached the extremes of alienation embodied in Phillip Marlowe and Mike Hammer, they have generally distinguished themselves from cops with their cooler, less manic attitude toward the struggle against crime. Compared with Broderick Crawford's messianic Capt. Dan Matthews (*Highway Patrol;* syndicated, 1955–59), James Garner's Jim Rockford is something of an existentialist. In terms of the TV western, the same distinction can be made between *Gunsmoke*'s Marshall Matt Dillon and *Have Gun, Will Travel*'s Paladin. Dillon (James Arness) is the sworn protector of Dodge City; his leadership of the community makes him more than just a man contracting to do a job. Chester, Doc, Kitty, and Festus provide him with a network of friendships that carries into every sphere of "legitimate" Dodge City life. On the other hand, Paladin (Richard Boone) is a free-lance San Francisco gun-fighter. A typical episode of *Have Gun, Will Travel* opens with him about to enjoy a decanter of fine French wine with an attractive, expensively dressed lady. He is interrupted, however, by his Chinese manservant, Hey-Boy, who presents him with a telegram on a silver platter. Slightly exasperated, he makes quick apologies to the lady and goes galloping off to Stinking Hole, Arizona, to save the paying customer who has requested his services.

71

In both police and private eye series, however, crime itself is made into a joke. It doesn't pay. It can't win. The criminals are sleazy misfits. Whatever heroic traits they manage to display early in an episode—courage, vision, intelligence—are quickly exposed as superficial affectations. Why do they even bother to try? They must be fools. Don't they watch television?

The TV networks did not quite burst into the world of cops and robbers with guns blazing. Gameshows, variety hours, sitcoms, wrestling, and The News were already established teleforms when Dumont broke the ice with *The Plainclothesman* in 1949, the fourth season of network telecast. NBC and CBS soon followed with *Martin Kane, Private Eye* and *Man against Crime*. These shows bear little resemblance to the expensive, filmed-on-location series produced in Hollywood today. Erik Barnouw writes of the early TV crimeshow:

> In 1949 all such programs were produced live. Produced in this way, *Man Against Crime* cost $10,000 to $15,000 per program; a writer usually got $500 to $700. The live production dominance was expected to continue. Both Sarnoff of NBC and Paley of CBS were said to be determined that it should.[6]

With radio divisions still bringing home the network bacon, the fledgling TV honchos were forced to keep a strict eye on production costs; expensive action sequences and filmed outdoor locations threatened the bottom line. Wrestling and boxing were much safer bets than car chases as ways to satisfy the public's hunger for "action." The crimeshows that did emerge during the period had to be barebones productions. Though producers tried to use proven radio formulas as models, the inevitable peculiarities of a new medium made this difficult. Time, for example, could easily be measured in radio scripts by counting the words on the page (the rule of thumb, according to Barnouw, was that 150 words equals one minute). The visual action intervals of TV made this system obsolete. Barnouw points out that *Man against Crime* contained an obligatory "search scene," which allowed the novice TV director to compensate for discrepancies in time. This scene would occur just prior to the denouement. Ralph Bellamy, the star, was cued from off camera on just how long to search for a salient clue. "If time was short, he could go straight to the desk where the clue was hidden; if there was need to stall, he could first tour the room, look under sofa cushions, and even take time to rip them open."[7] This was the brief age of forced experimentation in the genre. On *The Plainclothesman,* the Lieutenant (the otherwise unnamed protagonist of the series) was merely a disembodied voice, a rather thrifty device, given union rules that lower the pay scale for unseen television performers. This led to a unique narrative format:

> The technique was camera-as-actor, in which the viewer saw everything exactly as The Lieutenant would. If he lit a cigar, a hand (his) came toward the camera with a lighted match (even the tip of the cigar could be seen jutting out at the bottom of the screen); if he was knocked down, the viewer looked up from floor level; if he got something in his eye, the camera blinked, flickered and winked clear again. A punch in the nose provided the most spectacular effect for home viewers.[8]

Another money-saving device that helped shape narrative technique was the integration of commercials into the story line. In the days before TV time became prohibitively expensive, individual sponsors often owned whole shows. *Martin Kane, Private Eye* was under such sponsorship by a tobacco company, and commercials were worked directly into the script. In the middle of a murder investigation, Kane would make a ritual visit to Happy McMann's Smokeshop, located in the lobby of his office building, and find a few minutes to swap praises of Sano cigarettes with Happy, who was a series regular. Tight budgets also meant holding the line on actors' salaries, and surely an interesting effect was achieved by the constant replacing of the title player. William Gargan, Lloyd Nolan, Lee Tracy, and Mark Stevens all played the role of Martin Kane in less than five years.

While these early crimeshows, and others such as *Racket Squad* and *Front Page Detective,* achieved moderate success on prime-time schedules, it was not until midseason of the 1951–52 teleyear that crime found a formula and came into its own on network TV. NBC had been airing an experimental musical sitcom, *Ford Festival,* on Thursday evenings. The concept never took off, and the network decided to replace it with two TV versions of NBC radio crimeshows, which would alternate from week to week in the spot. *Gangbusters* had been airing on NBC Radio since 1936. Phillips H. Lord, its creator, producer, and host, appeared each week and introduced the episode in the manner of Rod Serling and Alfred Hitchcock. As in the radio *Gangbusters,* the episodes were primitive docudramas, "taken from actual police and FBI files."[9] Perhaps most spectacular of all was the show's distinctive trademark: "At the end of each telecast a photo of one of the nation's most wanted criminals was shown, and anyone having knowledge of his whereabouts was asked to phone the local police, the FBI or *Gangbusters.*"[10] The program was network television's first and only audience-participation crimeshow (though in recent years some local stations have revived the practice as part of The News). *Gangbusters* seemed to be an immediate TV hit, finishing Number Eight during its first full Nielsen season. However, it was canceled after only eighteen months on the air, leading Brooks and Marsh to speculate that "it probably was the highest-rated program ever to be canceled in the history of television."[11] The reason for the cancelation was significant. *Gangbusters* had been alternating in its thirty-minute prime-time slot with the genre's first full-fledged cultural institution—Jack Webb's *Dragnet.* Webb did for the crimeshow what Mr. Television had done for comedy-variety and what the Incorrigible Redhead had done for the sitcom: He made it a thoroughly familiar packaging formula.

Dragnet topped *Gangbusters,* finishing Number Four in the 1952–53 Nielsens, and thereby achieving the highest ratings ever for a crimeshow. A decision was made at NBC to provide Webb's Mark VII Productions with sufficient capital to produce expensive telefilm episodes of *Dragnet* for weekly telecast. *Gangbusters* was unceremoniously left to die a slow death with American radio drama, where it lasted until the bitter end, 1957.

74   *Dragnet* was not merely a hit. It was an ideology, a "look," and an object of satire that made it a household word even in households that did not necessarily tune it in. It was TV's first big crimeshow money-maker, drawing serious network attention—and cash—to the genre. According to A. C. Nielsen, only *I Love Lucy* and two of Arthur Godfrey's prime-time shows (*Talent Scouts* and *Godfrey and His Friends*) were rated higher in 1952–53.[12] *Dragnet* commanded consistent viewer loyalty, finishing among the Top 10 during each of its first four seasons before dropping to eleventh place in 1956–57. What is, perhaps, less well remembered about the series is that it was critically acclaimed as TV's first "realistic" cops and robbers show. It was the first such show to win an Emmy, receiving three consecutively as "Best Mystery, Action, or Adventure Program."[13] "*Dragnet*'s hallmark was its appearance of realism, from the documentary-style narration by Joe Friday, to the cases drawn from the files of a real police department ... to its careful attention to the details of police work."[14] Webb had moved the TV crimeshow from the thin artifice of tiny New York studios (most were hastily converted radio facilities) to the cavernous sound stages and spacious boulevards of Hollywood. Webb's purchase of an old Republic Pictures studio lot in North Hollywood, where he constructed a new TV production complex, was a sign of the times.[15] Cop, car, criminal, and TV camera would not be separated again.

Webb had created *Dragnet* for radio in 1949. As star, director, producer, writer, and narrator, he was already synonomous with the show when he brought it to television. He developed a distinctive style that would reverberate widely through the decades of TV police drama. Webb took the hard-boiled dialogue of Dashiel Hammett, Raymond Chandler, and James M. Cain out of the mouths of cynical, nonconformist private eyes and rootless drifters, boiled it a few minutes more, and put it into the mouth of a dour, laconic Los Angeles plainclothesman: "My name's Friday. I carry a badge." Brooks and Marsh claim that Webb was the first televisionmaker to bring the language of the stationhouse directly into the living rooms of America: "Can you give me an M.O.? Book him on a 358." Most importantly, however, Sgt. Joe Friday was a relentless crimefighting consciousness. Life on *Dragnet* was a corporate fight between Good and Evil, and Friday's boss was Good. The ferociousness of the battle left little room for sympathy for the twisted vermin who opposed the public order of the City of Los Angeles, the United States of America, and God Himself, all of whom Friday had sworn "To Protect and to Serve." Alex McNeil writes that Friday was "a cop who seemed to have no personal life and no interests other than police work."[16] A soldier enlisted in the war against evil, he simply did not expect the luxury of a personal life separate from duty. Friday's single-minded goal—the eradication of crime—often led him to interrupt even friendly witnesses with his monotone admonition of "Just the facts ma'am." He had no time for anecdotes or the personalities they revealed.

75

Webb constantly reminded the viewer that the criminals who preyed on the innocent citizens of his Los Angeles were real and were out there: "What you are about to see is true . . ." Narrative continuity was maintained in journalistic chronology: "10:51: I was working the graveyard shift at Homicide." At the end of each episode, sentence was pronounced upon the criminal as an iron hammer of justice pounded the point home. Perhaps it should not be surprising that this vividly paranoid vision of a Manichaean struggle for the American street was welcomed by many as "realistic."[17] After years of the highly stylized theatrical artifice of *Martin Kane* and *Man against Crime,* it must have seemed so. At the same time, Friday was a perfect, laconic all-American foil to the sneaky, double-talking (dream) Communists who were threatening American life from within and without. Barnouw has often made the point that TV came into being during the McCarthy Era and continues to have the birthmarks to prove it. *Red Channels* had been published by *Counterattack* magazine in 1949, providing the networks with their first comprehensive blacklist of "Red" performers and frightening them into meek submission with threats of product boycotts:

> Networks and agencies grew weary of being attacked and decided to take charge of the whole business themselves. Blacklist administration became a part of the built-in machinery of the industry. CBS, which in 1950 established a sort of loyalty oath, followed this in 1951 with the appointment of an executive specializing in security. At NBC the legal department assumed similar duties.[18]

The Red-baiters made no distinctions among television genres. Dancers, singers, and comedians were banned from *The Ed Sullivan Show*. Jean Muir was prevented from playing Mom on *The Aldrich Family*, Philip Loeb from playing Papa on *The Goldbergs* (he eventually took an overdose of sleeping pills). The blacklists of course included producers, writers, and technicians as well as actors. Caution became a by-word in the industry. The crimeshow, which is forced to deal with implicitly political issues to a degree that sitcoms and variety shows are not, had to be particularly sensitive to the pressures of the witchhunters. *Dragnet* was a series made in McCarthyite heaven. But there was also an abundance of evidence that the comic aspects of Webb's unabashed hyperbole were not completely lost. Takeoffs on *Dragnet* became a staple of American comedy. Radio comedians such as Stan Freberg and the team of Bob and Ray did sketches and made record albums based on the show. Daffy Duck and Porky Pig starred as Sgt. Joe Friday and Officer Frank Smith in a 1954 Warner Brothers cartoon by Chuck Jones. It is a testimony to Webb's powerful skill as an imagemaker that the scores of stand-up routines and variety shows inspired by *Dragnet* were instantly able to invoke the show with its four-note musical morpheme: *Dum*-de-dum-dum. (The show's theme music, "The Dragnet March," was composed by Walter Schumann; the piece is also known as "Danger Ahead.") The spontaneous comic imagery of those musical notes has been frequently used in commercials as well. In the early 1980s, for example, Tums, the heartburn remedy, transformed it to "*Tum-*

te-tum-tum." Pain-relief commercials are often tragicomic; the invocation of Webb, in this case, provides the comedy.

Dragnet of course had a tremendous influence within the genre as well. The Webb attitude toward crime provided a formulaic structure for such shows as *Highway Patrol, M Squad,* and *The Lineup.* Broderick Crawford's famous signature, his barking of "Ten-four! Ten-four!" on *Highway Patrol,* can be indirectly attributed to Webb's introduction of police jargon to television. Following in Webb's footsteps, Lee Marvin started his own production company and starred in and narrated *M Squad.* Desilu's *Lineup,* yet another half-hour crimeshow in the *Dragnet* mold, so closely followed the model that Webb was moved to quip, "It's pretty much a direct copy . . . *Dragnet* with the Bay Bridge thrown in."[19] Outside the immediate sphere of the crimeshow, other dramatic serial genres were affected as well. *Medic,* an early doctorshow written by Webb's friend and one-time collaborator, Jim Moser, was commonly referred to as "Drugnet."[20] Webb's rock-ribbed law-and-order conservatism even drew a response in kind from liberal quarters. No less a professional "progressive" than David Susskind produced a series called *Justice* (NBC, 1954–56), which followed the *Dragnet* docudrama formula but drew its "actual cases" from the files of the National Legal Aid Society. The series starred Gary Merrill as a socially conscious lawyer, a political and social mirror image of Sgt. Joe Friday.

Despite its unprecedented success, *Dragnet* seemed to go the way of all television programs at the end of the 1958–59 season. During its seven-and-a-half-year run, Webb's Mark VII Productions had managed to place only one other series on the air. This was *Noah's Ark,* the adventures of Dr. Noah McCann, a messianic veterinarian. In true Webb fashion, episodes were based on "actual cases" from the files of the Southern California Veterinary Association and the American Humane Society. After *Dragnet,* Webb's career went into an apparent tailspin. His *Pete Kelly's Blues* (the story of a 1920s speakeasy trumpeter) and *The D.A.'s Man* (an ex-private eye working undercover for the New York District Attorney's Office) both premiered in 1959; neither lasted a season. Though Webb had played Pete Kelly both on radio and in the movies, he appeared in neither of the two series. Perhaps he was attempting to solidify his position as an off-camera auteur. He commented to *TV Guide:*

> I have always been inclined toward production, but in the case of *Dragnet* it was necessary for me to direct. I'd always directed the radio show and I wanted the TV show to remain the same. No one does a good job wearing two hats. If anything, I am probably a better director than actor, but I don't consider myself a good actor. Acting and directing in the same show is a little like learning to pat your stomach and rub your head at the same time.[21]

After these failures, however, Webb was once again persuaded to appear on screen. *General Electric Theater,* a long-running CBS dramatic anthology package hosted by Ronald Reagan, was plummeting in the ratings in the early sixties as "The Golden Age of Television Drama" came to an abrupt close. In an attempt to rescue the series, GE yanked Reagan, altered the premise and name of the series to *General Electric True,* and hired Jack Webb to hammer home the point for the 1962–63 season. The show was not renewed.

Webb would not produce a major hit again until he resurrected *Dragnet* in the Age of Aquarius. *Dragnet '67* premiered just a few months prior to the Summer of Love; it was indeed a brilliant stroke. Now, not only could Sgt. Joe Friday contend with murder, robbery, and the banalities of traditional vice, but he could confront hippies, revolutionaries, marijuana, and LSD as well. Webb had never been shy about expressing his political opinions. *Red Nightmare,* a film he made with Jack Warner for the Defense Department in 1965, was a blunt attempt to keep McCarthyism alive during the Johnson administration. He frankly welcomed the increasingly political public rhetoric of the late sixties. In the years between the two *Dragnets,* shows such as *Naked City, The Defenders,* and *East Side, West Side* had at least introduced the notion to TV drama that it was psychosis and not the Devil that motivated crime. But Webb was having none of this. In what is probably the archetypal episode of the new *Dragnet,* an infant dies, drowned in the bathtub while his hippie parents revel in hedonistic decay at a pot party. It was the poetry of polarization: The "unhip" applauded this statement for decency; the "hip" laughed their heads off. *Dragnet* skyrocketed back from the graveyard into the Nielsen Top 20. Webb got hot. In 1968 he premiered a new series, *Adam-12,* keeping to his thirty-minute format long after sixty-minute episodes had become standard in the genre. The show was yet another terse rejoinder to the burgeoning counterculture, this time in the persons of two young policemen, Pete Malloy and Jim Reed, crimefighting examples for America's youth. Malloy was played by Martin Milner, who had appeared on television a few seasons earlier as Tod Stiles, a vagabond playboy who roamed the American road in a Corvette on *Route 66* with co-swinger George Maharis. Webb's transformation of Milner into the model of square propriety was politically didactic. Stripping Milner of flashy leisure clothes and sports car, he dressed him in a uniform and put him behind the wheel of a black-and-white. Webb's third (and final) comeback hit was his first hour-long series, *Emergency!*, which concerned the cases of two L.A. Fire Department paramedics. In both series, the traditional Webb voiceover narration is dropped. Instead, we follow the men in uniform through "a day in the life" of their jobs (i.e., one shift), as they monotonously go about the work of saving the pathetically vulnerable lives of wayward Angelenos. One case—the big case—acts as an anchor for each episode, but its development is punctuated by a series of minicases, or subplots, which are handled with bored professionalism by the Webb heroes.

Quinn Martin is another crimeshowmaker who has left an indelible signature on the genre. While Webb's hits were all Los Angeles cop shows done for NBC, Martin has produced both cops and private eyes for all three networks. His work is easily recognizable. No other TV seriesmaker has had the monumental show biz chutzpah to further punctuate the commercials in weekly TV shows with the titles "Act I," "Act II," "Act III," "Act IV," and "Epilogue" segueing the viewer back to the story line. If Webb's Joe Friday was an avenging proto Moral Majoritarian, Martin's Lew Erskine, Frank Cannon, and Barnaby Jones are more in the mold of upper-middle-class suburban Republicans. An early Webb influence, however, is evident in Martin's first show, *The Untouchables,* which he produced for Desilu just as *Dragnet* was completing its original run. Like *Dragnet, The Untouchables* was a raw, unmitigated struggle between good and evil. The cases were "real," adapted for prime time from Oscar Fraley's worshipful biography of Eliot Ness, the otherwise undistinguished G-man who nailed Al Capone for tax fraud in 1927. The barking, breathless narration of no less an institution of American journalism than Walter Winchell bestowed *Dragnet*-like legitimacy on Martin's narrative. Ness, like Friday, was simple and unpretentious in manner and dress, passionate only about his mission: to wipe out crime. *The Untouchables* was a notable event in American history in at least two ways: The show "was, by itself, almost entirely responsible for the Congressional investigation into the effects of television violence during the early 1960s. . . . the high rate of violence on the show (almost five violent deaths per episode, not counting various maulings, beatings and incidental gunplay) was roundly condemned and helped contribute to the show's eventual cancellation."[22] At the same time, the show drew critical fire from Italian-Americans. Having suffered through the Kefauver hearings and several spectacular Mafia busts during the previous decade, many were resentful of the weekly national focus on Italian-American mobsters. Frank Nitti, the turgidly evil capo who kept watch on Capone's Chicago *cosa nostra* while Big Al sweated at The Rock, was played by Bruce Gordon with a smirking hyperbole that gave the show a xenophobic touch. FBI agent Enrico Rossi, Ness's right-hand man, was little compensation. But the cancelation of *The Untouchables* was for the most part due to its ratings, the only truly respected critical barometer in a demography. Though the show managed to finish Number Eight during its second season, it otherwise finished out of the Top 20 altogether during its four-year run, the victim of such head-to-head competition as *The Jack Benny Program*, Groucho Marx's *You Bet Your Life*, *The Tennessee Ernie Ford Show*, and *Sing Along with Mitch*.

After the demise of *The Untouchables*, Martin left Desilu and formed his own QM Productions. The new company's first hit, *The Fugitive*, made QM a force to be reckoned with in TV crime for fifteen years. Robert Stack had played the brooding, tight-lipped Eliot Ness; an equally popular star was secured for the new series. David Janssen had already established credentials in the genre as *Richard Diamond, Private Detective* (CBS, 1957–59; NBC, 1959–60) when he was signed to play Dr. Rich-

ard Kimball, the title role of *The Fugitive* (ABC, 1963–67). The series was a unique one-crime concept, which Martin had bought from another producer. As the series narrator reiterated each week over the signatory montage, Kimball had been unjustly accused and convicted of the murder of his wife. On his way to the death house, he escapes from custody by grace of a railroad catastrophe. Exiled from the world of bourgeois respectability, the fugitive travels the American underworld searching for the one-armed man whom he had spotted leaving the scene of the crime. Martin went out of his way to qualify this seeming mis-   **81**
carriage of American law and order. The cop who pursues Kimball, Lt. Philip Gerard (Barry Morse), actually suspects that the doctor is innocent but pursues his man in single-minded, Webb-like service to his job. When *The Fugitive* reached the down side of its entropy curve, Martin took the unprecedented step of ending a long-running series with a climactic macrodenouement in which Gerard hears the one-armed man's confession and ends up shooting him to save Kimball's life. The American system may err at times, but with Quinn Martin on its side, ultimately it cannot help but render justice. With his ideology established in these two early series, Martin created a successful formula from which he varied little thereafter. Lew Erskine (Efrem Zimbalist, Jr.), the dapper G-man of QM's *FBI,* rid America of Commies, Nazis, and other assorted common criminals for no less than nine seasons. *Cannon,* the rotund private eye and man of taste, spent most of his five seasons on CBS waddling after athletic young murderers and petty racketeers. This show was QM's first private eye vehicle. Martin's conservatism is underscored by Cannon's excellent relationship with the police department. Martin added a third concurrent hit to *The FBI* and *Cannon* with *The Streets of San Francisco* (ABC, 1972–77). Karl Malden was brought to television as Lt. Mike Stone; Michael Douglas got his first national exposure as the hard-bitten veteran cop's young sidekick, Inspector Steve Keller. On a roll, Martin pulled yet another casting *coup de main* when he coaxed Buddy Ebsen out of post–Jed Clampett retirement to play the title role in his next private eye series, *Barnaby Jones* (CBS, 1973–80). Jones epitomized Martin's work in the seventies. The staid geriatric opponent of evil was omniscient and humorless, an upright pillar of the community with neither the time nor

the inclination for fun and games. Jones had come out of retirement after his son Hal was killed by criminals while working on a case. Though he quickly avenged the murder in the series' pilot episode, Barnaby could not help but remain on the front lines in the battle against evil. In one of Martin's few acknowledgments of changing times, he gave the grandfatherly crime-stopper a female protégé (Betty Jones, Hal's widow) and a young male sidekick (his nephew Jedediah). Jones, like Cannon, enjoys superb relations with the police. The trademark of all the QM protagonists—Feds, city cops, or private eyes—is a relentless seriousness, which is emphasized by their asexual lifestyles. Though the QM hero is not as manic as Joe Friday (and has been progressively less so since Eliot Ness), he is nonetheless engaged in an equally intense life-or-death struggle with the absolutely unmitigated evil of the modern criminal.

By contrast, good and evil are separated at a more differential threshold in the work of Roy Huggins. Huggins has been called "the most consistent and prolific TV creator,"[23] a title the record can support. He began his career as a middling novelist, screen writer, and director in Hollywood after World War II. Perhaps his best-remembered film was his last, *Hangman's Knot,* a 1954 western starring Randolph Scott. In 1955 he left the cinema to become a TV producer for Warner Brothers, which was making a late and desperate effort to establish itself as a network television supplier. Huggins scored huge successes for the studio with his westerns and crimeshows. *Cheyenne,* a western series assigned to Huggins, finished Number Twelve in 1957–58; it was Warners' first Top 20 show. Granted the opportunity to create his own series, he developed a private eye concept, *77 Sunset Strip,* from his novel of the same name. The series achieved popularity despite the fact that it ignored many tenets of the television treatment of crime that had become *de rigueur* in the *Dragnet* decade. The private investigators, Stuart Bailey (Efrem Zimbalist, Jr.) and Jeff Spencer (Roger Smith), were suave, urbane, and fun loving, a far cry from such feverishly consumed gangbusters as Joe Friday and Broderick Crawford. Their office abutted the driveway to the parking lot of a nightclub, Dino's Lodge, and the playboy sleuths were not above dropping in for a highball. The purviews of the sitcom and the crimeshow quietly intersected in the parking lot of

Dino's. A casting innovation that helped achieve this was the introduction of a regular character who functioned as the investigators' comic sidekick. Gerald Lloyd Kookson III, known to all as Kookie (Edd Byrnes), was the parking lot valet. Brooks and Marsh accurately describe the jive-talking Kookie, who obsessively combed his slicked-back hair, as "a kind of Fonzie of the 1950s."[24] Alex McNeil notes that "the character . . . was not intended to be a recurring one, but public reaction (chiefly from teenage girls) was so strong that Byrnes was given a regular role."[25] This of course is a rote procedure in demographic art. Sex—dealt with only as a crime by the police gangbusters—was introduced into the lives of the private eyes. Not only did they have a sexy female secretary, but beautiful women were bound to show up in the course of any case. Stu and Jeff even went out on dates. The rewards of battling evil are not merely spiritual in Huggins's L.A.

83

Warners Television had found its biggest hit to date; the self-consciously cool crimeshow finished Number Seven in its first season. In a mad dash to capitalize on what it hoped was the coming trend in the genre, Warners cloned a handful of replicas for equally anxious ABC, the perennial third-place network of the fifties (see table 1). Though only *Hawaiian Eye* came close to matching *77 Sunset Strip*'s success, Huggins had secured a new archstyle for the TV crimeshow. His private eyes were every bit as effective in capturing criminals as the hardtack gangbusters of the McCarthy Era, but their lives contained broader concerns as well. Stu Bailey held a doctorate in modern languages from an unspecified "Ivy League" university; Jeff Spencer had taken his degree in law. The change in styles is well summarized in the difference in theme music between *Dragnet* and *77 Sunset Strip:* The ominous "*Dum*-de-dum-dum" of "The Dragnet March" yielded to the white-jazzy finger-snapping of Mack David and Jerry Livingston's "77 Sunset Strip." Edd Byrnes even managed to put out a Top 40 single entitled, "Kookie, Kookie, Lend Me Your Comb." The theme music to *Hawaiian Eye* featured bongo drums, in cooptive homage to the beatnik underground. The McCarthy-inspired iceberg of law and order melted a bit in the glare of emerging Sunbelt glamour.

In 1963, after five successful seasons on the air, *77 Sunset Strip*'s ratings began to decline. In an ironic twist of demo-

84

Table 1.
Life of the Huggins Hip Private Eye Concept

SHOW:	77 SUNSET STRIP (ABC, 1958–64)	BOURBON STREET BEAT (ABC, 1959–60)	HAWAIIAN EYE (ABC, 1959–63)	SURFSIDE SIX (ABC, 1960–62)
HIP PRIVATE EYES:	Stuart Bailey Jeff Spencer	Cal Calhoun Rex Randolph	Tom Lopaka Tracy Steele	Ken Madison Dave Thorne Sandy Winfield
OFFBEAT SIDEKICK:	Kookie	Kenny	Kazuo Kim	Cha-Cha O'Brien
BEAUTIFUL SECRETARY:	Suzanne	Melody	Cricket	Daphne
SUNBELT LOCALE:	Hollywood	New Orleans	Honolulu	Miami

Crossovers: After the cancelation of *Bourbon Street Beat*, Rex (Richard Long) became a partner in *77 Sunset Strip* for a year. After the cancelation of *Surfside Six*, Troy Donahue, who had played Sandy, became Det. Philip Barton in *Hawaiian Eye*. Kookie graduated to detective status in *77 Sunset Strip* in 1962; he was replaced in the parking lot by J. R. Hale (Robert Logan), who matched Kookie's hip talk by speaking in initials (e.g., "C-U-L," meaning, "See you later."). There were many other crossovers among the Huggins shows.

graphic aesthetics, Warners hired none other than Jack Webb to save it. True to form, Webb stepped in and cleaned house, firing not only the politically suspect Kookie but the entire cast, save Efrem Zimbalist, Jr. Zimbalist, who a few years later would become Quinn Martin's no-nonsense FBI agent, Lew Erskine, obviously passed conservative muster with Webb. Beside the star and the title, little else familiar was retained in the series. The bad-but-not-evil underworld of bookies, loose women, and street types that was centered in Dino's parking lot was scissored by the puritanical Webb. Bailey was transformed into an international agent who traveled the world to foil dope smugglers and equally sinister subversives. The show quickly lost what audience it had and was canceled after just one season of its "new look." At about the same time that Webb was attempting to recast 77 *Sunset Strip* in his own image, another Huggins concept, *The Fugitive,* was bought by Quinn Martin, who produced it in his own distinctive style. One cannot help but wonder what the show would have looked like if Huggins had kept control of the project. Surely the high-sphincter pressure of the Gerard-Kimball chase would have been tempered by a modicum of glamour and romance. Huggins continued to remain active in other projects, even during the *Sunset Strip* years. The most important of these was *Maverick* (ABC, 1957–62) which he created and produced. In this western saga of a trio of good-hearted gambling brothers, Huggins developed the heroic *schlemiel* persona for James Garner that would later be updated and reprised in *The Rockford Files* (NBC, 1974–80). *Alias Smith and Jones* (a loose adaptation of *Butch Cassidy and the Sundance Kid*), which Huggins produced and wrote, was the only new western series to play on network TV for more than one season during the seventies. The Huggins touch is again apparent. The cowboy heroes are handsome, suave, and articulate. Former outlaws themselves, they debunk the white hat/black hat dichotomy. Like Jim Rockford, they often find themselves working for the law while the legal establishment works against them.

Before turning to a more detailed discussion of Jim Rockford, Huggins's antihero extraordinaire, it is first necessary to discuss what happened to the genre in the years between 77

Sunset Strip and *The Rockford Files.* That can best be summed up in a name and a decade: Aaron Spelling and the sixties.

Spelling synthesized and restyled the Los Angeles crime-world of Webb, Martin, and Huggins, integrating it racially and sexually and decisively shifting the measure of justice from "good versus evil" to "healthy versus sick." In the process, his name became synonymous with ABC crime drama for a decade, helping the network to become the programming—and ratings—leader in the midseventies. While The News had provided sensationalistic coverage of the Vietnam War and the Civil Rights Movement, representation of these historical phenomena in prime time did not get seriously underway until 1968 when Spelling's *Mod Squad* premiered on ABC. As Bob Schneider writes in his provocative essay, "Spelling's Salvation Armies,"

> By 1968 the Vietnam War, and its media-induced spinoff, the generation gap, had sorely divided the nation. It was in fact so divided that it was in the process of electing Nixon, the Gollum in a Brooks Brothers suit, who had, in a moment of zen inspiration, co-opted the militants' V-sign and subtitled it with the phrase "bring us together." It was . . . the news that had made a hit of the war and of the protests. It also fell to TV to "bring us together," to minimize the murderous potentials of the ideologically induced yet psychically sanctioned split in the generations. Within this context the mondo-jingo world of Webb was no longer tenable. . . . [Such] shows in fact became another in the series of constantly escalating provocations that were pushing both sides of the generation gap ever more deeply into the trenches of their media-manipulated Maginot Line. What became necessary were mediative shows. In the area of action/adventure this call . . . was answered by Aaron Spelling. His *Mod Squad* featured the best of both worlds in a visionary compromise. Youthful exuberance modified by adult [parental] pragmatism presented a paradigm of intergenerational cooperation in the post-60's world. At the same time it presented visions of the family affirmed.[26]

Not only had Spelling managed to stage a parent/child reunion right in the S.C.P.D. Metropolitan Division stationhouse, but he had fused the polar strains of the TV crimeshow as well. Huggins coolness met Webb messianism, and the result was hip law and order. Schneider describes the *Squad*:

> [Its] central characters were all ex-hippies who had decided to apply their searing social consciences to the saving of souls of a more muddled mettle—by joining them [the police] as undercover cops. They worked under Captain Greer, a strong father-figure, who always made the right decision at the psychologically proper moment. The squad was made up of Pete, a rich kid and frat member, who had [at one time] fallen into drugs; Linc, an appropriately named former black militant; and Julie, the show's sexual fulcrum ... [a] dreamy-eyed blonde with a long mouth and big heart, who had gone through some unspecified young adult trauma.[27]

87

This neo–Popular Front, consisting of a hip white male, a black militant working through the system, and a quasi-liberated woman, all under the direction of a father figure from across the generation gap, was not quite uniquely Spelling's. Cy Chermak's *Ironside* (NBC, 1967–75) contained a similar alliance of new wave policepersons. The difference was emphasis. Ed, Mark, and Eve (later Fran) were basically straight arrows. At the same time, they were so prone to youthful error that they repeatedly had to be saved by their wheelchair-ridden father figure. The Chief (Raymond Burr, straight from nine omniscient years of *Perry Mason*) was the center of the series, the source of wisdom and moral judgment, not unlike the father in a fifties sitcom:

> "What would you have done to those people in the Boston Tea Party?" asks the idealistic young policewoman Fran Belding.
> "I'd have arrested them; they broke the law," replies the Chief.

In *The Mod Squad,* the heroic focus was on youth. Captain Greer was not a "police genius" like Robert Ironside; he merely advised from behind a desk. The Squad went out and maintained law and order pretty much on its own.

The great theme of Spelling's work was rehabilitation—a

new theme for the TV crimeshow. Evidence of Spelling's obsession with the idea can be found in his first television show, a western, *Johnny Ringo* (CBS, 1959–60). Its protagonist, a one-time outlaw, becomes the crusading sheriff of Velardi, Arizona. As Schneider implies, Spelling recognized that Webb's tele-world, as it was recrystallizing in *Dragnet '67,* had become something other than seriously dramatic to a significant segment of American consumer purchasing power. How could "least objectionability" be achieved among a polarizing viewership? Spelling did for the crimeshow what Norman Lear would later do for the sitcom: He introduced The News into prime-time representation and established the emerging consumer power (18–34-year-olds) as the moral power. As Warners had done with *77 Sunset Strip,* Spelling-Goldberg Productions spun off its successful new formula for all it was worth. In Spelling's next ABC hit, *The Rookies,* the cooption process has evolved another step. *The Mod Squad* turns in its street threads and puts on police uniforms. Pete resurfaces as the painfully serious Mike Danko; Julie as the committed angel of mercy, Nurse Danko; and Linc as the community-minded soul brother, Terry Webster. They are all under the direction of *pater familias* Lieutenant Ryker. Webb's Friday is married, but his wife is never seen on screen, and Huggins's private eyes are unattached swingers. But in *The Rookies,* both worlds are brought together. Mike (Sam Melville) and Nurse Danko (Kate Jackson) are typical Spelling protagonists. They are young, good-looking, fun-loving, and idealistic, dedicated to law and order because of—and not despite—their "searing social consciences." To compensate for the fact that the white leading man was married, a new element was added: Officer Willie Gillis, played by male ingenue Michael Ontkean. Unmarried, he invited romance from the audience as he stood on a ravished ghetto street after a riot, wondering about the relevance of Thoreau's *Civil Disobedience.* As Quinn Martin had done in *The FBI,* Spelling branched out from the humdrum felonies of homicide and armed robbery to the more controversial crimes of terrorism and civil disturbance. In *S.W.A.T.,* Spelling's next effort, these Walter Cronkite crimes become the center of the narrative field. Here, the viewer is more likely to run into the PLO than into a pickpocket. The ex-hippies had indeed walked a long road; in *S.W.A.T.* they have become a crack paramilitary unit. Yet even here an element of social worker mingles with gangbuster. Crime, though no less wrong than it ever was, is more pitiable than contemptible. By the time we get to *Starsky and Hutch,* Spelling seems to be suggesting that it is downright uncool not to be a cop. Cruising the Strip in their pin-striped musclecar, flaunting their designer Lifestyle through every climactic collar, Starsky and Hutch clearly belong to different demographic taste groups than Webb's Reed and Malloy, their contemporaries in the fight against Southern California crime. Things have "progressed" so far in postrevolutionary America that the blond surfer-boy cop and his curly-headed Jewish partner find their father figure in Captain Dobey, an Afro-American. All through the early seventies, Spelling built a vision of an America that would continue to be America because of—and not despite—the idealism of its young people. The Spelling hero is a post–Charles Reich young American who has learned that the best way to save the world for Consciousness III is to become a cop. The next hit of this cycle was *Charlie's Angels,* Spelling's first venture into the private eye world. If hippies could fight crime, so could Farah Fawcett-Majors. In keeping with Spelling ideology, the show begins each week with an ascerbic swipe at the institutional sexism of the police department, which forced the three female supersleuths to leave their stereotyped jobs and become private eyes:

89

> the show's opening sequence depicts the "Angels" as unsuited for mundane duties as policewomen, and their subsequent transformation by Charlie who "took them away from all that" to give them glamor and status as private investigators with fashionable clothes, cars and money.[28]

Charlie's Angels began to close the page on the Spelling revision of the sixties. Hip idealism was decaying into egotistical glamour. By the midseventies, the sixties were finally coming to a close on prime time. In *Hart to Hart,* the last crimeshow of the cycle, the Spelling crimefighters are a conspicuously middle-aged—though rigorously glamourous—millionaire husband-and-wife team. Jonathan and Jennifer Hart practice crime detection as a leisure-time pursuit, not unlike hang gliding or weekend cross-country skiing. Earth-tone aristocrats, they do it for kicks—a release from the taxing tensions of their jobs (Jonathan is the head of a multinational, Jennifer an author). From the mainstreamed revolution of *The Mod Squad* to the Me-Decade voyeurism of *Hart to Hart,* the Spelling crimeshows are a kind of cultural historical story cycle of the baby-boom generation, told by means of the familiar cops-and-robbers metaphor. Spelling relentlessly pursued the concept of "hip" until it became diffuse beyond meaning. Perhaps tiring of the quest, he shifted the direction of his work toward a bizarre, as yet unnamed program genre; *The Love Boat* and *Fantasy Island* are both Spelling productions.

90

The end of the age of social consciousness in the TV crimeshow did not signal a return to strict law and order. The Pandora's box of the crimefighter's "feelings" had been opened. The preeminent TV crimeshow of the late seventies was *The Rockford Files,* a series created by Roy Huggins and Stephen J. Cannell and produced by Meta Rosenberg. Eschewing messianism, glamour, and social consciousness in favor of dogged, sometimes bumbling, but always determined individualism, Jim Rockford is the first detective to successfully emerge on TV from the American film tradition, a kind of postnuclear Sam Spade. Rockford lives in what appears to be a broken-down mobile home; inside, it is furnished like a state-of-the-art American single person's efficiency condo. He is the harried everyman of modern America, alienated from institutional bureaucracy, just staying alive, trying to make a living as a private eye. His retired father, Rocky (Noah Beery), wants him to give up this private eye nonsense and follow him into interstate trucking. The police are not much help; Rockford has already done five years for a crime he never committed. He has more trouble collecting fees from clients than capturing criminals. *The Rockford Files* takes a giant step past 77 *Sunset Strip* in the direction of the sitcom. Sitcomic scenes involving father and son in the tiny enclosed space of the mobile home share the hour with L.A. car chases. The host of semiregular characters in the series reads like a sitcom cast list: Beth Davenport, the slightly spaced-out, bleeding-heart lawyer; Angel Martin, the paranoid, double-crossing ex-con and con man; Lance White, the goody-two-shoes private detective; John Cooper, the unjustly disbarred lawyer; Dennis Becker, the overworked but sympathetic police detective. These characterizations give flesh to the conventional car chases, shoot-outs, and arrests that otherwise compose the setting of *Rockford*'s Los Angeles.

Like *Dragnet, The Untouchables, 77 Sunset Strip, The Mod Squad,* or any successful, long-running series, *The Rockford Files* has a clearly identifiable ambience and attitude, mood and cosmos. This, not cathartic release at the defeat of evil, is the experience of the TV crimeshow. A hypothetical episode of *Dragnet* opens:

> *Pan of Los Angeles harbor*
> *Friday* [*Voice-over*]: This is the city—Los Angeles. More cargo is handled by its piers than any other port on the Pacific coast. Sometimes people steal some of it. That's where I come in. I carry a badge.
> [*Music:* "*Dum*-de-dum-dum"]
> [*Full-screen close-up of L.A.P.D. badge*]

A *Rockford* episode opens:

> *Pan of abandoned solitaire game on cluttered table*
> *Telephone answering machine* [*Voice-over*]: Hello, Rockford? This is Acme One-Day Martinizing. If you don't pick up your shirts by Wednesday afternoon, 5:00 P.M., they will be donated to a reputable charity.
> [*Music: Synthesizer plays* "The Rockford Files"]
> [*Shot, from driver's seat, of freeway overpass*]

The "wiping out of crime" has become a moot point on *The Rockford Files.* Evil, a noncommittal bag of psychosis and sin, is here to stay, as much a fact of life as greed, lust for power, or any of a thousand human traits. Christopher Wicking and Tise Vahimagi, in their study of television directors, give much of the credit for the existential style of *Rockford* to Stephen J. Cannell, Huggins's collaborator: "Cannell [has the] ability to write convoluted plots in the Chandler manner, at the same time concentrating on human foible rather than darker evils."[29] A look at Cannell's career reveals his versatility in the genre and provides an insight into the incestuously small circle of individuals responsible for most network crimeshows:

If Roy Huggins is the King of light entertainment, Cannell must be the heir apparent. In his ten year career he has risen from a humble scribe to the executive producer, mainly through his connection with first, Jack Webb (*Adam 12, Chase*), then the Huggins empire (*Toma, Baretta, Rockford Files, City of Angels*), before striking out on his own with *Richie Brockelman* and *Black Sheep Squadron*.[30]

92

Having worked with both Webb and Huggins, Cannell clearly chose the more lighthearted path of the latter. In *Black Sheep Squadron,* he turns the battle for air supremacy in the Pacific during World War II into a wild, macho bachelor party starring Robert Conrad ("Knock these batteries off my shoulder; I dare ya."). Subsequent Cannell efforts include *The Greatest American Hero,* a tedious synthesis of *The White Shadow*'s ideology and *The Six Million Dollar Man*'s special effects, and *The A-Team,* whose macho vision goes beyond Robert Conrad to the precipitate of Mr. T.

If Cannell is indeed "the heir apparent" to Huggins, Jack Lord kept Webb's Manichaean tradition alive with *Hawaii Five-O* (CBS, 1968–80), "the longest continuously running police show in the history of television."[31] Though we see a share of sumptuous shots of Hawaiian beachscape, the day-to-day glamour of life in the Aloha State (which is harped upon in Huggins's *Hawaiian Eye*) is largely missing from the show. Asexual and messianic, Lord's Steve McGarrett suggests Joe Friday in the rhythm of his ritual climactic line, "Book him, Danno."

Though it can be argued that "serious" drama of any kind has always required comic relief, the balance lately has been so tipped in favor of the comic on most TV crimeshows that the crime often seems like a dreary appendage to the comedy. Whatever sense of foreboding the crime may inspire is instantly mitigated by a surrealistic certainty that the perpetrator will soon be removed from society; the malignancy will be extracted. Kojak will be back in the squadroom sucking Tootsie Roll Pops with Crocker, Stavros, and Captain McNeil. Rock Hudson and Susan St. James will be giggling about the case from under the covers. Columbo will stumble off in his ratty raincoat, having taught yet another millionaire criminal that the specter of proletarian common sense is haunting Southern California crime. Harry-O will gingerly hop a bus home after removing a criminal from behind the wheel of a sports car and sending him home to the joint. The portly, aging Cannon (William Conrad once played Matt Dillon on the radio) will sit down to a cardiac-arresting meal after running down yet another evil mesomorph. McCloud, having taught both the criminals and cops of New York City another lesson in Old West law enforcement, will ride his horse down Broadway into the New Jersey sunset.

The strict constraints of the TV crimeshow formula have led to increasingly absurd gimmickry in recent years. A genre that had prided itself on "Realism" seemed to be self-destructing during the late 1970s. Cartoon superheroes began to replace cops and private eyes. *The Six Million Dollar Man, The Bionic Woman, The Incredible Hulk,* and *Wonder Woman* achieved the same arrest records as *Joe Forrester* and *Police Woman,* but they allowed a chance for something "fresh and different"—special effects. With antiviolence protests from parents' groups on the rise,[32] the technical bravado of laser beam rays and miraculous transformations provided a safe avenue for the genre's expansion. Thus the crimeshow gradually lost its identity to the action/adventure show, a broader category that includes a variety of action-oriented series types. In 1978–79 not a single Newtonian cop or private eye made the Nielsen Top 20.

Given this trend, it is not surprising that cops and private eyes began showing up in sitcoms in the midseventies. *Barney Miller* premiered on ABC in 1975 and became one of television's most popular shows. Danny Arnold, the creator/producer of the show, has strict sitcom credentials; his credits include *The Real McCoys* and *Welcome Back, Kotter.* In *Barney Miller,* Arnold took *Kojak*'s multiethnic New York police squad, cut out the bullets and car chases, and built a strong, well-written, politically progressive sitcom out of stationhouse banter. In *Fish,* a *Barney Miller* spin-off, the detective played by Abe Vigoda retires from the force to run a home for a bunch of madcap juvenile delinquents. If international war could be fun (*M*A*S*H, Hogan's Heroes, Black Sheep Squadron*), so could the domestic war against crime. As is usually the case when a new variation on a proven formula is deemed sellable, a slew of ridiculous crimecom attempts followed. In *Holmes and YoYo,* John Shuck,

Rock Hudson's right-hand cop in *Macmillan and Wife,* becomes an experimental robot policeman. Randolph Mantooth (formerly of Jack Webb's *Emergency!*) starred in *Detective School,* a sitcom about "a low-budget school for fledgling gumshoes."[33] Yet another ill-fated sitcom, *Big Eddie,* featured veteran film heavy Sheldon Leonard as a reformed gangster bringing up a granddaughter (as if Meyer Lansky had replaced Brian Keith in *Family Affair*). Though none of these shows come close to the heights of comic farce achieved by Nat Hiken in *Car 54, Where Are You?,* an early classic of this type, they emblemize, in their numbers, the decisive turn toward the frankly comic representation of cops and robbers that prime time experienced in the late seventies. *Police Squad* (ABC, 1982), a frank, no-holds-barred satire of the crimeshow genre was, perhaps, inevitable. While it and most of the cops-and-robbers sitcoms were instant failures, humor has come to play an increasingly important role in the crime series of the eighties.

If the "serious" cop and private eye are not to go the way of the sheriff and the western gunfighter and disappear from prime-time television, their future is likely to be determined by the fortunes of the effusively celebrated copshow, *Hill Street Blues* (NBC, 1981–). Perhaps not surprisingly, the show is produced by a studio that made its name in sitcoms, MTM Enterprises. *Blues* is indeed an innovative blend of sitcom, soap opera, and traditional crimeshow. John Gabree, writing in *TV Guide,* reports that the concept for the show originated in a request by Fred Silverman, then president of NBC Television, for a series about Fort Apache, the Bronx police precinct famous throughout the world for its crime rate. The concept, however, went through many changes before becoming a show. Steve Bochco, executive producer and writer, recalls,

> He [Silverman] asked us to do a show about an inner-city precinct. We didn't want to do it. We were sick of doing cop shows. ... We said we couldn't do a good cop show if we were shackled by a lot of broadcast standards. We sort of got a promise from them to leave us alone.[34]

Curiously enough, the Bronx location was dropped. Though MTM had achieved its initial notoriety partially by stressing definite locales other than New York or Los Angeles (Minneapolis, Indianapolis, Cincinnati), *Hill Street Blues* was not located in any particular city. In a parody of the fifties sitcom device that placed families in the homogeneous suburban community of Anytown, U.S.A., Bochco and his partner Michael Kozoll placed their eighties police show in the high-crime streets of Any-innercity, U.S.A. Borrowing a technique from Webb, the show does not concentrate on any one particular crime but instead gives us "a day in the life" of the precinct. Each episode begins with the day shift receiving its assignments in the squadroom. This is followed by the signatory montage, which consists of shots of patrol cars speeding out of the precinct yard to tangle with destiny. The show departs radically from the Webb formula, however, in that the resolution of plot conflicts by the end of an episode is by no means assured. While there is little glamour in the lives of the policepeople (in the sense of the early Huggins private eyes), more narrative attention is given to the personal lives of the crimefighters than to the crimes. As in Joseph Wambaugh's *Police Story,* the cop is shown to be an unappreciated hero living between the rock of dangerous criminals and the hard place of public abuse. There is even a bit of Spelling idealism to be found in the series, particularly in the person of Joyce Davenport, the public defender who doggedly pursues Miranda cases by day and a meaningful relationship with divorced precinct captain Frank Furillo by night. The name "Davenport" may be a reflexive allusion to Beth Davenport, the liberal lawyer on *Rockford.*

95

Perhaps the most radical innovation of *Hill Street Blues* is the show's decentralization of personae. While this type of narrative structure has always been a formal element of daytime soap opera, it has never before been used in the crimeshow genre. Though Huggins wrought his private eyes in twin pairs and Spelling cloned his do-good cops in communal squads, Bochco and Kozoll have created a prime-time series with many centers, following the trend set by such recent family melodramas as Lee Rich's *Dallas* and *Dynasty.* Captain Furillo (Daniel J. Travanti) is the picture of 35–49-year-old success. His three-piece suits, trips to the gym, and capacity to make effective judgments under pressure with equal parts of pragmatism and morality, coupled with the tireless energy that allows him to put it to the public defender both in court and in the bedroom, make him a candidate for college-educated, middle-management-executive Man of the Decade. Sgt. Philip Esterhaus (Michael Conrad) is the show's slightly older, working-class hero. Not only is he possessed of a vast untutored intelligence, but beneath his blue collar lies a fifty-year-old body that can excite and satisfy both a forty-year-old woman and an eighteen-year-old cheerleader. His gentle concern for his fellow human beings is expressed each week in the opening squadroom sequence. After hearing the day's agenda, the cops begin to leave their seats to hit the streets. Esterhaus calls them back to order, as if to deliver an overlooked piece of important information: "Hey, ... be careful out there." All elements of *The Mod Squad* are represented in the Hill Street stationhouse; hipsters, blacks, and women abound, all capable of acts of heroism, all sensitive to insult. Ed Marinaro and Michael Warren, as two dashing young officers, should do for 12–17-year-old girls in the eighties what the Spelling heroes did so profitably in the seventies. There is even a S.W.A.T. team leader, thrown in for primarily comic purposes. Rednecks, Jews, Hispanics, and a member or two of virtually every demographic category are to be found among Hill Street's finest. Given what is for television the relatively "non-perspectival, non-centered, and radically de-symbolized" structure of *Hill Street Blues,* it might more accurately be titled "The Post-Mod Squad."[35]

The show's unabashed emphasis on police sexuality is self-consciously justified by its commitment to "realism." The cops live in the "real world" of the eighties—as it has been created by television. They are obsessed with psychological health and self-improvement. When personal dysfunction occurs, vocational dysfunction cannot be far behind. A similar justification is used for the show's portrayal of violence. When Bochco complained of being "shackled by a lot of broadcast standards," he was talking about the twin constraints on sex and violence that combine to form the perimeters of TV narrative. John Gabree writes,

> As with sex, so with violence. A policeman's life involves risk; and to be true, the producers say, their stories must be violent. They must also be accurate: death must come,

as it does to real cops, randomly, unexpectedly, *tragically*. In the first episode, for instance, two officers are suddenly blasted by a gunman in the middle of a gag about having their squad car stolen. In a later show, a troubled youth who is befriended by a gruff undercover cop hangs himself in his cell. Instead of the numbing throb of violence that is the pulse of most action shows, *Hill Street*'s violence erupts with the shocking impact of a police strobe on a bloody corpse. "Actually," says Kozoll, "there are few incidents of violence on the show and none of it is gratuitous."[36]   **97**

In the tradition of Emile Zola, Bochco and Kozoll have justified their frank portrayal of sex and violence on the basis that the show is, as the U.S. Supreme Court demands, "of redeeming social value." At first *Hill Street Blues* lived a tenuous existence on network television. The pilot episode premiered as a two-hour made-for-TV movie in the spring of 1981. A few episodes followed, and the series achieved a ranking of eighty-ninth in the 1980–81 Nielsens, a signal for routine cancelation. The show won an unprecedented eight Emmies, however, and last-place NBC renewed it, professing a concern for art (the opening squadroom sequence is shot with a hand-held camera). Grant Tinker, the head of MTM Enterprises, has since replaced Silverman at NBC; the executive producer demonstrated as much patience with the show as its conceptual artist, and the ratings improved handsomely. The show may have an important asset in terms of current trends in the television industry and in demographic theory in general: CBS carried the low-rated *60 Minutes* as a "prestige" albatross for years until it eventually built the show into a Top 10 finisher. Once the show's news-magazine format proved itself at the bottom line, ABC and NBC followed with similar efforts (*20/20* and *NBC Magazine*). More recently, NBC carried *Saturday Night Live* for a number of seasons until that show began to build a class, if not mass, audience. When weekend late-night satire attracted target advertisers, *Fridays* and *SCTV Comedy Network* soon followed. Continuing refinements in demographic wisdom are being made in the direction of creating "quality" audiences for the sale of Lifestyle products. If *Hill Street Blues* can deliver an identifiably upscale demographic viewership, it may not have to pull "forty shares" to stay on the air; it may bring the targeting technique right to the heart of prime time. Mercedes-Benz, for example, became a regular *Hill Street Blues* sponsor in 1983. The threat of cable "taste culture" channels has forced the networks to consider this alternative to "pure quantity." If successful, *Hill Street Blues* is likely to shift the direction of the crimeshow away from sitcomic gimmickry and toward the emotional distensions of the soap opera. John Gabree is correct if he is implying that tragedy (in the Aristotelian sense) is at least technically possible on the show; a heroic character indeed may die. If *Hill Street Blues* is to do this, however, it must first create a hero and then be willing to kill him or her. Thus far, only afternoon soap operas have voluntarily allowed such deaths.

Gleason's Push ★ 4

Translated to the big time, he began to press in all directions, a process known generally as throwing his weight around, which is an exact description of Gleason's most characteristic movements before the camera. He is a heavy man with the traditional belief of heavy men in their own lightness and grace, and he sashays and pirouettes with a faint and entirely inoffensive suggestion of effeminancy— he is so definitely one of the mob.

Gilbert Seldes, The Public Arts

I was in New York and I had a little dough and I wanted to gamble. I called a joint in Las Vegas and I said to the guy, "This is Jackie Gleason. Will you please put a hundred on the red for me?" and the man said, "Just a minute, Mr. Gleason. Hold the phone." I waited, and in a minute he was back. "Sorry, Mr. Gleason," he said, "You lost." "Thanks, pal," I said. "I wired the hundred to you half an hour ago." That's class.

Jackie Gleason, in Jim Bishop, The Golden Ham

The television personality develops in one or more of three general modes: the representational, in which he dons the mask of a frankly fictional character; the presentational, in which, as "himself," he addresses the audience within the context of theatrical space; and the documentary, in which his "real life"—

his exploits, his opinions on matters of public concern, his Lifestyle—becomes the subject of other television programs or presentations in other media. Gleason, like many of the early TV clowns, went the grand route of developing all three. Modern TV sitcom stars such as John Ritter, Robin Williams, and Henry Winkler are, by comparison, technicians in an age of specialization. The pioneers, having come to television from the four corners of the entertainment world, created personal vehicles for themselves; not needing a more precise term, they simply called them "shows." The specifics of such packaging formulas as "the sitcom" and "the variety hour" had not yet gained their current importance in the business world.

Jack Benny opened in front of the curtain doing stand-up and discussing the week's "show" in the presentational manner of Carson opening *Tonight*. After the first commercial, however, he reappeared miraculously transported into a sitcom in which he remained "Jack Benny" while an actor named Eddie Anderson played his valet, Rochester. Moreover, the subject of the ensuing sitcom narrative was often a problem encountered in preparing that week's "show." *The Burns and Allen Show,* which like *The Jack Benny Program* and *Tonight* was directed by Fred de Cordova, achieved a similar synthesis of modes. The "show" was transformed at will by George, who could at any moment call the narrative to a halt and shift into the presentational mode with long stand-up soliloquies, self-reflexive commentaries on plot, or even digressive non sequiturs. Like Fielding's authorial voice in *Joseph Andrews,* George Burns is an interlocutory narrator who casually intervenes in the story line for comic purposes. George and Gracie, like their contemporaries Gleason and Benny, carried their personae across the proscenium curtain: They live in a sitcom world with their neighbors Harry Morton (Hal March; later, John Brown; later, Fred Clarke; later, Larry Keating) and Blanche (Bea Benaderet); they close the "show" on a stage, performing one of their vaudeville routines. *The Abbott and Costello Show* was structured along similar lines. Red Skelton, whose comedy depended largely on caricatures of the inebriated and the mentally deficient, self-consciously returned from the sketch world at the end of each "show" to thank the audience for allowing him into the privacy of its homes. Declaring a halt to the willing suspension of disbelief, his clown makeup dripping out of place, he closed with his trademark line, "Good night . . . and God bless." Ernie Kovacs, perhaps the most self-conscious *artiste* yet transmitted by the network system, often showed videotapes of his "works," personally presenting these on camera from the director's chair of a studio booth. As often as not, he appeared as an actor in these blackout sketches.

The most interesting of the early TV comedians were artists who had sneaked in under the gun of the marketing formulas that would eventually come to dictate form. The same had been true of Chaplin, Keaton, and Lloyd in early Hollywood. Their films are exhilarating celebrations of what is possible in a technically complex mass medium before the bureaucracy of quality control has been established. They came upon a new technology and invented instruments to produce dreams. There is a joyful sense of tinkering in their work that stands in stark contrast to the gloom of modern Research and Development projects. There is an implicit hope—especially in Chaplin's work—that the world will finally get the joke and be moved to such uncontrollable outbursts of laughter that evil itself will die, broken and forgotten. The TV pioneers, having only recently witnessed World War II and its excruciating excesses of human cruelty, were understandably more jaded. TV stars, at least until Alan Alda, were more on the order of gratuitous tricksters than idealists. The specter of McCarthy hung over the business. Who *hadn't* played a benefit for some "antifascist" group during the thirties? There was little room for utopian vision in a medium where cast members and even technicians had to be approved on political grounds by network officials.[1] The television clowns had not been hired to draw people into the play world of a theater; their only job was to assemble millions for the selling of toothpaste and automobiles. The television industry had promised its customers "the great middle class." The object was its subject as well.

Benny's "cheapness," for example, was a studied middle-class spoof. There was a distance between artifice and reality; Benny overplays the joke and asks the audience to laugh at it with him. The star's philanthropic activities, including his many benefit concert performances, were public knowledge. Benny merged the representational and presentational but established

101

a separate documentary identity. In a similar vein, Gracie's astounding "stupidity" reveals itself as deep intelligence; her humor is based on a foundation of complex language play, Elizabethan in proportion and style. Milton Berle dressed as a woman and camped across the stage but took diligent pains to remind the viewer that he was laughing at "those people" and not acting out any organic fantasy of his own. He accomplished this distance by means of his unremitting hyperbole.

102   Gleason, of all the clown-auteurs of the fifties, put the least distance between himself and his "act." He worked so hard at this that it is meaninglessly reductive to call him a "primitive." He was Brooklyn's answer to *Le bourgeois gentilhomme*. Opening his show with a Busby Berkeley–style number by the June Taylor Dancers, entering from the wings amidst an entourage of his personally auditioned Glea Girls, daintily lifting a coffee cup from a saucer to take a sip of you-know-what, the Great One bellowed, "How sweet it is!" and mugged for the camera while his audience—often composed of old neighborhood cronies brought in from across the river—went berserk.[2] Ostentatiously displaying his expensive tastes in booze, broads, and life itself, the Cincinnatus of the Brooklyn tenements wallowed in the admiration of the masses. Gleason was a uniquely American comic original. In both life and art he projected the persona of the Depression-bred blue-collar ethnic who demanded the right to live like a king. Like a Damon Runyon mobster, he held daily court at Toots Shor's Times Square restaurant for the New York press. His car? An immense Cadillac, complete with bar and chauffeur—a personal gift to The Great One from Frank Sinatra himself. Given to a neurasthenic fear of flying (he had survived an emergency landing in the 1940s), Gleason traveled the country on personal appearance tours in private railroad cars. The compelling pathos of Ralph Kramden, Gleason's greatest mask, derives in large part from the painful spectacle of a Jackie Gleason rendered impotent by lack of money.

In 1948 Jackie Gleason was a thirty-two-year-old nightclub comedian whose career seemed stalled at a dead end. A rambunctious professional loudmouth who had been spawned in the fertile comic garden of Brooklyn railroad flats, Gleason had launched his career as a wisecracking teenage host of amateur night shows at the Halsey Theatre in his Bushwick Avenue neighborhood. His credentials from the school of hard knocks are impeccable. His father, John Herbert Gleason (for whom Jackie was named), was a hopeless alcoholic, a forlorn clerk working at an insurance company by grace of a successful brother. He failed to return home from work one day and was never heard of again; the case remains open in New York police files. Jackie, the family's only surviving child (a brother, Clemence, had died of consumption), was eight years old. Mae Gleason, a teenage bride who had never held a job, was forced into the work world. A local Irish precinct boss secured her a job as a token seller at the Lorimer Street station of the BMT Canarsie Line. Gleason was indeed a child of the streets. He dropped out of high school, and later vocational school, after just a few weeks, preferring to spend his time with the Nomads, a Bush-wick "athletic club." As a gang member, he gained a good reputation: "He would give or lend whatever he had to a friend; he had a spitting contempt for boys who did not 'belong.' "[3] He was a familiar figure on the Bushwick Avenue of the 1930s, known for his sharp tongue, "dandy" dressing, and virtuoso pool playing. Though a voracious eater ("He ate more than Mae could afford to have him eat"),[4] Gleason was something of an athlete and not fat as a youngster. As a teenager, he developed a reputation as a ladies' man.

103

Mae Gleason died in 1935 when Jackie was nineteen. At this time he was making about six dollars a week hosting amateur shows at various spots around the New York area:

> A sensible boy would have gone to see the nearest politi-cian and asked for a job on a WPA project at $25 a week. Or he might have gone to a grocery store and offered to work days for $20 a week. But Jackie Gleason was not sensible economically; he would never understand the value of money.[5]

Under the tutelage of Sammy Birch, a local comic who acted as his agent, Gleason developed an act as "Jumpin' Jack Gleason." He achieved his first important success as master of ceremonies at a rowdy Newark saloon, the Club Miami, where he was known to mix it up with hecklers in dark alleys after the late show. What seemed to be a real break came in 1941 when Jack Warner caught his "off-color" act at Manhattan's Club 18. Perhaps a bit drunk, Warner signed Gleason—by now a twenty-five-year-old "fat-man comic"—on the spot. The ensuing early adventure in Hollywood ended disastrously. As a contract player at Warner Brothers, Gleason simply failed to impress the brass. Jack Warner couldn't even remember who he was. He was buried as a third banana in such forgettable movies as *Navy Blues, Larceny, Inc., Orchestra Wives,* and *Springtime in the Rockies* and was let go barely a year later. Back in New York, minor roles in minor Broadway musicals led nowhere. Even his nightclub bookings were beginning to dry up. Jim Bishop, a Broadway gossip columnist for the *New York Daily Mirror* who wrote a 1956 biography of Gleason entitled *The Golden Ham,* called 1948 the low point in the star's life:

> On the personal side, he had lost his wife, his manager, his valet. On the professional side, he was a funnyman whom no producer took seriously; an artistic bum who could be substituted when a better man was sick; a comedian of no particular character; a theatrical personality who was almost a star. This was bad, because Gleason was too big for the small clubs and not big enough for the $5000-a-week places. It added up to unemployment.[6]

Less than four years later, he was living in a Fifth Avenue penthouse duplex, his name had reached coveted "household word" status, and Jackie Gleason was generally acknowledged to be among the hottest properties in show business, an institutionalized star who was rapidly approaching the level of Bob Hope. The *deus ex machina* that had saved Gleason from the obscurity he so deeply feared was of course television.

As Bishop indicates, Gleason had a history of making pinch-hit appearances for bigger-name comedians who were unable to fulfill bookings. The crowning moment of his early career had been a two-week engagement substituting for Milton Berle at Greenwich Village's Carnival Club in 1946. His first television break came under similar circumstances. Pabst Blue Ribbon Beer had decided to bring its successful NBC Radio sitcom, *The Life of Riley,* to NBC Television for the 1949–50 season. William Bendix, who had played The Working Stiff from Brooklyn for a decade in such Hollywood films as *Guadalcanal Diary* and *Kill the Umpire,* had created the radio role of Chester A. Riley, a blue-collar Brooklynite who follows the booming postwar aircraft industry to the suburban reaches of Los Angeles. Bendix, however, was enjoined from performing on television by his movie contract, and a new Riley had to be found. Having been recently dropped by his New York agent, Gleason had come under the management of Bullets Durgom, a West Coast promoter with connections in the embryonic Hollywood telefilm industry. Durgom got him the part, and though Gleason was apprehensive about the role he was in no position to refuse it. **105**

Gleason's apprehensions were well founded. Bendix had created Riley as "a lovable dope who was always making the wrong moves with the best of intentions."[7] Gleason's nightclub act had been based on sharp-tongued insults and wisecracks. He was able to exhibit little of his talent during his short tenure as Chester Riley. Gleason had always been much more of a "personality" than an actor. He had failed utterly in representational cinema. Though convincing of course as the displaced Brooklynite, his attempt to portray a dim-witted schlemiel is dismal. He wanders around in front of the camera, ill at ease, with little to do but look "bug-eyed."[8] The show was often stolen from Gleason by second banana Sid Tomack, who played next-door neighbor Jim Gillis. Tomack, in the role of the smart aleck—the role in which Gleason excelled—subjects the dumbbell Riley to psychic torture, conning him into ridiculous schemes. In *The Honeymooners,* this is precisely what Gleason would do to Art Carney's Ed Norton. After producing only twenty-six episodes, Pabst dropped the sitcom in favor of boxing. Three years later, after Bendix had played out his film contract, NBC revived *The Life of Riley* with the show's old radio star and a completely new cast; it was a hit that played five seasons in prime time. In a tribute to Gleason's subsequent phenomenal success, the old Gleason *Riley* still enjoys a life in syndication. Reruns of it are especially popular in New York, which has always been Gleason's stronghold.

For the second time in less than a decade the comic returned home to New York from Hollywood, having come up empty in his push to become a national star. The television industry, however, was rapidly expanding in New York in 1950, and another opportunity soon presented itself. That year, as Brooks and Marsh write, "big-budget variety shows seemed to be taking over television."[9] Milton Berle, who had been Gleason's early idol from his nightclub days, reigned as Mr. Television on *The Texaco Star Theater.* Eddie Cantor, Jimmy Durante, and Fred Allen were among the many stars preparing to take the plunge. In 1949 the DuMont Network, the American Motors of the early TV oligarchy, was struggling to keep up with the competition. One of its few bona fide successes had been a

comedy-variety package known as *The Cavalcade of Stars.* The show had premiered in 1949, starring Jack Carter, a loudmouth Brooklyn comic of the Berle variety. As soon as Carter began showing impressive numbers, however, corporate giant NBC stole him away to host its *Saturday Night Revue,* a similar show that aired opposite *Cavalcade.* Plucky DuMont moved *Cavalcade* to Friday night and countered with Jerry Lester, a veteran New York burlesque comedian. When Lester began to build an audience, once again NBC stepped in and cheated DuMont of its success; Lester became the host of *Broadway Open House,* the original late-night desk-and-sofa show, which prefigures *The Tonight Show.* Whelan Drug Stores, *Cavalcade*'s sponsor, expressed a willingness to stay with the series, and yet another host had to be found. The show's producer, Milton Douglas, chose Peter Donald, a radio personality with a reputation as "a wit and raconteur,"[10] but Donald refused the job, describing himself as a "low-voltage guy" who was not compatible with the manic pace of TV comedy-variety. Once again Gleason got a break as a second-choice substitute. Producer Douglas was so doubtful of Gleason's talents that he offered him only a two-week contract, hoping to find someone better in the interim. Bullets Durgom, after tough negotiations with DuMont, was able to persuade the network to stretch the deal to a whole month. For four one-hour shows, Gleason was to be paid $3,000; he actually turned down a higher-paying nightclub gig to take the job. The comedy-variety show was too great a temptation to refuse. It offered many of the freedoms of the nightclub stage before a national audience (though Gleason's tendency toward off-color ad libs would have to be held in check). In Bishop's estimation, this was the chance he had been waiting for:

he . . . knew that there was some sort of mist between him and the people. He reached for them, but they couldn't see him. Always when his big chance came to appear before multitudes of them, he was somebody else; he was not Jackie Gleason. Someone handed him a sheaf of pages and said, "Say this," and he said it, but the words were alien and the laughter was distorted and he took the money and went back to his hotel and sent some to his wife and some to the landlord and saved some for a party and wondered if this wasn't the end of the road.[11]

Despite the *Riley* fiasco, Gleason continued to have a gut feeling that he was made for television. The audience—unlike that of the nightclub or the Broadway stage—was grandly infinite. He would not be bound to represent some "artificial" character, as in the movies. He would finally get a chance to give "himself" to the masses.[12]

The Cavalcade of Stars starring Jackie Gleason premiered on DuMont's quasi-national television network on Saturday, 8 July, 1950, in the 9:00 P.M. (EDT) spot. The guest star was the perennially inimitable Rose Marie. Gleason rose to the occasion, breaking up the studio audience and even the crew in a parody of Italian neorealist cinema entitled "Stromboli" after Roberto Rossellini's film. After the second show, the four-week contract was torn up and Gleason was signed for the season. During his two years on DuMont, Gleason created the masks and the trappings that were to become his stock in trade. The show was telecast live each Friday night from the stage of the Adelphi Theater on West Fifty-fourth Street. Gleason assumed complete charge of the production and divided his four writers into two groups working on alternate projects, all subject to the collaboration, editing, and final approval of the star. In form, *Cavalcade* did not differ significantly from Berle's *Texaco Star Theater;* it was the star's vehicle. He developed an almost ritualistic format of presentation, which became his forever. The show began with a dance production number, followed by Gleason's royal entrance. After doing five minutes in front of the curtain, the star called for "a little travelin' music" and flew into a crazed Egyptian belly dance to the burlesque music of

Ray Bloch's orchestra. Freezing his 260 pounds at the stage's edge in a storklike pose, he announced, "And awa-a-ay we go . . . ," leading the viewer into the sketch world. The show's most popular continuing sketch was "The Honeymooners." According to Bishop, Gleason "had an idea for a sketch that would revolve around a married couple—a quiet shrewd wife and a loudmouthed husband."[13] Various titles were suggested, including "The Lovers," "The Beast," and "The Couple Next Door"; Gleason finally came up with "The Honeymooners." The irrepressible auteur even designed the set:

108

> They got a little flat in Brooklyn. Flatbush Avenue, maybe.
> Cold-water flat. Third or fourth floor. Hell, I lived in these
> joints. I know where the sink should be, the icebox—and
> don't forget the drip pan underneath—the sideboard and
> the round table. The little gas range. You know? Maybe we
> got something.[14]

Gleason personally selected Pert Kelton to play the wife, Alice, and Joyce Randolph for the part of Trixie Norton. Art Carney, already a regular in the show's repertory troupe, became Ed Norton.

Other *Cavalcade* creations include Reginald Van Gleason III, Joe the Bartender, and The Poor Soul. All these characters are undisguised fantasies of a childhood in the Brooklyn slums. Reggie Van Gleason, the deliberately magnificent millionaire in high hat and cape, is a pungent working-class satire of pretentious American gentility. Joe the Bartender was based on Jimmy Proce, in whose Bushwick saloon Gleason had spent much of his youth. Mr. Dennehy (pronounced "Dun-a-hee"), the unseen barfly with whom Joe converses in the sketch, takes his name from Pop Dennehy, the father of young Gleason's first girlfriend. Dennehy was a tenacious drinker who had opposed Gleason's courtship of his daughter Julie, predicting that the neighborhood kid's show business aspirations would leave him a worthless bum. The Poor Soul, played in pantomime, was a down-and-out loser of the Brooklyn streets. This nameless character was a projection of the pathetic image that haunted every slumkid who held self-conscious ambitions—the image of "the bum." The Bachelor, another character created on *Cavalcade* (which later disappeared from the star's repertoire), was also drawn from experience. In 1936 Gleason had married a former showgirl, Genevieve Halford, when he was working regularly at the Club Miami. The marriage had flourished while Gleason had steady work in New Jersey, and the couple had two daughters during this period. Things fell apart, however, after Gleason left Newark to go on the road. Gen refused to accompany him, and the comedian's frequent romances became regular items in the New York papers. Both practicing Catholics who refused to divorce, the two were separated for years (Gleason would finally divorce and remarry twenty years later). As a consequence, Gleason had lived most of the last decade as the Bachelor: "Typical routines, all in pantomime, were 'The Bachelor Gets His Own Breakfast,' 'Doing the Laundry,' and 'Dressing for a Date,' all to the soft music of 'Somebody Loves Me.' "[15]

109

During this fertile creative period, the orphaned prodigal son maintained close ties with the old Bushwick gang. Television had made him the hero of the neighborhood. He delighted in making spectacular appearances in the streets, sitting in the back of his Cadillac, chatting with "his people." Becoming a kind of show business godfather, he contributed generously to local charities, especially Saint Benedict's Church, and "loaned" money to old chums (notes that were never called). For those who couldn't make it over to the Adelphi to cheer on the pride of Bushwick Avenue in person, Jimmy Proce installed a television at his bar. When NBC programmed *The Gillette Cavalcade of Sports,* a boxing series, against Gleason, Proce was forced to put in a second TV set at the other end of the bar and play the two programs simultaneously.

Meanwhile, back at the front office, DuMont once again became the victim of its own success. This time CBS raided its number one star. Network chairman William Paley, taking note of the fact that Gleason's *Cavalcade of Stars* had knocked off CBS competition in every market in which DuMont was able to compete, more than quadrupled the $1,600-per-week salary Gleason was receiving from DuMont, offering him $8,000 a week to star in *The Jackie Gleason Show.* The CBS deal meant more than cash. On Columbia, his show would reach beyond the string of big cities covered by DuMont to virtually every HUT in the country. Moreover, CBS was the network of Edward

R. Murrow, Arthur Godfrey, Frank Sinatra, Jack Benny, and Burns and Allen; CBS meant "class." Gleason jumped at the chance.

Subscribing to the adage, "If it works, don't fix it," Gleason brought with him as many members of his DuMont cast and crew as contractual obligations would allow. Art Carney, Pert Kelton, and Joyce Randolph were all retained for the CBS show. Kelton, who had created the role of Alice Kramden, fell victim to a heart attack during the summer before the premiere, however, and a new Alice became a sudden priority. "The Honeymooners" had been the anchor of his success, and Gleason worried about the effect of a new Alice on the "magic" of the skit. Audrey Meadows, an actress Gleason had briefly dated a few years earlier, was suggested for the role, but Gleason rejected her as too glamourous to play the haggard hausfrau. Meadows wanted the role and paid a photographer to come to her home at six o'clock in the morning and capture her *au naturel.* As much impressed by her pluck as by the photographs, Gleason overruled his initial instinct and hired her immediately. Though he had been the de facto auteur of *The Cavalcade of Stars,* Gleason's new CBS contract institutionalized his position:

> Jackie agreed to devise a one-hour network show, for which he would hire the writers who would write the sketches; retain the orchestra to play the music and tell them what music to play; do the casting and hiring of the actors, be responsible for the lighting, the director, the producer, the camera work, the properties, the electricians, the stagehands, the carpenters, the dancing girls, the dances, the guest stars, the sets.[16]

In addition to his salary, he was given the lavish budget of $120,000 a week to produce the show. Despite the costs, major sponsors, including Schaeffer pens, Schick razors, and Nescafé coffee, instantly lined up to foot the bill. The Great One had arrived.

Because of the relatively small number of DuMont affiliates, it was almost impossible for any of the network's shows to achieve Nielsen Top 10 status. CBS shows, of course, had no such problem. However, *The Jackie Gleason Show,* airing Saturday evenings in the eight-to-nine spot, was given no easy task in the ratings war of 1952–53. Its chief competition came from NBC's *All-Star Review,* a rival comedy-variety hour that featured Jimmy Durante, Martha Raye, Georgie Jessel, and Tallulah Bankhead, among others, as rotating hosts. The stiff competition, especially on weeks when Durante was featured, kept Gleason out of the Top 20 during 1952–53. The two comedy-variety packages split the audience; each was held back from "hit" status. Gleason, however, managed to hold his own, outpointing *All-Star Review* and knocking it off the air. From then on, it was clear sailing. *The Gleason Show* skyrocketed into the top 10, finishing Number Eight in 1953–54 and Number Two in 1954–55 (this was *I Love Lucy*'s third consecutive Number One season). **111**

With superstardom achieved, Gleason began to expand his efforts in directions he had previously only dreamed about. Though he did not read music, he always believed he could be a composer and arranger. In 1953 he created "Melancholy Serenade," which has been his theme song ever since. He hummed out the tune while an unnamed composer "wrote it down." His next project was a record album. Selecting a group of popular standards that he felt had done well for him during personal seductions, Gleason rented a recording studio and the services of a large orchestra. Entitling the collection *For Lovers Only,* The Great One wielded the baton at the recording sessions. The tunes included "I'm in the Mood for Love," "Body and Soul," and "My Funny Valentine," all arranged by the maestro to include "violins dripping tears of love."[17] Several major recording companies, including Decca, from whom Gleason had leased his studio space and orchestra, laughed at the idea of marketing an album of romantic music by an overweight TV comedian. Capitol Records finally bought the album for $1,000—it had cost Gleason $8,000 to produce—in the hope that the television star could be persuaded to book Capitol recording acts on his CBS show. Gleason even had to pay the company an extra $3,500 to get the record pressed. Needing sales of 60,000 to break even, *For Lovers Only* sold 500,000 copies. Any doubts in the marketing world about the golden touch of The Great One were thus dispelled. More records, Hollywood film offers (how sweet that must have been), and even Jackie Gleason dolls followed. Rich-

ard Gehman, in a three-part *TV Guide* retrospective of Gleason's career, wrote in 1962:

> Gleason is so many different people, he makes Steve Allen
> seem simple as a paramecium. . . . ridiculed for fat, unable
> to live in a marriage his Catholic conscience would not
> permit him to dissolve, Gleason nevertheless has survived
> exuberantly because he has been able to train his troubles
> into helping afford him the energy he requires to be not
> merely a TV comedian but a superb actor, a conductor, a
> writer, a talent scout, a businessman, an 11-handicap golfer,
> a student of psychic phenomena, boozeophile and bon
> vivant.[18]

TV, of course, remained the wellspring of Gleason's incredible
rapport with the public. Like most of the comedians of his day,
he was not a sex symbol who could be sold to the public on his
good looks alone. Yet, unlike many of his contemporaries on
TV, neither was he a long-time "institution" whose career had
been established in other media (e.g., Bob Hope or Jack Benny).
Aside from Gleason's gaudy presentational and documentary
personae, his greatest life in the public imagination was as
Ralph Kramden, the hapless Brooklyn bus driver. "The Honeymooners" segment of the comedy-variety hour was its most
popular feature; sometimes as much as half the comedy-variety
hour was given to the sketch. It was so popular, in fact, that for
the 1955–56 season "The Honeymooners" was repackaged as a
separate representational sitcom. Donning the mask of Ralph
Kramden, Gleason left behind the pomp of his vaudeville theater to come home to the bottom circle of blue-collar Brooklyn,
where he suffered the indignities of pre-food-stamp working
poverty while dreaming American Dreams deluxe. The Kramdens' tenement walk-up apartment, located at 328 Chauncey
Street (an address that had once been the Gleasons'), was a
bare-bones flat the likes of which the consumer medium has
not seen since. By contrast, Archie Bunker, Norman Lear's working-class antihero of the seventies, would live in bourgeois comfort. Gleason's own life had mirrored history; he had climbed
the ladder of success from the bottom rung of the Depression
to the pot of postwar gold. Though *The Honeymooners* was

nominally set in "the present," Kramden poverty eternally bore the mark of the thirties. Alex McNeil describes the apartment:

> Almost all of the action took place on a sparsely furnished set: the Kramdens' living room contained little more than a bureau, table and chairs, sink, stove, and icebox. Rarely did additional characters appear (Joyce Randolph [Trixie] did not even appear in some sketches), and rarely were any needed; the timing and interaction of the regulars worked almost magically.[19]

113

The Honeymooners was filmed before a live audience in the ballroom of the Park-Sheraton Hotel in New York, world headquarters of Jackie Gleason Enterprises. Like most sitcoms even today, the show was televised theater, but there is a distinctly theatrical, almost "Broadway" flavor to the program. The audience, for example, applauds the first entrance of each of the principal players. Double takes—of which there are many— are held for extra seconds to squeeze the maximum reaction from the live audience and clear the noise for subsequent dialogue. The set functions in much the same way as an eighteenth-century French neoclassical stage; in fact, some episodes adhere to Aristotelian unities of time and place. The Kramdens' kitchen/living room is the locus. It contains three entrances: the front door (up center), through which most entrances and exits are made; the bedroom door (down right; that is, to the viewer's left), which serves the function of isolating characters from dialogue without sending them out of the apartment; and the kitchen window (up left), leading to the fire escape, which serves both as an avenue for comic escapes and as a means of communication with neighbors. Though the "unities" are not strictly observed, whole episodes often take place in this single setting, and time even occasionally correlates directly with the length of the teleplay. As in Corneille's *Le Cid* or Racine's *Phèdre,* major actions do not take place on the stage itself; instead, the characters' discussions of actions are the body of the drama.

The Honeymooners characteristically opens with Ralph's return from work. Decked out in his bus driver's uniform, carrying his lunch pail in hand, having just survived yet another rush hour behind the wheel of a Madison Avenue bus, he demands his dinner in no uncertain terms. Wife Alice, forbidden by the King of the Castle from pursuing a career outside the bare walls of the two-room flat, looks down at her apron, waits for Ralph to finish his latest tirade, and snaps out of her stoic trance just long enough to cut him down to size with a fat joke:

"You know why I deserve that promotion, Alice? I'll tell you why I deserve that promotion, Alice: Because I got it here," bellows Ralph, pointing at his head.

"And here . . . and here . . . and especially here," responds Alice, pointing to each of her hips and her stomach.

Then—video poetry—the Gleason explosion:

"Pack your bags, Alice. You're goin' on a trip—right to the moon. Bang, zoom, smash—right to the moon, Alice."

Art Carney, as upstairs neighbor Ed Norton, provided Gleason with the perfect foil. Sewer worker Norton possessed the patience of the dull, which the manic, irritable, hyperactive Ralph simply could not bear. Another supreme Gleason moment is his slow burn as Norton takes impossible seconds to remove gloves, shuffle cards, or limber his fingers to play the piano.

"GET OUT," roars Ralph, desperately gesturing at the door.

Two narrative subjects dominate *The Honeymooners:* Ralph's attempts to become rich and his attempts to assert authority over Alice. The dream of Ralph Kramden is not so much to move to Park Avenue as to impress Alice and Norton with the potency that only money emblemizes. For example, when he finds a suitcase containing a million dollars in the back of his bus, he merely redecorates the tenement flat with gaudy new furniture and fills it with expensive appliances. He has a telephone installed, fulfilling one of Alice's long-time dreams. He hires Norton as his chauffeur and then buys a car. Not satisfied just to quit his job, he calls Mr. Marshall, president of the Gotham Bus Company, to tender his resignation:

"Hello, Mr. Marshall?" he says in his calmest voice. "You may or may not remember me, but this is Ralph Kramden, one of your bus drivers. For the past fifteen years I've worked for you, never missing a single day, never getting a raise or a promotion. I just called to tell you that I have decided to terminate my employment at the company. [*Pause*] Oh yes, and just one other thing, Mr. Marshall: YOU ARE A BUMMMM."

The money of course turns out to be counterfeit.

The Honeymooners remains one of the few genuinely urban sitcoms to have appeared on American television. In the seventies, MTM Enterprises made a practice of producing flashy signatory montages to establish urban settings for its shows: Mary parading around Nicollet Mall in downtown Minneapolis; vistas of the Loop at dusk introducing *Bob Newhart;* portraits of the Cincinnati riverfront opening *WKRP.* None of these expensive location shots accomplishes the job nearly so well as the minimal expressionist gesture of Brooklyn tenements and clotheslines barely visible through the small square of 'the Kramdens' kitchen window. The MTM characters are for the most part upper-middle-class suburbanites who choose to live in the city because of their taste for urban Lifestyle; the Kramdens are creatures of the urban world.

115

Ralph is a lonely dreamer of get-rich-quick schemes. Alice is a fatalist, convinced that only hard work can lead to success, and if it doesn't, the matter is settled. Her puritanical intuition tells her that something is fishy when Ralph finds the money on the bus; as usual, she is right. Norton is more than satisfied with a sewer worker's lot in life. He buys what he wants on credit, and when it is repossessed, he goes to another store and starts all over again. But Ralph demands something more out of life. His schemes include investing in a New Jersey uranium mine, opening a chain of "diet pizza" parlors, and marketing downstairs neighbor Mrs. Manicotti's "beef stew" (it turns out to be homemade dog food). These schemes of course must be kept secret from Alice, and a reluctant Norton must be conned into partnership.

The other desire of Ralph's heart is prestige. This usually comes at Alice's expense. Ralph likes to go out with the boys, to spend his evenings bowling or drinking with the guys down at the Raccoon Lodge. But Alice, who subsists without the aid of a vacuum cleaner, washing machine, television set, or any other modern convenience, expects some attention when Ralph returns home. Demanding a TV set in one episode, she says, "I'm tired of looking at these four walls all day. I want to look at Liberace." Ralph adamantly rejects Alice's demands as self-indulgent or, worse, attempts at female domination. He blusters at Norton for kowtowing to Trixie, but, as in his attempts to get rich, he must eat crow at the episode's conclusion. In one of the few episodes that contains an "outdoor" sequence (a stage set), the Raccoons decide to go on a fishing trip. Shooting off his mouth, Ralph demands that wives be banned from the outing and humiliates the lodge brothers into agreeing. Alice and Trixie stow away in the back seat of the borrowed car. In another episode, a telegram arrives, saying, "I'm coming to visit. Love, Mom." Ralph explodes, demanding that Alice prevent her mother's visit. She refuses, and in a fury Ralph leaves the apartment and moves in upstairs with the Nortons. The visitor turns out to be Mother Kramden, whom Alice treats with the utmost warmth and respect. As usual, Ralph must face Alice in humiliation at the episode's end, embrace her, and admit, "Baby, you're the greatest."

There is a ritual, ceremonial, almost kabuki-like flavor to *The Honeymooners*. Each story is told by means of a series of twenty or thirty highly stylized morphemic units. At the same time, the show is not without its moments of spontaneity. Gleason was a quick study with a notorious reputation for refusing to rehearse. He felt rehearsal hurt his spontaneity and took the edge off his performance. Since the show was filmed before a live audience, missed cues were not uncommon, and the actors carried on in Broadway "trouper" style. Gleason's flamboyant personal habits (Lifestyle had not yet been invented) were another source of concern. Al Stump of *TV Guide* writes:

> Shortly before another show, Gleason hadn't been seen at CBS for several days. And again script delivery was "delayed." [Gleason had to personally approve all scripts.] Walking into Jackie's penthouse hotel suite, Audrey found him presiding over a party for 80, and well-buzzed on martinis. On the next *Honeymooners*, Gleason was to hit Audrey in the face with a pie. And few in the company gave him a better than a 6-1 chance to do it with accuracy. "I knew he'd miss by two feet," she says, "so when he wound up, I stumbled, managed to fall in front of his wild throw and saved another scene."[20]

By the mid-1950s, Gleason signed a three-year contract with CBS for $11 million, then the highest price ever paid for any series. He moved to an $800,000 Hudson River mansion in Peekskill, New York, that was built to his personal architectural specifications and contained twelve bars and a basement television studio so The Great One could make filmed commercials for the show without having to go down to the city. Unfortunately, however, his most creative period was behind him. What followed was a series of restless attempts to transcend his proven talents and achieve status as an artist.

Despite the artistic success achieved in *The Honeymooners* during the year it was liberated from variety-show packaging, Gleason was forced to return to the comedy-variety format for the following TV season. The problem was in the ratings and was probably due to scheduling. The half-hour *Honeymooners* aired at 8:30 on Saturday evenings, the second half of what had been the old Gleason hour. NBC counterprogrammed the hour-long *Perry Como Show,* which started at 8:00. Como, an old friend of Gleason's who had shared nightclub stages with him at Jersey shore resorts, was a huge success. Apparently, many viewers were unwilling to cross over from Como to Gleason at the midway point of the singer's show; *The Honeymooners* finished only twentieth in the 1955–56 Nielsens, a steep drop from the ratings of previous seasons. The return to the old format in 1956–57 did not solve the problem. *The Perry Como Show,* now head to head with *Gleason* for a full hour, climbed to Number Nine, while Gleason dropped out of the Top 20 altogether for the first time since his slow start in 1952–53. Como, whose slow-motion style is an early incarnation of the "mellow sound," was becoming a "personality" to be dealt with in his own right. The "Perry Como sweater," a loose, long-sleeved sweater that buttons at the waist, was becoming *de rigueur* in the sportswear world, and a weekly segment during which Perry sang a requested song drew millions of letters ("Letters, we get letters / We get stacks and stacks of letters"). Como's victory over Gleason was a sign of the times. Lawrence W. Lichty and Malachi C. Topping have shown that the number of network quarter hours (their bizarre unit of measurement) devoted to "Variety" declined from 278 in 1955 to only 161 in 1958; during the same period, quarter hours devoted to "Music" increased from 52 to 99.[21] Berle himself would feel the programmer's ax at the end of the 1958–59 season. I have speculated earlier on the cause

117

of the sudden decline of presentational comedy; suffice it to say that not only Gleason but his entire school of telecomedy was in the process of decline. NBC and CBS, the industry giants, were both stuck with "obsolete" vaudeville-style comic personalities whom they had signed to long-term contracts during the fifties boom. At least CBS did not put Gleason through the indignity of hosting *Jackpot Bowling,* as NBC had done to Berle, but Gleason was actually forced to sit out the 1957–58 season before Paley offered him another chance:

> Jackie was back in the fall of 1958 with a modified half-hour comedy-variety format. Gone were all the regular cast members from previous seasons and Buddy Hackett was added as Jackie's second banana. The chemistry wasn't there and after three months on the air, this short version of *The Jackie Gleason Show* expired.[22]

Thus began a four-year hiatus in The Great One's television career. Despite his setbacks, however, Gleason had built an F-score during the years on the tube that had made him a star of enormous proportions. He had moved product before, and a track record is never taken lightly in demographic circles.

Gleason ached to settle his old score with Hollywood and immediately headed for the Coast. The only success he had ever achieved in California had been as a nightclub entertainer at Slapsie Maxie's on Beverly Boulevard, but now the film industry welcomed him with open arms. His first role was as Minnesota Fats in *The Hustler* (1961), directed by Robert Rossen. Though the film was a vehicle for Paul Newman, then at the peak of his career, Gleason did well as a "natural" in the character role. Newman plays the title role of a young pool shark out to defeat "The Greatest." Gleason was tailor-made for his part as a streetwise champion who defends his supremacy in a billiard parlor. Having spent a good deal of his youth in Brooklyn pool halls, Gleason was able to perform many of his own shots for the camera. Most important in terms of his new career goals, he had played a noncomic role successfully in a hit movie and had been given featured billing with such movie stars as Newman and George C. Scott. Few believed he had the talent to do it. Gilbert Seldes, the most intelligent and sympathetic TV critic of the 1950s, had loved Durante and even found many good things to say about Berle, but he had rejected Gleason as gnawing and aggressive. He would admit no more than this: "I find Gleason distasteful and prodigiously skillful, and the combination is irritating."[23] Though now a millionaire and a superstar, Gleason's lifelong desire "to go first class"[24] was pushing him toward what he felt were greater things. Acting, which Gleason had once disdained as too constraining on his "personality," offered an avenue that led beyond stardom to the hallowed halls of artistry. The following year, Gleason found a film vehicle that he hoped would establish the "seriousness" of his talent: *Gigot*. The film was directed by Gene Kelly, and according to Bosley Crowther, John Patrick's script was "from a story provided by Mr. Gleason."[25] *Gigot* smacked of more "artistry" than most critics—or moviegoers—could bear. The story concerned a dirty, unshaven mute of the Paris streets who befriends and protects a prostitute and her young daughter. "Is this beginning to sound like an old Charlie Chaplin film?" Crowther asks. He answers his own question, writing of Gleason:

119

> it is evident that his characterization of a lonely, unspeaking vagabond, who hungers for social acceptance and the warmth of somebody's love is modeled after Chaplin. . . . But, unfortunately, Mr. Gleason, for all his comic skill when it comes to cutting broad and grotesque capers, as he does now and then, does not have the power of expression or the subtleties of physical attitude to convey the poignant implications of such a difficult, delicate role.[26]

Far from becoming the "classic" it self-consciously set out to be, *Gigot* is hardly remembered at all; it is rarely even shown on TV. Gleason was simply unable to translate the short TV blackout sketches of his Brooklyn bum, The Poor Soul, into a feature-length Parisian *clochard* for the cinema. The critics would not grant him the genteel pedigree he was seeking. One cannot help but think of subsequent great television comedians—especially Dan Aykroyd and John Belushi—forsaking their medium to make mediocre movies in search of the cinema's greater status.

Gleason's best performance during his Hollywood renaissance was as Maish Rennick, the double-dealing manager of Mountain Rivera (Anthony Quinn), an over-the-hill fighter. The film, *Requiem for a Heavyweight,* was adapted for the large screen by Rod Serling from his original *Playhouse 90* teleplay. Maish sells out his fighter, telling him to take a dive in the fifth, but the punch-drunk Mountain, like Hemingway's Jack Brennan in "Fifty Grand," is unable to reverse the instincts of his lifelong career in the ring; he doesn't go down until the seventh. Maish is beaten by thugs and given a few days to recover the mob's losses. Despite the admonitions of Mountain's cut man, Army (Mickey Rooney), Maish signs Mountain to take on the role of a wild Indian in a professional wrestling show. Returning to his familiar cosmos of cheap rooms, bars, and New York streetlife, Gleason is powerful in the role. Reviewing the film for the *New York Times,* A. H. Weiler wrote: "As the manager, Jackie Gleason contributes a brilliantly underplayed role of a ruthless, yet realistic and terrified man ready to rob the dignity of the fighter to whom he is basically devoted."[27]

During this period, Gleason made two more films: *Papa's Delicate Condition,* in which he plays a small-town turn-of-the-century alcoholic (a role originally written for Fred Astaire)[28] and *Soldier in the Rain,* in which he plays an army sergeant opposite Steve McQueen. Both pictures were "light dramas" laced with doses of comedy. Though Gleason had not broken any box office records, he was apparently satisfied that he had rectified Hollywood's earlier impression of him:

> They love me here. We came in with it [*Papa's Delicate Condition*] five days ahead of schedule, saved about $120,000, and they could throw it out in the gutter and still make money with it. Every studio in town is after me: "Produce, write, direct, write your own ticket, my boy!"[29]

One can only guess at Gleason's motives for returning to the television grind. In the 1956 biography, Bishop had claimed that "a passion for constant approval" was Gleason's deepest priority.[30] Perhaps the contracting film audience could not satisfy his need; his hunger for recognition on every street corner won out over his desire for "class." Gleason attempted to achieve both in his return to television by following a master.

Groucho Marx had come to television, like many famous film and radio comedians, in the gold rush of the early 1950s, but his vehicle differed radically from those of his fellow pioneers. *You Bet Your Life* (NBC, 1950–61) was neither a variety hour nor a sitcom but a low-budget quiz show that acted as a frame for Groucho's piercing wit. The camera focused on the famous cigar, moustache, and glasses as the band struck up "Hooray for Captain Spaulding," Groucho's theme from *Animal Crackers.* George Fenneman, the show's announcer, like Margaret Dumont before him, stood by, at the mercy of Groucho's relentless wisecracks. The famous duck, in Groucho disguise, descended from above bearing the weekly "secret word." Fenneman ushered in the contestants ("Won't you please come out and meet . . . Groucho Marx?"), and it immediately became apparent that they were handpicked straw men for the great raconteur. Even during the era of *The $64,000 Question* and *Twenty-One,* the prizes on *You Bet Your Life* rarely added up to more than a few thousand dollars; the "game," in fact, was changed in format from year to year. So thoroughly did this show depend on the unique phenomenon of Groucho's personality that the networks were unable to duplicate its success by means of a structural formula. Groucho had not only conquered television with a decade-long series, he had done it with "class."

The cancelation of *You Bet Your Life* was slated to take place at the end of the 1960–61 season, and perhaps it seemed logical to both CBS and Gleason that The Great One could fill what would soon be an empty space in teleculture. In any case, a quiz show vehicle was developed for Gleason. *You're in the Picture* premiered as a midseason replacement for an ill-fated half-hour adventure series on 20 January 1961.

The four celebrity panelists on the show were situated behind an oversized comic cutout of the kind found in amusement park photography booths. They had no idea what the picture through which they had stuck their heads, and sometimes their hands, represented. The object was for the panel to guess what the picture was by asking questions of the host/emcee Gleason. When they had successfully identified the picture, a new one would be substituted and they would start over. Jackie's wit was supposed to add to the humor of the show, which was played primarily for laughs.[31]

Gleason had indeed returned to television in grand style; the show was canceled after only one telecast. Though the following week's *TV Guide* listed *You're in the Picture* for Friday, 27 January 1961, at 9:30 P.M., viewers who tuned in saw "only a bare stage containing an armchair in which 'The Great One' sat. 'I apologize for insulting your intelligence,' Gleason told his astonished viewers. 'From now on I promise to stick to comedy.' "[32] Like Ralph Kramden begging Alice's forgiveness at the conclusion of a *Honeymooners* episode, Gleason shuffled before the camera with pathetic humility. He did not exactly keep his promise, however. Though the title of the program reverted to *The Jackie Gleason Show,* for the next three months the half hour became a talkshow during which Gleason philosophically engaged such guests as Jayne Mansfield, Mickey Rooney, and Bobby Darin. Ironically, Groucho Marx, the inspiration for *You're in the Picture,* returned to television the following fall with a similar talkshow format. But *Tell It to Groucho,* like Gleason's interview vehicle, lasted only half a season. It was becoming apparent that the Nielsen families were losing their taste for the big-name comic "personalities" who had dominated early TV. NBC's *Saturday Night at the Movies* had premiered in September of 1961, offering made-for-theater feature films—in color—to the prime-time audience. Its success led NBC to program another two-hour block of prime-time air for Hollywood films on Mondays. ABC soon followed with a Sunday night movie series. The star comedians of the fifties were disappearing as fast as the two networks could purchase blockbuster films from the studios.

CBS, probably due to its leadership in the ratings, was slower to join the movie bandwagon; the network would not program a weekly movie package until 1966. Columbia's pioneer stars— Red Skelton, Lucille Ball, Danny Thomas—were still finishing in the Top 10 in the early sixties. Gleason's contract stipulated that he collect $100,000 a year in compensation if CBS did not use him in a series. Network officials were thinking in terms of occasional Gleason specials (or "spectaculars," as they were then called), but the star yearned for a weekly series: "I guess you have to put it this way," he told *TV Guide,* "I'm just too much of a ham to stand by and watch all the action goin' on. I got to get into it."[33]

Gleason was given yet another chance in the 1962–63 season. Still somewhat anxious to transcend his status as a "lowbrow" entertainer, he entitled his new Saturday night series *Jackie Gleason's American Scene Magazine,* promising an hour of topical satire, a commodity that was indeed sorely lacking on American television. In fact, however, the new show contained little that could be called either topical or satirical. Instead, for the first time in five years, all the old Gleason trappings were brought out of mothballs: The June Taylor Dancers opened the show, and the traditional overhead shot of the dance formation again appeared. The Glea Girls were back as well. The star entered, "coffee cup" in hand, and did five minutes in front of the curtain. The old trademark lines that had been developed more than a decade earlier at DuMont ("How sweet it is," "A little travelin' music," "And awa-a-a-y we go") were once again heard on Saturday evening network air. Reginald Van Gleason III, Joe the Bartender, and The Poor Soul returned from the grave. What was missing, of course, was Ralph Kramden. Gleason attempted to develop a new sketch, "Agnes and Arthur," with Alice Ghostley in the role of the wife. It bore a pale resemblance to "The Honeymooners" and was unceremoniously dropped. But during this era of contracting comedy-variety fare, the show was able to find an audience and finished a respectable seventeenth in the ratings during its first season. Gleason would hold down his time slot for a total of eight seasons; his most mediocre effort would be his longest-lived Nielsen success. "American Scene Magazine" was dropped from the title after a few seasons, and Gleason settled in for season after season of shadowy reprises of his once vibrant comedy. The kid from the Brooklyn slums had long ago lost touch with the old neighborhood, and his attempts to play street characters became more and more stylized.

In 1964, like many successful Brooklynites, he left New York for Miami Beach, where CBS created a complete new production facility for *The Gleason Show.* Traditionally, announcer Johnny Olsen had introduced the show with the dramatic line, "From New York, the entertainment capital of the world";

123

now the show emanated "From Miami Beach, the sun-and-fun capital of the world." The tough kid from Bushwick Avenue became a golf-playing Sunbelt millionaire.

Whereas once Gleason had played only "himself," he now played a series of paper-thin imitations of his old creations. Nowhere was the decay of his artistic persona more evident than in the painful revival of "The Honeymooners" in 1966. After a nine-year absence, Gleason persuaded Art Carney to rejoin him. Audrey Meadows, however, now married to an airline executive and retired from show business, was no longer interested in the part she had once coveted. Sheila MacRae became the third Alice Kramden; Jane Kean played Trixie. The "magic" was gone. Though the audience whooped and hollered at every threat to send Alice to the moon (and the nostalgia of the Gleason-Carney reunion propelled the series to a Number Five finish in the ratings that season), the hour-long sketches simply lacked the manic intensity of the fifties *Honeymooners*. Gleason's weight fluctuated wildly. He kept three complete wardrobes: for 260 pounds, 220 pounds, and 180 pounds. At times he displayed less spare tire than the aging Carney, and this created what were perhaps the revival's funniest moments. Ever the *artiste*, Gleason came up with the innovation of playing "The Honeymooners" as a musical comedy, and he commissioned songwriters Lyn Duddy and Jerry Bresler to compose original songs for the weekly episodes. They were, quite simply, awful. Worst of all, the once immutable cosmos of the original "Honeymooners" was tampered with. At one point, Ralph won a trip around the world, leading to a series of musical theme episodes ("Gay Paree," "Jolly Olde England," etc.). The eternal loser was traveling the world in distinctively "first-class" style. The final destruction of Gleason's greatest creation took place in the last episode, in which Ralph Kramden receives his long-awaited promotion to dispatcher at the Gotham Bus Company.

The cancelation of the final *Jackie Gleason Show* took place at the end of the 1969–70 season. According to television historian Les Brown, Gleason—like Paul Henning—was a victim of CBS's plan to "modernize" its schedule and capture a greater share of the 18–34-year-old audience with "hip" and "relevant" programming.[34] The string had run out on Gleason nostalgia; his audience was large, but too old to interest the CBS brass.

Red Skelton, the only other pioneer still holding down a comedy-variety series, was likewise dropped by CBS that year. (Skelton was picked up by NBC but after one season was again given
his walking papers.) Gleason was furious. He had turned his
back on the potential he had shown for a "serious" acting career in *The Hustler* and *Requiem for a Heavyweight* in favor of
weekly television. Though he would continue to collect $100,000
per year in forced exile, his career was in limbo. In a December
1970 *TV Guide* article entitled "Jackie Gleason's Plea: Why Pay
to Keep Me off the Air?" which featured a drawing of The Great **125**
One in prison uniform with a CBS "eye" shackled to his ankle,
Gleason told reporter Robert Musel:

> I've no way of getting through to the public if I'm without
> a network. They say I can't appear on television other than
> with CBS because they're paying me a sum of money. I
> consider this to be something wrong. I don't think they
> should be able to keep me off the air. Contracts with net-
> works are like romances. It's like going with a broad. Some-
> times the relationship between the network or the broad
> and yourself is reasonable. But in my case it isn't. They have
> control over me for four more years. In other words they
> are emasculating me from appearing before a TV audience.
> I could have gone to ABC or NBC, but I'm tied to CBS.
> Suppose CBS kept me off four years? They could destroy
> my career.[35]

Reporters, who had always been fond of the loose-talking
Gleason, kept rumors flying about the star's imminent return
to television. Robert K. Doan, whose "Doan Report" was for
many years a regular feature of *TV Guide,* seemed to be waging
a personal campaign to get Gleason back on the air. In September of 1970 he reported that "inside gossipers insisted" that
Gleason would soon be made host of a new CBS late-night
desk-and-sofa show that would compete directly against Johnny
Carson's *Tonight Show.*[36] Nothing came of it; CBS opted for
movies and reruns of police shows. In 1973, with Gleason's
CBS contract finally approaching expiration, Doan announced
that Gleason had already signed a long-term pact with NBC to
do made-for-TV movies. An excited Doan reported, " 'We're

going after Gleason as an actor,' an NBC spokesman exulted."[37] No such deal was ever made. In fact, Gleason would not appear in prime time again until 1976, two years after he had gained his "freedom." On the twenty-fifth anniversary of the creation of Ralph Kramden, ABC aired a one-hour special, "The Honeymooners—The Second Honeymoon." Though Audrey Meadows emerged from retirement to play Alice, the show was yet another dreary, misplayed revival.

It is often said that any personality—and especially any comedian—who becomes a star on television is apt to "burn out." An entropy curve may be drawn on which to plot the life of a TV program or star. Gleason, always larger than life, leaves us two such careers to consider. As an advertising vehicle for the sponsors who bought time on his programs, he generally delivered in yeoman fashion. He faltered, even faltered badly, and recovered, and this in its own way is remarkable in an industry notorious for discarding yesterday's headliners. As an artist, he achieved superb moments in front of the television camera, moments that are likely to outlast the hours of mediocrity that were the product of the second half of his career. The bare walls of the Kramdens' tenement apartment linger as an image of the sitcom at its most powerful: a tiny door into a world at once exotic and banal. Reruns of the thirty-nine half-hour episodes of *The Honeymooners* made during the 1955–56 season are always a treat. The viewer is sure to recognize the plot in a matter of moments or may even know the lines of dialogue by heart. But the place can only be visited by television. The place is too tiny a physical space for slapstick, yet not a stage for stand-up monologues. With the noise of the wildly appreciative studio audience cluttering the sound track, it is too artificial a place to be believable, yet the emotional highs and lows created within it are too piercing to ignore. Gleason had failed in his early attempts at the cinema because "he was made to play somebody else." As Ralph Kramden, he offers the viewer the pungency and poignancy of naked psychodrama. Without the gaudy, vulgar *nouveau* who paraded the prizes of conspicuous consumption in front of the curtain, Ralph Kramden is emptied of his most compelling dimension.

Gleason still emerges from his Florida estate to take on character roles in Hollywood films. A generation born after the cancelation of the final *Jackie Gleason Show* knows him as Sheriff Buford T. Justice of *Smokey and the Bandit I* (1977) and *II* (1980). The *Smokey* films, which star Burt Reynolds and Sally Field and are built on a foundation of car chases and CB lingo, are set along the highways between Florida and Texas. This may seem a curious setting in which to find the pride of Bushwick Avenue. But after a dozen years as a southerner, Gleason—who has always based his best characters on his "real life" experiences—has achieved some notoriety in the role of a corrupt, overweight redneck sheriff. Lawrence Van Gelder of the *New York Times* writes, "With Mr. Reynolds playing it cool and Mr. Gleason doing his burns and investing the film with a certain raunchy humor, the rest is up to the vehicles."[38]

Despite the longevity and general success of his show business career, Gleason was never able to achieve the critical success that would enshrine him in the comedy pantheon as "a classic clown." Horace Newcomb, the so-called "guru of the academic critics,"[39] avoids him completely in his major work, *TV: The Most Popular Art;* Gleason's name does not even appear in the book's index. In *Television: The Critical View,* a large collection of critical articles by various writers edited by Newcomb, not a word about The Great One is to be found. Russel Nye mentions Gleason but once in *The Unembarrassed Muse,* as part of a list of "early fifties" comedians, despite the fact that Gleason's show was still on the CBS Saturday night schedule when Nye's book was published. "Radio's 'comedy hour' format fitted television perfectly," Nye writes, "all that had to be done was to film it."[40] Apparently Fred Allen never figured this out.

"The Gleason Case," as Gilbert Seldes entitled his 1956 essay, is a fabulous American Dream, the story of a 260-pound Gatsby seeking the love of 200 million Daisies. Like Fitzgerald's tragic hero, The Great One had been driven by his heart's desire to rise from poverty and obscurity to the heights of boom-time America:

> He had come a long way to his blue lawn, and his dream must have seemed so close that he could hardly fail to grasp it. He did not know that it was already behind him, somewhere back in the vast obscurity beyond the city, where the dark fields of the republic rolled on under the night.[41]

Perhaps more to the point is the epigraph to Fitzgerald's novel, lines credited to Thomas Parke d'Invilliers (actually the author's friend John Peale Bishop):

> Then wear the gold hat, if that will move her;
>   If you can bounce high, bounce for her too,
> Till she cry, "Lover, gold-hatted, high-bouncing lover,
>   I must have you!"[42]

Self-Reflexive at Last ★ 5

Suchlike I love . . . I loosen myself and pass freely . . . and
   am at the mother's breast with the little child,
And swim with the swimmer, and wrestle with the wres-
   tlers, and march in line with the firemen, and pause and
   listen and count.
                 Walt Whitman, "I Sing the Body Electric"

I say to myself, "Of the innumerable effects or impressions,
of which the heart, the intellect, or (more generally) the
soul is susceptible, what one shall I, on the present occasion, select?"
   Edgar Allan Poe, "The Philosophy of Composition"

Whitman and Poe were the major urban poets of nineteenth-century America. Their visions are diametrically opposite. Whitman saw a new beginning for humankind in the teem-
ing polyglot masses of the new nation; Poe was horrified by its
chaotic formlessness. The imaginative agenda of identification
that Whitman chants in the lines above may be answered in a
broadcast day consisting of *Nova, The Wide World of Sports,
Georgia Championship Wrestling,* and a rerun of *Emergency!*
One imagines an America without television, an America mutat-
ing the ideas, customs, styles, religions, genotypes, and leisure
habits of the world, yet unable to "normalize" these creations
instantly by representing them to every citizen in every corner

of the Republic. Whitman's call for an indigenous American art was surely motivated by an impulse to share news of the great experiment in democracy with those whom he called "the Americans of all nations."[1] The key to heterogeny—and therefore to the success of democracy itself—was the power of identification, the power to imaginatively merge self and other. Malcolm Cowley writes of Whitman:

> The poet sees far into space and time; . . . he ranges over the continent and goes speeding through the heavens among tailed meteors. His secret is the power of identification. Since everything emanates from the universal soul, and since his own soul is the same essence, he can identify himself with every object and with every person, living or dead, heroic or criminal.[2]

One hundred years before Gleason, Whitman walked the streets of Brooklyn. The array of characters he encountered at this gate to the New World ignited in him an electric charge of identity and gave birth to a new poetry. The poet saw himself as Adam in the Garden, naming Creation. Poe, by contrast, was a magazinist. His method and work contain an explicit rejection of Whitman's panoramic stream of consciousness. Poe writes of his *modus operandi,* "In general, suggestions, having arisen pell-mell, are pursued and forgotten in a similar manner."[3] Instead, he sees the writer as a grand manipulator of a "susceptible" audience.[4] The magazine industry, which had been engaged in a kind of proto-demographic marketing since the rise of Grub Street in eighteenth-century London, demanded a literature that would sell in mass quantity, or that at least could be targeted at specific readership groups. It is therefore not surprising that Poe's detective and horror fiction should have had so profound an influence on popular American film and television narrative. Whitman wrote that Poe's works, "by final judgment, probably belong among the electric lights of imaginative literature, brilliant and dazzling, but with no heat."[5] Emerson called Poe "the jingle man."[6] Whitman, once a successful newspaperman, dropped out of "the market" and published the idiosyncratic *Leaves of Grass* (1855). With the *Leaves,* he offers himself to the reader as a lover, pledging his body and soul. Poe, on the other hand, is a master technician whose chief concern is sensation. Both artists seek to seduce the reader; the difference is that of the *amateur* and the pro.

The television viewer, a rough number, a jerking knee in the voodoo poetry of Madison Avenue, sits, reclines, makes love, eats, fondles a handgun, smokes marijuana, snores in front of the set. Convenient and eclectic, television is a crisis of consciousness. Confronted with everything the cultural traffic will allow, the imagination engages or avoids. Engagement means completing the circuit of transmission through the neural system to mind and emotion; avoidance constitutes abortion of the image, isolation of the senses, satisfaction with mere relief, and a surrender of cognitive capacity at the hands of an increasingly ugly world.

131

NBC initiated daily network radio service on 16 November 1926, with a broadcast anchored from the grand ballroom of the Waldorf-Astoria Hotel in New York, where a thousand invited guests in formal attire danced to orchestra music and listened to crooners.[7] They were joined by half a continent in various states of undress. To emphasize the miracle of "the network" to a public that had become more or less familiar with radio over a period of twenty years, remote pickups were featured in the show. Will Rogers stood at a microphone in Kansas City, then the westernmost frontier of network coverage, and did stand-up comedy for thirty states from the shores of the Missouri River. Did minds skip across the continent with those electric waves from New York to Chicago to Kansas City and back again? Or had the multitudes been manipulated through a voyeuristic evening at the Waldorf? Forty-three years later, network coverage had become audiovisual and had been extended to the Moon. *Das Fernsehen,* the German word for the television set, means "the thing to see far with." The rest is up to the viewer.

On the premiere episode of *See It Now* (CBS, 1951–55), Edward R. Murrow presented live images of the Atlantic and Pacific oceans. "We are impressed by a medium," he commented, "through which a man sitting in his living room has been able for the first time to look at two oceans at once."[8] The passage to India that had eluded Columbus, Hudson, and the others was achieved by a feat of communication. Sylvester ("Pat")

Weaver, an early NBC programming strategist who is the conceptual auteur of such shows as *Today* and *Tonight,* had a similar vision of television as "the window on the world." "Weaver," writes Alex McNeil, "saw the *Today* show as a program that few people would watch from beginning to end; instead, it was to be designed so that viewers could eat breakfast and get ready for school or work without devoting all of their time to the television set."[9] It originated from a studio on the ground floor of the RCA Building in Rockefeller Center; windows allowed viewers the spectacle of a midtown Manhattan street during morning rush hour. An entourage usually waved and mugged for the camera, like a family celebrating its new 8-mm home-movie kit. Behind these "actors," the imperturbable streetlife of New York paraded past, a continuous, evolving event, recorded in its earlier stages by Whitman's pen. *Wide Wide World,* another Weaver concept, developed this mode of presentation even further: "On the October, 1955 premiere the topic was 'A Sunday in Autumn,' and reports were made from Lake Mead, the Grand Canyon, Weeki Wachee (Fla.), Dallas, San Francisco, St. Louis, Gloucester (Mass.), Cleveland, Omaha, and New York City."[10] The list is Whitmanian, and the concept as well. Steve Allen, the first host of Weaver's *Tonight* show, delighted in training a camera on the street and verbally extemporizing a narrative frame to suit whatever personalities and events the urban moment might yield. Dave Garroway stood in front of a large painting of a magic carpet, anchoring a series of transcontinental pickups. One edition of *Garroway at Large* (NBC, 1949–54) originated from the rooftop of NBC's Chicago studios and consisted of long pans of the evening skyline.[11]

Recently, however, the casual "window on the world" has all but disappeared from network television. *Sunday Morning* with Charles Kurault is perhaps a notable exception. Kurault delights in Weaver-like pans of regional landscapes, especially during seasonal splendor. Otherwise, "firsthand reports" have become an almost exclusive province of "hard news." Whitman claimed, "The United States themselves are essentially the greatest poem."[12] This is the supposition of a show such as "A Sunday in Autumn" and of Weaver's work generally. But the dramas of international egos, crime, cruelty, death, and disaster offer dependable narrative continuity, and this has made them more suitable for contemporary marketing. The economic stakes have become too high to trust Whitman's open-collared Muse on network air. The schlockumentaries (*Real People, That's Incredible!*) actually debase the window-on-the-world concept. They are composed of segments that are window-dressed to resemble firsthand images but are so painstakingly staged and edited that they are actually disguised representational dramas. In 1981 *That's Incredible!* began adding a disclaimer to its final credits, which, in the space of a second or two, informs the viewer that what he or she has seen are "actual events" that have been "reenacted" for the camera.

133

Local stations, especially those with remote minicam units, still occasionally express the primal video urge simply to "show things." In the spring of 1980, for example, station WMT-TV, Cedar Rapids, Iowa, used its new minicam to present the longest freight train to ever pass through town. As the six o'clock edition of *Action News* opened, the anchorman cut to a reporter who stood in the foreground while the freight train rolled past. At intervals of approximately six or seven minutes throughout the half-hour telecast, the anchor returned to the trackside scene. The train kept up its steady pace as the sign-off credits rolled vertically across it. Neither the engine nor the caboose ever appeared.

Perhaps the event that violated the innocence of network TV's "window on the world" was the first Kennedy assassination. Its status as the heaviest event that had happened to America since Pearl Harbor was secured by the fact that it precipitated the extended suspension of all regular network programming. The relentless representationalism of daily transcontinental TV ceased for the first time since the medium had achieved ubiquity. Furthermore, it remained unclear for days as to when or even whether traditional proscenium distance would be reestablished. But even this regimen seemed to normalize, establishing a loose taxonomy of dramatic genres of its own: the long commentaries by patriarch anchormen such as Cronkite and Huntley; "The Funeral," marked by John-John's made-for-TV salute; "The Assassination of Oswald," network television's first snuff film; the endless biographies of Oswald and Ruby, each inspired by the revelation of a new "fact" ("Oswald *had* lived in the Soviet Union"; "Ruby *did* have underworld connections"). During all of this, the mystique of the U.S. Constitution notwithstanding, television was in charge of the country. The possibilities of coup d'état or some other radical development of the assassination were controlled by network telecast. The mere fact that Walter Cronkite was narrating the event suggested that no serious damage had been done to the structure of the state. After three days of such programming, TV turned the reigns of power over to Lyndon Johnson, and *Perry Mason* came back on the air. Television had demonstrated its central position in American culture to a degree that was no casual matter.

134

A more recent example of the political significance of a national television transmission system can be found in the failed Spanish coup d'état of 1981. Armed members of the Civil Guard entered the chambers of the Cortes, sprayed the ceiling with machine-gun bullets, and took the legislators hostage. Informed of the attempt, King Juan Carlos appeared on national television in support of the constitutional monarchy, effectively isolating the Fascists in the parliament building.

As Enzensberger has written, "control of capital, of the means of production, and of the armed forces . . . is no longer enough." He continues:

When an industrially developed country is occupied or liberated today, whenever there is a coup d'état, a revolution, or a counterrevolution, the crack police units, the paratroopers, the guerilla fighters do not any longer descend on the main squares of the city or seize the centers of heavy industry, as in the nineteenth century, or symbolic sites, like the royal palace; the new regime will instead take over, first of all, the radio and television stations, the telephone and telex exchanges, and the printing presses.[13]

The implication of Enzensberger's statement is that power has become a matter of information. The "fact" (or normalcy) of state control is more effectively established by a television screen viewed by millions than by the barrel of a gun pointed at a mere crowd. Television's greatest power, as I have suggested earlier, is its ability to select and legitimate the "normal." The importance of normalcy cannot be overestimated in the modern political state. It is the principle that regulates the character of all mass-produced consumer goods and services. It is the state of affairs that defies unbearable paranoia and allows business-as-usual to be conducted even under the hydrogen threat. The daily collection of horror stories selected as The News is pointedly anormal; it is The News. On the other hand, the representational theater of familiar characters solving recognizable problems in conclusive ways is normal; it happens continuously every day, every hour, every minute. Repetitious announcements of "gangland slayings" and "guerrilla kidnappings" flatten such events into slightly dissonant rhythms that are absorbed by the monolithic wall of normalcy. Would the same be true of the "shows" that would be telecast on a channel whose programming consists of permanent live coverage of the Times Square subway station or a suburban shopping mall's videogame parlor? It is no wonder that the television industry has shied away from the dangers of discovery and committed itself to the ideology of demographic magazinism. Network researchers would certainly agree with Poe's assertion that the relationship between audience and art is "the desire of the moth for the star,"[14] a determined reaction, a tropism. Their jobs depend on it. Poe writes of art, "With the Intellect or with the Conscience, it has only collateral relations. Unless incidentally, it has no concern whatever with Duty or with Truth."[15] It is hard to imagine a bolder manifesto for the American television industry.

135

Cradle to Grave

The lives of the vast majority of Americans born since the defeat of the Axis forces have been accompanied by a continuing electronic paratext to experience. This shadow memory is interactive with individual memory; it provides images that function as personal signifiers (e.g., the music or TV show that played during a certain sexual experience) and at the same time serves to document and redocument collective experience. TV is the central source of this companion record to experience, but it would be naive to minimize the contributions of other media. Radio, which was once a primary delivery system offering broad ranges of representational and presentational programming, gradually yielded many of its functions to television during the decade following Hiroshima and became a thoroughly formatted medium. Most radio stations gave up the broadcast of diverse programming. Each station adopted a single program that became congruent with its identity: all-Top 40, all-C&W, all-AOR, all MOR, all-Muzak, all-Classical, all-News, all-Talk, et cetera. Today, only a handful of eclectic commercial radio stations exist.[16] The demographically successful radio station adopts a single format which makes it a cultural locus in its market; this is as true of "Top 40" as it is of "Classical." This change parallels the shift in the magazine industry from "general interest" periodicals (*Life, Look*) to "target interest" periodicals (*Skiing, Apartment Life*). Though radios that receive TV sound, and even televisions that plug into automobile cigarette lighters, have become generally available, driving continues to be one of the few conscious activities that is structurally isolated from telecast. Since almost all Americans live in areas served by poor or nominal mass transportation systems, the car radio fills an important coverage gap in the message distribution system. Competition for listeners is particularly intense in the radio industry during what is termed "drive time," a period roughly equivalent to what used to be called "rush hour." Radio also holds a special significance because of its role in the national puberty rite. McLuhanites often describe television as a modern hearth, the center of domestic life in the homes of the global village. This is more than a metaphor at times. In New York City, for example, a local independent station offers its viewers what Jim Hoberman describes as "a three-and-a-half hour Christmas Eve telecast of a log burning in the Gracie Mansion fireplace, accompanied by seasonal Muzak. This epic transmission (actually a 10-second loop repeated 1200 or so times) was conceived by the WPIX chairman of the board 'in the hope that viewers would make a tradition of coming together as a family on Christmas Eve.'" Hoberman concludes that "*The Yule Log* is evidence that daily life in America has surpassed surrealism and broken through into science fiction."[17] Though television has recently been criticized by the Fundamentalist Right as a force divisive to family life, watching television together is an important family activity in many American households. As teenagers enter sexual awareness, they rebel against television to some degree, as they do against all symbols of family authority. A. C. Nielsen reports that Females 12–17 and Males 12–17 (in that order) are the demographic age units that watch the least television.[18] All adult groups, as well as children below the age of twelve, watch more. The taboos surrounding sexuality become associated with the taboos inherent in a "special music" that parents cannot share with teenagers. Though sitcoms such as *The Partridge Family* (ABC, 1970–74) and *The Brady Bunch* (ABC, 1969–74) have attempted to make rock and roll a wholesome family activity, an implicit rejection of family order accompanies the search for sexual identity, and television, as a center of family life, must bear a share of adolescent resentment.

137

Rock and roll has come closest of all the electronic arts to fulfilling the dream of an indigenous American art, an art severed from the umbilical cord of European culture. It is a music that takes place in what Jack Kerouac called "the great American night." Its moments of unabashed celebration of racial, gender, and class integration, and its pervasive obsession with sexual expression, rival Whitman's. Rock music is such an organic component of the American cultural landscape that, if one has grown up in the U.S.A., it is possible to compose one's autobiography by listing a series of all-time personal favorite songs. By means of radio, each rock and roll subgenre develops its own archive of golden hits; these are periodically recycled into contemporary play lists. While driving around, the listener may spontaneously encounter a song that compellingly suggests a particular time, place, event, or person; this is one of the great pleasures of North American civilization. Until quite recently, television was unable to present music—rock or any other kind—in an attractive way. For a public well-equipped with stereo components, the tiny monaural speakers of TV sets offer little satisfaction. This may partially explain the demise of the musically oriented TV variety show, which was popular until the mid-sixties, the era of mass stereoization. The TV industry, however, having conquered its own parent, owns the radio industry, and the hits just keep on coming—in stereo, on cable, etc.

The American cinema, which shared mass message distribution responsibilities with radio during the years between the first two world wars, has also become a relatively peripheral, though still important, medium of American mass culture. Except for a dozen or so blockbusters each year, movies can usually hope only to break even at the box office; profit margins are established by sales to television. This situation has affected not only the subject matter of films but the editing technique as well. Narrative continuity must be planned for commercial interruption in almost all major studio releases. Ironically, every time a moviegoer "gets away from the TV set for a night" and lays down as much as five dollars for a ticket at the box office,

138

he or she is paying for the privilege of participating in a market test that will be used to determine the price of the film's sale to television: If so many people are willing to pay to see a picture, then so many more are presumed to be willing to watch it for free. Whereas once all feature-length films were completely dependent on the sale of tickets directly to the public, direct marketing is now only a component of a larger marketing strategy. The made-for-TV movie forgoes direct marketing completely. Like radio, the cinema plays an important role in the teenage puberty rite. In a nation where live theater, in the relatively few places it is available, is outlandishly expensive, the movie has become the definitive date, rivaled only by the more expensive rock concert. The darkened theater is a free zone for petting; the privacy of the car at the drive-in is convenient to coitus. But after the erotic problem of parental restraint is solved, the movies become less important and the convenience of television reasserts itself. Nielsen's "National Audience Demographics Report" shows that from the age of eighteen until death time spent watching television steadily increases.[19] Even the once unique experience of "the great screen" is challenged by home video projection systems.

The carefully coordinated relationship of television, radio, the movies, the audio and audiovisual recording industries, the print media, and all the components of what Enzensberger calls "the consciousness industry" is underscored by the interlocking directorates and lateral agreements that control them. Competition among media is nominal; it is the same kind of competition that exists among the Chevrolet, Pontiac, Oldsmobile, Buick, and Cadillac divisions of the General Motors Corporation. Everyone must drive, and everyone must imagine; the market has been carved up according to rational marketing theories. The early antagonisms between the radio and recording industries, and later between the television and movie industries, have been replaced by an industrially mature relationship that establishes a collaborative, productive role for each medium in the total marketing blitz of American culture. The result is complete coverage of the population. On the Left, Herbert Marcuse has damned this phenomenon as a brainwashing system that leads to "one-dimensional man." Ernest van den Haag, a conservative, bemoans the "monotony" of the media blitz but blames it on "the mounting political power of the poor," who **139** demand constant semiliterate recreation.[20] Yet viewers who cannot find it in their souls to become thoroughly alienated from the images that have filled their senses since before the advent of their consciousnesses, or who lack the wealth to protect themselves from media ubiquity, are likely to find little useful in either of these politically motivated analyses. Memory—the sensual recall of image—is too valuable a resource to discard. Artful uses for this cultural heritage can be found.

The Stars Come Out at Night

Each week, the A. C. Nielsen Company publishes *Fast Weekly Household Audiences Report* for its corporate customers. It contains, among many things, a chart entitled "% TV Households Using TV (Average Minute)," which catalogs each hour of the previous television week by the quarter hour, indicating the percentage of households with televisions that Nielsen believes is watching (anything) during an average minute of each fifteen-minute period. The following information is taken from the report issued for the week of 12–18 December 1977 (eastern time): At 6:00 P.M., only about 50 percent of households with television sets in the United States were playing at least one of them. By 9:00 P.M., the percentage had risen to approximately two thirds of all HUTs. At 11:00 P.M., as prime time ended, the percentage of households watching had returned to the level of about one half of the population. By 1:00 A.M., less than 20 percent of Americans were "using TV." The sharp drop-off of viewership that normally occurs during the period following the late local news has traditionally defined "late night" as a marginal period. This has occasioned a relatively greater degree of programming experimentation than has occurred in the economically crucial hours of prime time. For many years, only NBC bothered to program network telecasts after 11:30. The relative lack of interest in the time period was of course a direct result of its reduced potential for assembling large audiences. Sponsors pay by the head; each one that falls to the pillow diminishes the pot of gold by another speck. This is easily demonstrated by comparing the performances of a prime-time show and a late-night show: On 13 December 1977, both *Laverne and Shirley* and *The Tonight Show* "won" their time periods. Garry Marshall's sitcom achieved a rating of 34.6; more than one third of all U.S. HUTs (i.e., 25,220,000 households) were tuned in to this prime-time tale of the two Milwaukee brewery workers. *The Tonight Show Starring Johnny Carson* also led its competition but with a rating of only 10.0 (or 7,290,000 households). Furthermore, Nielsen reports that total television viewership steadily declined during *The Tonight Show*'s 11:30–1:00 time period, while it increased during *Laverne and Shirley*'s 8:30–9:00 period.[21] Finally, it is taken for granted that the size of each household steadily diminishes as sleep comes to individual members of the unit. As the evening dissipates into the wee hours, the television audience gradually loses some of its "mass" characteristics and takes on a more demographically specific profile. "Who is watching at 1:00 A.M.?" is not as difficult a question to answer as "Who is watching at 9:00 P.M.?"

Traditional show business wisdom, predating television, has always held that the "late show" can be a bit raunchier (i.e., more "sophisticated") than the early show. Indeed, NBC hired none other than a burlesque comedian to host *Broadway Open House* (1950–51), network TV's first late-night show. Jerry Lester, a veteran of the New York bump-and-grind scene, based much of the show's humor on his lewd physical and verbal reactions to the fifty-inch chest of Dagmar, "the show's biggest star next to Jerry."[22] Dagmar, actually an actress named Jennie Lewis (née Virginia Ruth Egnor), had been cast and rechristened by Lester to play the burlesque role of the buxom blonde airhead to the comic emcee's lascivious wiseguy. Her "part," in what otherwise appeared to be a presentational show, called for her to read "inane poetry with a deadpan delivery" while

Lester heckled. But television played strange tricks on burlesque tradition. The camera lingered longer on the zaftig Dagmar than on funnyman Lester. "She was an instant hit and became a regular feature, her salary rising quickly to the point
where only Jerry made more."[23] Lester resented being upstaged
by a second banana and tried to undercut Dagmar by adding
another blonde bombshell, Barbara Nichols, whom he rechristened "Agathon." Still distraught by Dagmar's throbbing celebrity, Lester demanded that his own creation be given her
walking papers. The network refused. Used to having his own **141**
way on the runway, Lester quit the show, leaving the upstart TV
executives to stew in their own juice. TV, after all, seemed a
shaky proposition in 1951; burlesque would never die.

NBC did not attempt another late-night network venture
until three years later. This time, a carefully groomed TV personality was made host. Steve Allen, first host of *The Tonight
Show*, singlehandedly invented the art of desk-and-sofa as it is
still practiced today. A stand-up comedian, composer, musician,
author, and actor, Allen brought a range to the role that has
never quite been matched. Johnny Carson still does characters
invented by Allen; David Letterman pays homage to "Steverino"
each time he throws a pencil at the phony window behind him
and sets off the sound effect of glass being broken. Allen's
comedy is a synthesis of vulgar erudition and erudite vulgarity.
He is equally at home ad-libbing with guests or taking a pie in
the face. Allen often opened his show with outrageous physical
stunts, such as diving into a giant vat of Jell-O or stuffing his six-
foot frame into a front-loading automatic washer for a turn.
Settling down at his desk, he might conduct intelligent discussions of jazz or even books, yet he could not resist punctuating
these with wild outbursts of adolescent noises (his seagull imitation, "Shmock, shmock," is memorable). He had broken into
national TV as cohost, with Jan Murray, of *Songs for Sale* (CBS,
1951), a talent scout vehicle in which the songs of unknown
composers were performed by name vocalists and judged by a
panel that included Duke Ellington and Mitch Miller. In 1953
he became host of another amateur show, *Talent Patrol* (ABC),
which featured acts by U.S. armed forces personnel. That same
year, NBC selected him to host Pat Weaver's experimental New
York late-night talk/variety show known as *Tonight*. This pilot

market test yielded positive results, and the show went network the following season. True to his talent scout origins, Allen "discovered" many new stars while behind the *Tonight Show* desk, including comedians Don Knotts, Louie Nye, Tom Poston, and Bill Dana (who unveiled José Jimenez to the world as a *Tonight Show* sketch). But in the midfifties, *Tonight Show* audiences rarely numbered as high as half a million households. For Allen, the show was merely a stepping-stone to the more desirable heights of prime time, and in 1956 NBC granted him **142** a conventional comedy-variety show. Allen took many of his *Tonight Show* regulars with him and created one of the funniest comedy shows in prime-time history. Its mixture of continuing sketches (Allen's "Man on the Street Interviews" with Knotts, Nye, Poston, and Dayton Allen are perhaps the most widely remembered) and stand-up comedy make it a prototype for the late-night comedy shows of the eighties. Unfortunately, *The Steve Allen Show* faced no less an opponent than *The Ed Sullivan Show,* and it lasted only three years.

When the prime-time show went into production, Allen did not quit as *Tonight Show* host but cut his appearances down to three times a week (a precedent Johnny Carson would eventually follow). On Mondays and Tuesdays in late 1956, *Tonight* was given over to Ernie Kovacs. In the vast junkpile of television history, perhaps no individual stands out as so original an artist as Kovacs. The mustachioed, cigar-puffing performer/writer/director/producer was the master of the nonnarrative television comedy blackout sketch. He was the first commercial television artist—perhaps the only—to significantly scratch the surface of the unique visual possibilities of a medium effectively ruled by techniques borrowed from radio, stage, and cinema. Tuning in to a Kovacs show, the viewer might be treated to four or five minutes of a man sucking a single strand of spaghetti to the tune of Beethoven's Fifth, or a woman gingerly enjoying a bubble bath while a procession of midgets emerge from beneath the suds. Narrative resolution, the burden of much televised comedy, was never as important to Kovacs as achieving sublime moments of beauty on the ugly little black-and-white screen. Kovacs's work shares more spiritually with the avant-garde theater of Richard Foreman than with the comedy-variety of Caesar, Gleason, or Berle.

Allen left *The Tonight Show* altogether in January of 1957, just four months after the rotating Allen-Kovacs arrangement had been initiated. Kovacs disappeared from the show as well. It is worth noting that Kovacs managed to stay on the air (on a succession of ABC shows, which included a stint as a prime-time gameshow host) until his death in an automobile accident in 1962. He has the distinction of being the only popular comedian in television history whose work has been aired on PBS. A ten-part retrospective of Kovacs's sketches was shown in hour-long episodes in 1977.

143

In 1957 NBC attempted to redesign *The Tonight Show* completely. It was renamed *Tonight! America after Dark* and was brought closer to the concept Pat Weaver had envisioned in 1953:

> Its original host was *Today* veteran Jack Lescoulie. There were reports by contributing columnists in New York, Chicago, and Los Angeles, and live coverage from all three cities and elsewhere via remotes. Interviews with personalities in the news, in politics, or in show business were interspersed with live visits to night clubs, Broadway openings, or such places as research hospitals and planetariums. Regular features were Bob Considine's summary of the news of the day, "The World Tonight,"; a Hy Gardner interview segment, "Face to Face,"; and news commentary, human interest stories and interviews on "Considine's Corner."[24]

Taking a quick nose dive in the ratings, the show was canceled less than six months after its premiere. Of the four late-night styles that had been tried, Allen's had clearly been the most successful. NBC returned to the desk-and-sofa format with a new host, Jack Paar.

As Jack Gould of the *New York Times* wrote, Paar was "not the traditional trouper" but "a creation of television."[25] Indeed, Paar had no discernible show business talent; he was neither actor, comedian, singer, dancer, animal trainer, nor ventriloquist; nor did he have any kind of "act" that people, over the centuries, have paid to see. What he could do was talk—often right at the camera. He talked mostly about his friends and his enemies. An early booster of both Fidel Castro and John Kennedy, he occasionally made forays into politics. He looked tear-fully into the camera to quit his job on three separate occasions on issues ranging from salary to censorship. In the preface to his autobiography, *I Kid You Not,* Paar describes himself this way:

> I've never been a Communist or alcoholic and I've never been psychoanalyzed. Actually I'm a pretty ordinary guy. I'm just like any other fellow with a wife and daughter, pleasant suburban home, a Mercedes-Benz convertible, twenty-seven pairs of imported sunglasses, and who has an hour and three-quarters TV show every weekday night.[26]

144

Surrounding himself with a clique of midcult raconteurs (Hugh Downs, Alexander King), second-rate ingenues (Genevieve, Florence Henderson), and third-rate comedians (Joey Bishop, Peggy Cass), Paar constructed a remarkably banal fantasy world of angry feuds and sentimental affections that became the sub-ject of the show. He used the show as a soapbox from which to denounce his enemies, who included Dorothy Kilgallen and Ed Sullivan and almost anyone who wrote for a newspaper. In the context of pre-Kennedy assassination television, Paar's *Tonight Show* was a sophisticated glimpse into the petty world of New York show biz life. No other network star has ever used a show in quite this way.

Under Paar, the desk-and-sofa show emerged as an impor-tant showcase for the American entertainment industry at large. While variety show hosts were forced to pay big-name stars thousands of dollars to appear on their prime-time shows, the same comedians and singers gladly appeared on *Tonight* for minimum union scale (less than $500). The reason for this lay in a formal aspect of the desk-and-sofa arrangement. While being "interviewed" or "chatting" with the host, the performer could freely plug his or her concert and club dates. These de facto advertisements were worth far more than the few thou-sand dollars sacrificed by agreeing to appear at scale. Ed Sulli-van, the dean of variety show hosts, angrily accused Paar of exploiting entertainers; the two became mortal enemies over the issue. The conflict also points to an interesting distinction between the presentational and documentary modes on television.

One regrettable Paar innovation, which would affect late-night television for decades, was to change *Tonight* from a "live" to a "live-on-tape" show. The live-on-tape concept is a remarkable television original. It purports to document an in-studio performance "as it happened" but gives network censors the opportunity to "bleep out" objectionable material. It also allowed Paar to cut production to four shows a week. The price was the loss of television's only daily, live, nonrepresentational show outside the purview of The News. On Friday nights, *Best of Paar* reruns were shown, establishing *The Tonight Show*'s painful and ever-expanding tradition of reruns. While the cosmology of a representational series is enriched by the rerun, the desk-and-sofa episode becomes drearily dated by it.

145

Like Steve Allen, Paar "graduated" to prime time with *The Jack Paar Program* in 1962. During the spring and summer of that year, while the host-designate, Johnny Carson, played out the string on his ABC contract as emcee of the daytime game-show *Who Do You Trust?,* two dozen temporaries played musical chairs on *Tonight*. This was perhaps the show's most interesting period. Groucho Marx (who had turned down an offer of the permanent job) did a week, along with such diverse comers as Art Linkletter, Joey Bishop, Merv, Soupy Sales, Arlene Francis, and Jan Murray. Jack E. Leonard explored the commercial limits of insult humor that Don Rickles would later violate. The C&W crowd was offered Jimmy Dean; beatniks, Mort Sahl. The country club set was even offered Peter Lind Hayes and Mary Healy. Jerry Lewis, just in the process of making an important career move from the cinema to the charity drive, brought his special psychotheater to *Tonight*.

The night of 2 October 1962 marked the establishment of *Tonight Show* normalcy: Johnny Carson took over. Carson's success was immediate. Kenneth Tynan writes:

> With the public, Carson's triumph was . . . non-pareil. Under the Paar regime, the show had very seldom been seen by more than seven and a half million viewers. . . . Under Carson, the program *averaged* seven million four hundred

and fifty-eight thousand viewers per night in its first six months.[27]

John Horn, TV critic of the *New York Herald Tribune,* was not as impressed by Carson as the Nielsen families: "He exhibits all the charm of a snickering small boy scribbling graffiti on a public wall."[28] Whereas Steve Allen, Ernie Kovacs, and Jack Paar, each in his own way, strove for a TV species of eastern gentility, Carson's persona is strictly Middle America, a midwestern core with a touch of California thrown in for style.

146

The modus operandi of Carson's humor seems to involve an invitation to the audience to see things from his point of view. Once accepted, this becomes a license to tell self-consciously weak jokes. These jokes then become objects of derision, which both Johnny and the audience laugh at from the perch of sound common sense. It is fruitless to try to compare Carson to any other comedian in history. His continuous, almost daily appearance before millions for over twenty years puts his work in a genre of its own. No one has done it before, and no one is likely to do it in the future.

Carson's consistent ratings have enabled him virtually to dictate the terms of his contract—and the form of *The Tonight Show.* In 1972 he moved the show from New York to Burbank out of personal preference. The network had opposed the move, but Carson proved to be bigger than the show. The official title has been changed to *The Tonight Show Starring Johnny Carson,* and this is used even on the many nights when guest hosts occupy The Prince's chair. In the show business world, an appearance on *The Tonight Show* has become as important for a performer as an appearance on the evening news is for a politician with national aspirations. Mel Brooks, who rarely appears on other TV shows, has said of him: "From the word go, Carson could tell when you'd hit comic gold, and he'd help you mine it. He always knew pay dirt when he saw it. The guys on other shows didn't."[29] Even Woody Allen, who has had little flattering to say about television or the TV industry, remarked of Carson, "He loves it when you score."[30]

The strikingly negative effect, however, of Carson's twenty-year triumph on *Tonight* has been precisely his longevity. With yeoman energy he has succeeded in robbing the late-night period of the specialness (non-prime-timeness?) of its early extremes. Carson is not as vulgar as Lester, as erudite as Allen, as visionary as Kovacs, or as emotional as Paar. His sparingly used masks—Carnak (derived from Allen's "Answer Man"), Art Fern (Allen made the name "Fern" famous), Aunt Blabby (Jonathan Winters's "Maude Frickert"), and Floyd Turbo (a shotgun-toting redneck, Carson's only original)—can be funny, but the viewer has no hope of seeing established limits transcended.

As an interviewer, he is neither a witty raconteur nor a brainless praiser of guests. In 1969 the other two networks attempted, for the first time, to compete directly with *The Tonight Show.* ABC tried to go over Carson's head with Yalie Dick Cavett; CBS attacked from beneath with Merv Griffin. Cavett was packed off to PBS. Merv was exiled to permanent syndication. Johnny is the Chevy of late-night TV, the Quarter-Pounder, the 65 percent polyester white shirt. Expectations are low enough that mere efficiency is appreciated and failures are easily forgiven. The best the other networks are willing to offer against him are Ted Koppel and reruns of *Quincy.* Maybe one of the guests will be good tonight. Why not at least watch the monologue?

Johnny Carson, like Walter Cronkite, has been a potent totem in the iconography of American normalcy. Having spent the fifties dutifully building their F-scores—Johnny as a daytimer, Walter as a goody-two-shoes reporter in the shadow of *enfant terrible* Edward R. Murrow—they captured the desks of *Tonight* and *The CBS Evening News* in 1962, creating a presentational frame around prime time that would last from the Kennedy moment to the first Reagan budget. A grand videotape or even transcription of the thousands of daily Carson monologues and Cronkite news scripts would offer a comprehensive guide to the boundaries of culturally acceptable subjects, political positions, and tastes that defined institutional (official?) American culture for twenty years. According to *Performer Q,* the annual survey of the recognizability and popularity of media personalities (it is used by the networks to make casting and salary decisions), photographs of Carson and Cronkite were correctly identified by 88 percent of the American population; the two had exactly that same F-score in 1977.[31] Walter opens the television evening with a story on the increasing hydrocarbon content of air in metropolitan Los Angeles ("The Environmental Protection Agency revealed today ..."); Johnny closes with a story on the air pollution in Burbank ("How thick was it?"). Tragedy, the lesser form in the canon of demographic aesthetics, precedes comedy, which gets the last word. The events of history—from Oswald to Stockman—are reduced to mere content by this monumental form. Walter is the frown, Johnny the smile, on the great icons at the left and right margins of the American proscenium. Cronkite's retirement in March of 1981 and Carson's gradual retirement, which progresses with each new contract, bring this era to an end. Who will replace these emigrants from the Old World of Radio/Cinema who came as young men to the Golden Land of Television and made it so big? Whoever they are, they will be native-born. David Letterman and Ted Koppel are apparently among them.

Boomers

Television's growth and development as a mass medium, industry, and art form have occurred more or less simultaneously with the nuclear threat against all life as we know it. The unspeakable horror that palpable Armageddon conjures for the rational mind makes comedy particularly appealing. Under the threat of faceless end-of-the-world button pushing, there is an honest urge, if not a responsibility, to be a wiseguy, to find a use for the static energies of cynicism. The bomb itself is best written into daily consciousness as a kind of punch line to history. The imagination tires and shrinks from exploring the tragic possibilities of the latest reports, whether they are presented on ABC's *World News Tonight* or in the *New York Review of Books*. Laughter is a control of the hysteria that deeper contemplation of existing conditions causes. A well-wrought joke is a welcome reminder of the heroic possibilities of the imagination. The young Faulkner wrote *The Sound and the Fury* and *Absalom, Absalom!;* facing death, he wrote *The Reivers* and adapted short stories for *Lux Video Theatre* (CBS, 1950–57). A new generation of artists, brought up in a culture of doom, has produced notable works of comedy and is promising more. In contrast, representational TV tragedies, usually packaged as made-for-TV movies, rarely reach the midcult "heights" achieved by Paddy Chayefsky and Rod Serling on *Playhouse 90* a quarter of a century ago.

The first glimpses of baby-boom comedy on national television were seen on *NBC's Saturday Night Live* during the late seventies. The show premiered in October 1975; it marked an experimental effort by NBC, the late-night leader, to expand into the Saturday late-night period, long a preserve of local movie showcases. In 1973 the network had made its initial foray into weekend late-night programming when it launched *The Midnight Special,* a rock-variety package hosted by bubble-gum radio disc jockey Wolfman Jack. The show aired after Johnny Carson on Fridays. *Don Kirshner's Rock Concert* premiered in syndication that same year, and the fight for post-Vietnam 18–34-year-old consumers had come to the marginal hours of the late-night weekend time period. Visions of relatively educated, moneyed, and ready-to-spend boombabies, hungry for motorcycles, water beds, and an extra can of Mountain Dew, attracted advertisers who had been priced out of the spiraling prime-time head-count market. The problems of music on TV, however, remained. While the PBS television network and National Public Radio have simulcast many programs, allowing viewers with TV sets and FM receivers to watch operas and symphony orchestras and listen to the performances in stereo, this option is limited in commercial network broadcasting. For example, an NBC simulcast of *The Midnight Special* was not likely to be carried by an NBC radio affiliate that maintains an all-Muzak or all-News format. (This problem can be readily avoided on cable TV; MTV offers permanent simulcast of rock music in video and FM cable stereo to subscribers.) Furthermore, Wolfman Jack and Don Kirshner were hardly credible as "hip" personalities. The late-night rockshows had used stand-up comedy acts as tangential features. *Saturday Night Live* was an attempt to climb farther up the demographic scale by reversing the ratio of music and comedy. Media-child good taste would always prefer the stereo system to monaural TV music; on the other hand, TV performance of stand-up comedy can compare favorably to the comedy record album. What other than music might draw the rock audience?

The early episodes of *Saturday Night Live* were erratic. The

149

show seemed to be intended as a revolving showcase for up-scale target group draws. One early episode, guest-hosted by Paul Simon (no "guest stars" on this earth-toned show), was more a musical concert than a comedy show. Richard Pryor, George Carlin, and Buck Henry, comedians once considered fringe mass audience performers but now in the boomer mainstream, were among the early guest hosts. The fact that the show had a repertory troupe, the Not Ready For Prime Time Players, was itself no guarantee of innovation; one need only recall the painful horrors of the Ace Trucking Company. But as the show developed, the Not Readies gradually transcended their initial supporting role. Their send-ups of TV shows and commercials, which appeared with increasing frequency, were something more than the blind distensions of the comedy spots on *Donnie and Marie* and *The Flip Wilson Show.* Lorne Michaels, *Saturday Night's* producer, was bringing about a renaissance of the TV blackout sketch. Marc Eliot has compared *Saturday Night Live* to Max Liebman's *Your Show of Shows* starring Sid Caesar and Imogene Coca (NBC, 1950–54):

> *Saturday Night Live* brings live TV variety full cycle. Its ensemble cast is no less effective than Caesar's, sometimes better, willing to go further out on a limb. Whereas Caesar's humor was equally effective when dealing with suburbia, the movies, or television, the *Saturday Night* crew is, at best, uneven. When they are good, they're great, when they are bad, they're awful. Their only legitimate realm of satire was television itself.[32]

Chevy Chase, who quickly developed the highest F-score in the ensemble cast, emerged as the de facto "star" of the show in its first two seasons. He was the most visible regular, having been given the plums of delivering the show's trademark opener ("Live from New York . . . it's *Saturday Night!*") and the anchor position on the obligatory newsshow satire, "Weekend Update." Chase's pratfalls and his institutionally offbeat humor often turned the show into an FM version of *The Tonight Show.* His Nielsen textbook good looks repeatedly stole the camera from the cast's superior comic talents. When Chase left the show to become a respectable Hollywood movie star in 1976, however, the writers

and performers of *Saturday Night Live* were freed of the albatross of showcasing a "next Johnny Carson." They created a
shadow play of cultural memories that is capable of exquisite
power.

Having passed through the looking glass, comedians who
had grown up watching television offered the first art to emerge
from this definitive experience of the postbomb world. In one
episode, Desi Arnaz plays Frank Nitti in an *Untouchables* sketch.
His wife turns out to be Lucy (Lucille Ball played by Gilda
Radner). She has left Little Nitti with Mrs. Trumble to come
down to the club with his machine gun. Upon finding that
Lucy—ever the zany redhead—has brought him a machine gun
loaded with blanks, Desi/Nitti/Ricky explodes in anger. Gilda/
Lucy then unleashes a resounding morpheme on American te-
lecultural consciousness, Lucy's epic surrender to deep and
unavoidable trouble: "Whaaaaaa!" The "total television" of the
performance is enriched by Lorne Michaels's thoughtful production. Like *The Untouchables,* the sketch is telecast in black
and white, which itself is a vehicle for time travel when inserted
into a color show; Nielsen estimates that 85 percent of American HUTs are color equipped.[33] The show closes with Arnaz
offering an inspired rendition of Ricky Ricardo's legendary theme
song, "Ba-ba-lu," and leading the cast off the stage in a samba
line.

For the lifelong viewer, this technique simulates the effect
of the *nekyia,* the ancient Greek passage into Hades, where the
ghosts of the past are conjured and consulted. In *The Dream
and the Underworld,* a psychological study of the daily human
relationship with the dead, James Hillman writes:

> Our culture is singular for its ignorance of death. The great
> art and celebrations of many other cultures—ancient Egyp-
> tian and Etruscan, the Greek of Eleusis, Tibetan—honor
> the underworld. We have no ancestor cult, although we are
> pathetically nostalgic. We keep no relics, though collect
> antiques. We rarely see dead human beings, though watch
> a hundred imitations on the television tube. The animals
> we eat are put out of sight. We have no myths of the *nekyia,*
> yet our popular heroes in films and music are shady under-
> world characters.[34]

151

The *nekyia* myth that Hillman feels is absent may be buried beneath the "hundred imitations" he mentions. The "dead" of TV are not the guest criminals blown away by Eliot Ness, Kojak, or T. J. Hooker; they are, rather, the canceled series and their characters. They rise from the grave regularly—on reruns, in conversation, and through impersonation. Only a few hours, days, or weeks before seeing the Desi Arnaz sketch on *Saturday Night Live,* the viewer may have seen the ghost of Lucy—dressed in toreador pants, chatting with Ethel in the kitchen—walk through any one of a hundred familiar rituals. To then see the ghost resurrected to video flesh, reacting to new situations, revealing new aspects of her intimately familiar persona, is a giddy experience, a redemption of a thousand Lucy-watching hours.

Dan Aykroyd emerged as a virtuoso of teleshadow comedy. Never decisively committing his technique to either hyperbole, naturalistic imitation, or understatement, he often uses all three to create a single character. His imitation of Tom Snyder is a performance that not only reviews the experience of watching Snyder on television but urges the imagination to appreciate the existential dilemma of having nothing else to watch at one o'clock in the morning. Snyder, a living testament to Roman Hruska's famous defense of mediocrity, has let it be known publicly that he is offended by Aykroyd's imitation. In itself, this points toward the radical innovation of Aykroyd's work; it has traditionally been considered an honor to be mimicked by a fellow performer, regardless of the imitation's content. Similarly, Barbara Walters has complained of Gilda Radner's "Baba Wawa," and Elizabeth Taylor of John Belushi's finger-licking imitation. These impersonations tend to strip their objects of "normalcy" by filtering out the blindingly glossy rays of network slickness. At their best, they break the trance of stardom.

Performance telerealism of appearance, voice, gesture, and camera address constitutes one of three essential elements of this comedy. The degree to which the image is convincing also depends on the excellence of television theatercraft—makeup, costuming, lighting, set design—in suggesting the object of imitation. These characters, scenes, et cetera, are themselves largely the products of network artifice; with care—and the same technology that created the originals—the imitators can compellingly reconstruct them. And yet, as is the case with all art, technical brilliance alone is not satisfying. Fully realized boomer telecomedy demands a narrative context in which the image can achieve animation and complete resurrection. The third element is often achieved by means of hyperbolic incongruity. Kenneth Burke, discussing literature, describes this method of recontextualization as "perspective by incongruity."[35] In the best sketches, the dazzling technical achievement of "perfect imitation"—the goal of most TV—self-destructs by placing itself in an impossible context that undermines and tests belief. For example, Snyder/Aykroyd appears with his mother (played by Jane Curtin); they are guests on a special Mother's Day episode of *The David Susskind* (Bill Murray) *Show.* The other panelists are Henry and Mother Kissinger (John Belushi and Laraine Newman) and Leon and Mother Spinks (Garrett Morris and Gilda Radner). Mrs. Snyder, like her son, chain smokes and is dressed in a white leisure suit. She is a fantasy inspired by Aykroyd's imitation of Snyder. What begins as mimicry develops a germinating cosmos of its own, which not only is more interesting than the original but gives watching the original new depth. Snyder's distinctive laugh, a cornerstone of the Aykroyd imitation, has been indelibly underlined; this costs Snyder a measure of his manipulative power, which he derives from an ability to make his point of view normal.

153

One of the show's finest sketches made excellent use of guest host Ricky Nelson, who had grown up on television in front of the current primary consumer group. The sketch's black-and-white image—now as much a signifier of the fifties as Eisenhower or Edsel—is a baroque fifties sitcom kitchen. Ricky Nelson enters through the back door to what will obviously be a spoof of *Ozzie and Harriet.* He goes to the refrigerator for some milk and brownies, but the mother who enters is not Harriet Nelson but June Cleaver (Curtin). *Leave It to Beaver* music—the original—plays on the sound track. The camera swings over to Dan Aykroyd, who is Rod Serling. In a turgid recuperation of Serling's painstaking voice inflections ("Submitted for your approval . . ."), he informs us that Ricky Nelson, a sitcom son in search of his sitcom home, is actually lost in *The Twilight Zone*. The ancient *Twilight Zone* audiovisual signature takes over, descending from outer-space bongo drums back to the sitcom kitchen. Ricky Nelson enters and goes to the refrigerator for milk and brownies. This time he has landed in *Father Knows Best,* complete with Robert Young (holding a coffee cup!), a Bud/Belushi, and a classic simpering breakdown from Betty Anderson (Laraine Newman). Aykroyd/Serling reappears, offering further commentary. Descending once again from the *Twilight Zone* heavens, the camera picks up the empty kitchen. Ricky Nelson enters, and this time it's the *Danny Thomas* home. After appropriate homages to Uncle Tonoose (Bill Murray) and Louise the Maid (Garrett Morris), Belushi, as Danny Thomas/Danny Williams, spits his coffee all over the table. Aykroyd meanwhile has gone to makeup; he comes back as George Burns (an astounding performance) and offers vaudeville *explication de texte*. Sitcom action resuming, Ricky Nelson this time finds himself in no less a shrine of sitcom ancestor worship than the Ricardo home. "You're not *my* Ricky," shrieks Lucy/Gilda at Nelson. Ricky is bringing home Cesar Romero for dinner, and she's burned the roast! "Whaaaa!" Aykroyd, now Alfred Hitchcock, steps forward from the line-drawing profile to pronounce the hopelessness of the situation.[36]

These direct imitations of personalities and programs were complemented by indirect imitations—or epitomizations—whose objects were television forms. The sitcom, center of longitudinal television consciousness, is consistently invoked by use of archetypal sets. *Saturday Night Live* developed a number of ur-sitcoms that pushed the genre to thoughtfully absurd precipitates. "The Coneheads" was perhaps the most popular of these sketches. An alien family from the planet Remulak, the Coneheads take up residence in a suburban American housing tract. Their foot-high coneheads notwithstanding, they explain their lack of knowledge of local culture to their naive Earthling-American neighbors as stemming from the fact that they are emigrants from France. Their mission—to scout Earth culture as a prelude to Remulakian invasion—includes participant-informant anthropological duties. While Beldar and Primat nostalgically pine for the Old World, daughter Connie is seduced by American culture, developing a taste for male humans and rock and roll (in one episode she dates Frank Zappa, exclaiming, "Oh, bay-bee, oh bay-bee!"). Undercover as a typical American family, the Coneheads appear as contestants on *Family*

Feud. They defeat a family of romaine lettuce enthusiasts from Delmar Ray Vista, California. "The Wide-ends" is in some ways the most interesting of these sketches. Vintage fifties sitcom dialogue and plot are played with poker faces; however, the backsides of the family members are overstuffed to enormous proportions. This single physical sight gag explodes all sitcom convention. The audience is treated to the spectacle of the genre making an ass of itself in no uncertain terms.

Saturday Night Live reached full flower during the 1977–78 and 1978–79 seasons. Though, as Eliot contends, television memory art was the show's chief source of power, other features were artfully cultivated as well. The show offered parodies of hit movies. Original short films were presented. Continuing sketches such as "We Are Two Wild and Crazy Guys" and "Cheeseburger, Cheeseburger" are related to television memory only in the sense that they are images of modern American culture and social structure. Many of the best comedians in show business—Steve Martin, Rodney Dangerfield, and Lily Tomlin among them—did their best TV work in the relatively "liberated" atmosphere of the show. Musicians who rarely appeared on TV—the Band, the Rolling Stones, Peter Tosh, Patti Smith, and others—found no image problems in performing on *Saturday Night Live*. One need only see a kinescope of Elvis Presley rolling his eyes in embarrassment as Milton Berle hugs and praises him on the 1956 *Berle Buick Show* to understand the reluctance of some musical artists to appear on TV comedy shows.

Though *Saturday Night Live* had no formal commitment to the comedy of television memory, the show brought it before a mass audience and used it as the centerpiece of an eclectic review of life in contemporary America. Navigating the Scylla and Charybdis of preachy intellectualism and blind distension, the writing and performance in Lorne Michaels's show found a path between the two. The gross-out joke (e.g., John Belushi's Elizabeth Taylor choking on a chicken bone) emerged as baby-boom slapstick. Bill Murray, who joined the show in 1977, demonstrated a mastery of American wiseguyisms, especially while dealing out nuggies as Lisa Lupner's boyfriend, Todd Delamuca. His Nick the Nightclub Singer, a sublimely third-rate postmodern crooner who works airport lounges, Arctic airbases, and

Pocono hotels, is a fabulous embarrassment to professional entertainment. Murray rarely achieves photorealism in his television imitations in the manner of Aykroyd or Radner; he is, rather, a consummate suggester of moods and styles. Jane Curtin took on the role of the beleaguered straight arrow, struggling to maintain dignity amid the show's endless procession of gross-out jokes. She is the foil, for example, for the phlegm-ball ecstasies of Radner's Rosanne Rosannadanna. Laraine Newman rarely strayed from her California burnout persona, wandering listlessly through the fallen postsixties world. Garrett Morris, the cast's only black member, self-consciously performed a comedy of tokenism, playing all black roles, male and female, and even doing duty as Hispanic baseball player Chico Esquillar. John Belushi's drug jokes and physical comedy made the show palatable to some of the less sophisticated elements of the burgeoning pot-smoking community. Belushi became the comiculture's first martyr since Lenny Bruce when he died of a drug overdose in 1982; with a Jimi Hendrix, one wonders, can a Janis Joplin be far behind?

At the end of the 1978–79 season, Aykroyd and Belushi left *Saturday Night Live*—and television—for Hollywood feature films. This was an unfortunate mistake for both their careers—and for TV. Excellent video comedians who were capable of using the medium's mythology and technology to great advantage, they went to Hollywood to make a series of bland, mediocre movies, such as *The Blues Brothers, 1941,* and *Neighbors. The Blues Brothers,* an attempt to make a two-hour movie out of a solid five-minute TV blackout sketch, squandered the power of the original. The few good moments in the film are the musical performances of Aretha Franklin, Ray Charles, and James Brown. *The Blues Brothers* offers a lavishly produced car chase through the middle of an enclosed suburban shopping mall; *Saturday Night Live* had done a far better job of destroying malls in its series of sketches about one that contains a Scotch Tape Boutique and a franchise of the Barry White Big Man's Clothing Store chain. Aykroyd in particular is wasted on the large screen. His remarkable talents as a mimic and his thorough mastery of TV language, both verbal and physical, go completely unused. As long as TV's most talented artists are seduced by the easier money and relative respectability of the cinema, TV comedy is not likely to transcend the familiar horizons of David Brenner or Ruth Buzzi.

Woody Allen, who first gained national attention for himself as a performer of stand-up comedy on *The Ed Sullivan Show* in the midsixties, seems to have set a standard of gentility for video comedians. *Annie Hall,* Allen's tour de force, contains among its many themes an indictment of television for crimes against art. In *Manhattan,* Allen plays a loosely veiled *Saturday Night Live* writer who quits the show in disgust at its sell-out mediocrity. Allen's well-deserved success in the movies is un-derstandably a far more attractive vision of the future for a TV comic than ending up as the host of *Jackpot Bowling* or, like Gleason, beating to death twenty-year-old routines. Few, how-ever, have been able to make the transition as gracefully as Allen has.

157

Looking back in television history a few more years, one finds that George Schlatter's *Rowan and Martin's Laugh-In* (NBC, 1968–73) suffered a similar fate at the hands of the movies. At a time when *The Dean Martin Show* and *The Glen Campbell Goodtime Hour* passed for comedy-variety, Schlatter attempted to rethink prime-time presentational comedy. Dan Rowan and Dick Martin, the show's title players, did not function as its stars in the traditional sense. Instead, they were hosts for a strong repertory troupe that performed lightning-quick blackout sketches ("Sock It To Me," "Here Come de Judge," "The Party"). Though Lorne Michaels slowed Schlatter's blistering pace considerably and invested his material with a far keener intelligence, the shape of *Saturday Night Live* in some ways is foreshadowed by *Laugh-In,* especially its no-star, repertory style. *Laugh-In*'s de-mise also foreshadows the end of *Saturday Night.* One by one, *Laugh-In* lost its funniest comedians to the movies, including Lily Tomlin, Henry Gibson, and Goldie Hawn. Only Tomlin has been equal to the test. Curiously, *Laugh-In*'s Eisensteinian ed-iting pace, the very aspect of Schlatter's work rejected by Mi-chaels, survives in such shows as *Hee-Haw* and *Sesame Street.* Schlatter finally gave up on comedy-variety after an aborted attempt to revive *Laugh-In* in 1978; he went on to produce *Real People,* the first of the modern schlockumentaries.

Despite its premature death, the concrete innovations in video performance art achieved by the actors, writers, and technicians of the original *Saturday Night Live* were in accordance with avant-garde demographic aims. The show's audience was discernibly young, upscale, and hedonistic. It was an audience that institutions as diverse as Tampax, Honda, Memorex, and the United States Army wanted to talk to. The show eventually received the ultimate demographer's stamp of approval—it inspired imitators. In 1980, ABC premiered *Fridays*, a ninety-minute late-night comedy show telecast "live" from Los Angeles. It soon revealed itself as an AM version of *Saturday Night*. Bill Lee, who coproduced the show with John Moffitt, promised *Rolling Stone* magazine that *Fridays* would be built on "ground-breaking humor that's hopefully an extension of what *Saturday Night Live* has done."[37] *Fridays'* weak writing, erratic performance quality, and, most of all, its self-congratulatory, ain't-we-artists tone made it a painful reminder of how fragile a commodity originality is in a mass medium. NBC, showing even less class than a television network is supposed to, has retained the name "Saturday Night Live" for two new shows (new producers, new casts) since the original died of Hollywood fever. *Saturday Night Live II* (1980–81), produced by Jean Doumanian, seemed to be based on a theory of viewer inertia that held that the loyal "Saturday Night" audience would not notice that the new show was not funny and would just continue to watch out of habit. *Saturday Night Live III* (1981–), produced by Dick Ebersol, is something of a rebound from Doumanian's quick disaster. However, only two of its players, Joe Piscopo and Eddie Murphy, are capable of getting laughs. When they are off camera, the show is every bit as bad as *Saturday Night Live II*. While these shows have made the original *Saturday Night Live* their model—and failed to greater and lesser degrees to live up to that standard—another late-night comedy show, *SCTV Comedy Network* (NBC, 1981–83), committed itself completely to the comedy of television memory and defined the frontier of commercial video art.

A Light from Melonville

For the most radical and elaborate American media theory, one must look to the work of . . . Canadians.

Daniel J. Czitrom, *Media and the American Mind*

It's the community contained within the station *cum* network itself that really matters. *SCTV* builds on the recognition that we don't so much watch TV as live with it, and anyone who refuses to invest a few weeks simply living with *SCTV* is unlikely to develop a real taste for the show. After that, it's either addiction or signing off permanently.

Richard T. Jameson, *Film Comment*

As the central collective image bank of national culture, television has been a natural subject for lampoon among both professionals and amateurs since American homes became HUTs, but the monologues and improvisations of the baby-boom comedians who began to come of age during the third decade of telecast have been obsessed with it. Whereas once, perhaps (if Hollywood films are to be trusted), nascent clowns sneaked into tent shows and vaudeville houses to watch the pros, the rookie crop of boomer stand-ups who cracked the nightclub circuit in the early seventies had, in the privacy of their own homes, spent their lives witnessing the greatest barrage of nonstop entertainment in history. In *The Age of Television,* Martin Esslin calls this phenomenon "the drama explosion."[38]

Second City, a nightclub that has enjoyed a reputation for fostering avant-garde mass comedy ever since Mike Nichols and Elaine May appeared there in the fifties, became an early commercial testing ground for television-age humor. In addition to Second City's original Chicago club, "an enterprising Torontoite named Andrew Alexander ... bought the Canadian rights to the Second City monicker and set up shop in a disused firehouse."[39] The Chicago and Toronto Second Cities became the salons of telememory comedy. Dan Aykroyd, Gilda Radner, John Belushi, and Bill Murray were all Second City graduates when they came to *Saturday Night Live.* They demonstrated that the revery of memory to which an audience could be brought by means of live imitations on a bare nightclub stage could be augmented and intensified by use of an actual TV network's arsenal of artifice. To imitate Eddie Haskell was one thing; to bring that imitation to a *Leave It to Beaver* set and present it on the tube to the nation was quite another: total teletheater. Furthermore, the commercial success of *Saturday Night Live* showed that the Muses of Art and Demography were in rare harmony.

While *Saturday Night Live* was making headlines in both the trade papers and the rock and roll magazines, a group of Toronto-based Second City comedians began a syndicated show of its own. Andrew Alexander produced it right in the old firehouse. The original *Second City Television,* which premiered in 1977, was a thirty-minute program that many local stations scheduled immediately following *Saturday Night Live.* Baby-boom comedy was establishing the wee hours of the weekend as its programming ghetto. Though *Second City* was shown across Canada, no more than fifty-five U.S. stations were carrying it (some of these PBS affiliates, who inserted public service announcements in the commercial slots). In 1981, however, NBC picked up *SCTV* for U.S. network telecast. The show was hyperextended to ninety minutes and given a 12:30–2:00 A.M. slot on the Friday night schedule, replacing the canceled rock showcase, *The Midnight Special.* The big mouth had won an impressive, if temporary, victory over the electric guitar in the battle for the boomer consumer; the rock 'n roll video revolution was yet to come.

When a rather ragged NBC peacock is pushed aside by the gleaming, statuesque SCTV logo, there is an acceleration of imaginative pace that does not occur elsewhere on television. The split-screen montage of SCTV's own history—scores of flashing TV impersonations, televisions flying out of apartment house windows, tableaux of SCTV station personnel—warns the viewer that any show, commercial, event, gesture, style, or moment that has gone out over the air since there has been television may suddenly reappear. SCTV, a beleaguered network, a station found beyond the UHF band at Channel 109, a show with a shamelessly phony laugh track, is an entrance into the modern Hades of televised civilization. The chaos of this underworld is familiar enough to suggest order. In the tradition of professional wrestling and *The Burns and Allen Show,* constant tension is maintained by the integration of the presentational and representational modes. "The station *cum* network," as Jameson calls it, is an epic synthesis of all TV genres. SCTV president Guy Cabellero, riding his wheelchair like Chief Robert Ironside, is part Fred Silverman and part Don Corleone. Johnny La Rue, in monogrammed bathrobe, wanders the halls of network corporate headquarters dreaming of concepts *(Johnny*

La Rue's All-Girl Pajama Party), pining for crane shots ("*Poly-nesiantown* could have been a great film!"). Bob and Doug Mackenzie, though possessing the hoser soul of Canada itself on *The Great White North*, envy smarty-pants Brian St. Johns, who is blessed with a respectable topic for his show: money. Lola Heatherton, who greets most men on camera by exclaiming "I want to BEAR YOUR CHILD!" attempts to transcend the prison of her fabulous body by interviewing Sister Theresa in a Bombay Hospital; she is angered when a dying untouchable fails to recognize her. The spirit—and vocal cords—of Ethel Merman lives beneath the leopard-skin pillbox hat of station manager Edith Prickly.

161

The seven comedians who performed and wrote *SCTV* at the show's peak—John Candy, Joe Flaherty, Eugene Levy, Andrea Martin, Rick Moranis, Catherine O'Hara, and Dave Thomas—are all superb masters of television nuance. Collectively, the cast may play as many as a hundred roles in one ninety-minute episode. "Among them," writes Jameson, "they constitute a repository of pop-cult incunabula embracing decades of film and television, and some of their best concepts have flowered as a result of lunatic cross-pollinations."[40] There are three major types of SCTV characters: frank imitations of actual TV personalities (Ricardo Montalban, Walter Cronkite, Brooke Shields); epitomizations of TV types (Count Floyd, host of *Monster Chiller Horror Theater;* Libby Wolfson, host of *You!,* a daytime SCTV women's program; Bob Wink, host of many gameshows); and the frankly fictional SCTV personnel (Cabellero, Prickly, La Rue). These three dimensions—television history, television myth, television fiction—are, in the best episodes, seamlessly textured into a rich drama of life with the medium. The performers only appear as "themselves" briefly in the opening credits, yet they manage to carry core personae through their endless transformations.

The three elements of electronic shadow memory comedy are brought to optimal synthesis during the show. The re-creation of TV mise-en-scène is painstakingly photorealistic. Performance portraiture is of equal quality, mixing elements of hyperbole, naturalistic depiction, and understatement to resurrect audiovisual images. Moreover, *SCTV*'s peculiar structure, its double life as a representational narrative and a presentational comedy show, allows it to create intricate and fantastic recontextualizations. James Wolcott of the *Village Voice,* one of the few TV critics to appreciate the show's richness, describes one of these:

> With a giant typewriter serving as a backdrop, bushy-browed Gene Shalit (Eugene Levy) opened his first variety special by kicking his feet and shaking his bottom like nobody's business, belting out the lyrics from *Misteroger's Neighborhood.* . . . Joining Shalit on his special were guest critics Roger Ebert (Dave Thomas) and Gene Siskel (Joe Flaherty), who did a fingersnapping version of "Jeepers, Creepers" which ended with Siskel pointing to Shalit's atomic afro and asking, "Jeepers, creepers—where'd you get that hair?" Also on hand was Miss Rona herself, played to a devastating "T" by the superlative Catherine O'Hara. Praised by Shalit for her stirring rendition of "I've Grown Accustomed to His Face," Miss Rona replied, "A definite dichotomy of feelings come into play here Gene, on the one hand . . ."—as easily accurate a rendering of Barrett's pretentious diction as one could dream of.[41]

162

G. Gordon Liddy appears as a guest on *Mrs. Falbo's Tiny Town* to favor the children with a fairy tale about frontal assault on a defended position.

Indira Gandhi and Slim Whitman appear in a commercial for their touring Broadway smash, *Indira* ("Don't cry for me, Rawalpindi . . .").

The Solid Gold Dancers and Divine make guest appearances on *Dusty Towne's Sexy Christmas Special.*

Bob Hope (Dave Thomas) and Bing Crosby (Joe Flaherty) are actually two rock and roll stars who go to *Fantasy Island* to become comedians. Mr. Roarke (Ricardo Montalban/Eugene Levy) puts them in "The Road to Casablanca," where they meet Humphrey Bogart (John Candy) and Ingrid Bergman (Catherine O'Hara).

Sylvester the Cat appears as a corpse on *Quincy, Cartoon Coroner.*

David Brinkley hosts a science special, *Walter Cronkite's Brain.*

The epitomizations or stereotypes of TV functionaries are broad-stroke caricatures. Mrs. Falbo (Andrea Martin) is Mister Rogers gone berserk. Instead of quietly entering the studio and putting on a cardigan sweater, she zooms up in a fuel-injection Dodge Charger. Billy Sol Hurok (Candy) and Big Jim McBob (Flaherty), the farmer-critics of *Farm Film Review,* show an aesthetic bias toward movies where people "get blowed up real good . . . real good." *The Sammy Maudlin Show* is the epitomization of epitomizations. Sammy (Flaherty) is the sum of the Hollywood Ratpack, equal parts Dean Martin, Joey Bishop, and Sammy Davis, Jr. Maudlin and his Ed McMahon, William B. (Candy's homage to an obscure New York disc jockey), are alternately moved to gales of laughter and streams of tears by the funny stories and humanitarian accomplishments of their guests. Jameson writes:

163

> One of the severest cases of hyperventilation I ever experienced followed Bobby Bittman's guest appearance on the Sammy Maudlin talkshow to promote his dramatic TV-movie debut, a remake of *On the Waterfront.* Now, Bobby Bittman is Eugene Levy's masterpiece—a rampantly loathsome singer-comedian who comes out flashing rings, chains, smiles and inane how-are-yas, invariably interrupts his act to pontificate "in all seriousness" about something, and more often than not ends up berating the audience for failing to appreciate that he's "giving 110 percent up here!"[42]

In another of Bittman's appearances on the *Maudlin Show,* the comedian brings kid brother Skip along to make his TV debut. Skip, however, blows his monologue and, back at the sofa, insists on calling Bobby "Herschel," his pre–show biz name. The two lapse into an argument in Yiddish, creating "dead air," the ultimate sin of any talkshow. Sammy, a master of normalcy, is put to the test; he recaptures control by proclaiming that such a stirring event as two brothers arguing in their "native ethnic language" on national television could happen "only in America."

The SCTV station personnel are used to create representational narrative superstructures for a typical episode's collection of shows, commercials, and promos: CCCP-1, a Soviet television network, is jamming SCTV with its racist anti-Uzbek sitcom *Hey Gorgi!* and its big-rubles gameshow *Uboscrabblenik;* aliens have infiltrated SCTV through the body of Conrad Bain's brother, who has recently been signed to star in a rip-off of *Diff'rent Strokes* (NBC, 1978–); a gang war has broken out between SCTV and the "Big Three" networks over SCTV's refusal to back Ugazzo Home Vision, a Mafia-controlled pay-TV system. Despite all this, the SCTV broadcast day must continue as normal. The absurd representational framework is forced to cohere by the compelling telerealism of the inpersonations and the aesthetic truths of the epitomizations:

> Catherine O'Hara, one of the few comediennes who can doll herself up to mock glamorousness, slipped on a jungle-mane wig and did a killing parody of brat nymphet Brooke Shields. As the host of *The Brooke Shields Show,* O'Hara petulantly played with her feet as her mother (Rich Moranis in drag) nudged her on the arm, hoping to draw Brooke's attention back to her guests. Brooke's first guest was Speaker of the House Tip O'Neill, played by John Candy in a toupee that looked as if it had been dipped in sugar frosting. "Tip O'Neill, that's a really silly name," said Brooke, idly toying with her toes. "Can I call you Tip Toenail?"[43]

While other late-night comedy shows sacrifice sketch continuity to dutifully "present" their "all-time-great" rock and roll acts, SCTV works the music right into its narrative framework. Wendy O. Williams and the Plasmatics go to the woods with Gil Fisher on *The Fishin' Musician;* Al Jarreau plays the Jolson role in the final remake of *The Jazz Singer;* violinist Eugene Fodor even appeared in *New York Rhapsody,* a send-up of the John Garfield/Joan Crawford film, *Humoresque.*

"Friends call me now and say, 'I can't believe you're doing what we used to do when we were kids,'" Rick Moranis told *Rolling Stone.*[44] Indeed, *SCTV* is the ultimate trivia game, acting out a pageant of television history as a dare to the viewer's memory. It is a farce in the sense that it is "stuffed" with jokes from beginning to end; yet it goes against all previous industry wisdom in that it is full of unexplained allusion. The remarkable quality of *SCTV* is that enough of it is available to a large enough audience to sustain it as a commercial venture. The critics who claim that television has given the American public nothing are proved wrong; television has given us itself. When Rick Moranis appears as Merv Griffith, a simultaneous impersonation of Merv Griffin and Andy Griffith, and interviews Floyd the Barber (Eugene Levy), a mythological event takes place that is intelligible only to the faithful. Wolcott describes Levy's Floyd the Barber as "a mythic bore," "a comic monster out of Ring Lardner."[45] Wolcott's jump from American television to American literature is well made; the two are branches of the same tree.

165

When *SCTV* returned for 1982–83, its third season on NBC, it was without the services of Rick Moranis, Catherine O'Hara, and Dave Thomas. Once again, the lure of *le cinéma*—or perhaps the odiousness of TV itself—had cheated American television of its best video artists. Martin Short joined the cast, but his astounding impressions (especially of Jerry Lewis in *Martin Scorscese Presents Jerry Lewis Live on the Champs Elysée*) and the new set of original characters he added to the show's repertoire could not balance the losses. The equilibrium of Catherine O'Hara's wildly sexy energy and Andrea Martin's studied neuroses was broken. Without Moranis and Thomas, Bob and Doug Mackenzie, probably the show's two most popular characters, were lost; this dealt the show's chances to stay on network air a fatal blow. At last word, *SCTV* was bound for a fall 1983 premiere on HBO's deluxe upscale cable target service, Cinemax.

Perhaps it should not be surprising that the rise of electronic shadow memory comedy on television occurs as the Network System we have become accustomed to goes into decline. As NBC, CBS, ABC, PBS, and the big-city independents are joined by HBO, ESPN, ART(!), CBN, WHT, USA, CNN, and the rest yet to come in the alphabet soup of the cable converter, the forty years or so during which scores of millions of people watched the same TV shows day in and day out are likely to be remembered as a quaint, naive period. Cable innovations will allow the demographer marketeers to decentralize structure and even to isolate and attack pockets of aesthetic resistance (the highly educated are among the early prominent target groups). But whatever television's future, Paul Henning, Jack Webb, Jackie Gleason, and their contemporaries will remain television's past. Evolution inevitably breeds an interest in primitive beginnings. In an article for *The Critic* in 1884, Whitman wrote: "That America necessitates for her poetry entirely new standards of measurement is such a point with me, that I never tire of dwelling on it."[46]

Notes ★

Preface

1. William Carlos Williams, *In the American Grain* (1933; rpt., New York: New Directions, 1956), p. 75.

2. John Fiske and John Hartley, *Reading Television* (London: Methuen, 1978), p. 14.

3. Stan Wilk, "Coming of Age in Sonora," *American Anthropologist* 79, no. 1 (1977): 84.

4. See Michael R. Real, "Cultural Studies and Mediated Culture," *Journal of Popular Culture* 9, no. 2 (1975): 81–85.

5. See Malcolm Cowley, ed., *Walt Whitman's "Leaves of Grass": The First (1855) Edition* (New York: Penguin Books, 1976), including Cowley's introduction.

6. Robert Sklar, *Movie-made America: A Cultural History* (New York: Vintage Books, 1975), p. 86.

7. Tylor defined "culture" as "that complex whole which includes knowledge, belief, custom, art, law, morals, and any other capabilities and habits acquired by man as a member of society"; *Primitive Culture: Researches into the Development of Mythology, Philosophy, Religion, Art, and Custom* (New York: Henry Holt and Company, 1877), 1: 1.

Chapter 1: Beginning to Begin Again

1. As cited by Christopher H. Sterling and John M. Kitross, *Stay Tuned: A Concise History of American Broadcasting* (Belmont, Calif.: Wadsworth Publishing Company, 1978), p. 372. Minow coined the phrase

in this passage: "I invite you to sit down in front of your television set when your station goes on the air and stay there without a book, newspaper, profit-and-loss sheet or rating book to distract you—and keep your eyes glued to that set until the station signs off. I can assure you will observe a vast wasteland."

2. *Nielsen Report on Television, 1981* (New York: A. C. Nielsen Company, 1981), pp. 3, 6.

3. Hans Magnus Enzensberger, *The Consciousness Industry* (New York: Seabury Press, 1974), p. 9.

4. Edward Shils, "Daydreams and Nightmares: Reflections on the Criticism of Mass Culture," *Sewanee Review* 65 (1957): 568–69.

5. James M. Cain, *The Postman Always Rings Twice* (1934; rpt., New York: Vintage Books, 1978), p. 96.

6. "A mass medium can only achieve its great audience by practicing ... cultural democracy ... by giving a majority of the people what they want"; Dr. Frank Stanton, the president of CBS, as cited by Gilbert Seldes, *The New Mass Media: Challenge to a Free Society* (Washington, D.C.: Public Affairs Press, 1968), p. 17.

7. Walter Benjamin, "The Work of Art in the Age of Mechanical Reproduction," in *Illuminations,* ed. Hannah Arendt (New York: Schocken Books, 1969), p. 218.

8. In *Skyscraper Primitives* (Middletown, Conn.: Wesleyan University Press, 1975), Dickran Tashjian writes, "While Waldo Frank's despair that America is Dada may have been exaggerated, the chaos of Dada illumines America's essential conflict with tradition and may even lend intelligibility, if not significance, to our contemporary chaos in the arts." See also Waldo Frank, "Seriousness and Dada," *1924* 3 (1924).

9. See Marshall McLuhan, *The Gutenberg Galaxy: The Making of Typographic Man* (Toronto: University of Toronto Press, 1962), esp. pp. 255–63.

10. Sterling and Kitross, *Stay Tuned,* p. 147.

11. Robert Warshow, *The Immediate Experience* (Garden City, N.Y.: Doubleday, 1962), p. 128.

12. Dwight Macdonald, "A Theory of Mass Culture," *Diogenes,* no. 3 (1953), pp. 1–17; reprinted in *Mass Culture: The Popular Arts in America,* ed. Bernard Rosenberg and David Manning White (New York: Free Press, 1957), pp. 59–73.

13. Roland Barthes, *Mythologies,* trans. Annette Lavers (New York: Hill and Wang, 1972), p. 17.

14. Tim Brooks and Earle Marsh, *The Complete Directory to Prime Time Network TV Shows, 1946–Present,* rev. ed. (New York: Ballantine Books, 1981); see "Prime Time Schedules."

15. Barthes, *Mythologies,* p. 15.

16. David Chagall, "Reading the Viewer's Mind," *TV Guide,* 7 Nov. 1981, p. 48.

17. Barthes comments on this subject: "The public knows very well the distinction between wrestling and boxing; it knows that boxing is a Jansenist sport, based on a demonstration of excellence.... A boxing-match is a story which is constructed before the eyes of the spectator; in wrestling on the contrary, it is each moment which is intelligible, not the passage of time. The logical conclusion of the contest does not interest the wrestling-fan, while on the contrary a boxing-match always implies a science of the future"; *Mythologies,* pp. 15–16.

18. Jack Gladden, "Archie Bunker Meets Mr. Spoopendyke: Nineteenth Century Prototypes for Domestic Situation Comedy," *Journal of Popular Culture* 10, no. 1 (1976): 167–80.

19. A notable exception to this is the silent "Mr. and Mrs. Jones" series made by D. W. Griffith for Biograph in 1908–9. Robert Sklar describes these films as "situation comedies" in *Movie-made America,* p. 106.

20. Groups 4 and 5 are sometimes constituted as "35–49" and "49 + "; in recent years, "35–55" and "55 + " have been increasingly in use.

21. Daniel Czitrom, *Media and the American Mind: From Morse to McLuhan* (Chapel Hill: University of North Carolina Press, 1982), p. 190.

22. See Northrop Frye, *Anatomy of Criticism: Four Essays* (Princeton, N.J.: Princeton University Press, 1957).

23. Dorothy Rabinowitz, "Watching the Sitcoms," in *Television: The Critical View,* ed. Horace Newcomb (New York: Oxford University Press, 1979), p. 55.

24. Roger Rosenblatt, "Growing Up on Television," in Newcomb, *Television,* p. 351.

25. In 1961 Saudi Arabian State Television refused to show *I Love Lucy* on the grounds that Lucy dominated her husband. This misinterpretation of the text was later revised, and *I Love Lucy* was shown on Saudi Arabian TV in the seventies. See Bart Andrews, *Lucy and Ricky and Fred and Ethel: The Story of "I Love Lucy"* (New York: Fawcett Popular Library, 1977), p. 13.

26. For a review of the changes in the image of the American woman signaled by the popularity of *The Mary Tyler Moore Show,* see Carol Traynor Williams, "It's Not So Much 'You've Come a Long Way, Baby'—As 'You're Gonna Make It after All,'" in Newcomb, *Television,* pp. 64–73.

Notes

27. R. P. Blackmur, "A Burden for Critics," in *Lectures in Criticism*, ed. Elliot Coleman (New York: Harper and Brothers, 1949), p. 189.

28. Ibid., p. 188.

29. Walt Whitman, *Democratic Vistas* (1871; rpt., London: Walter Scott, 1888), p. 83.

30. Ibid., p. 5.

31. Allen Ginsberg, "Howl," *Howl and Other Poems* (San Francisco: City Lights Books, 1956), p. 11.

32. Barthes, *Mythologies,* p. 15.

33. Alex McNeil, *Total Television: A Comprehensive Guide to Programming from 1948 to 1980* (New York: Penguin Books, 1980), p. 112.

34. Ibid.

35. "Ratings," in *TV Guide Almanac,* ed. Craig T. Norback and Peter Norback (New York: Ballantine Books, 1980), p. 546.

36. Ibid., pp. 547–48.

37. I am including neither *The Ed Sullivan Show,* which was a "straight variety" show, nor *The Jack Benny Program,* which was an eccentric self-reflexive sitcom, in the comedy-variety category.

38. Seldes, *New Mass Media,* p. 143.

39. Ibid.

40. Brooks and Marsh, *Complete Directory,* p. 496.

41. Ibid.

42. Sterling and Kitross, *Stay Tuned,* pp. 528–29.

43. Brooks and Marsh, *Complete Directory,* pp. 692–93.

44. McNeil, *Total Television,* p. 647.

45. Ibid., p. 502.

46. Cheryl Bernstein, "Performance as News: Notes on an Intermedia Guerrilla Group," in *Performance in Postmodern Culture,* ed. Michel Benamou and Charles Caramello (Madison, Wisc.: Coda Press, 1977), p. 79.

47. *The Random House College Dictionary,* 1975 ed., p. 441.

48. Gunther Anders, "The Phantom World of TV," in Rosenberg and White, *Mass Culture,* p. 365.

49. Whitman, *Democratic Vistas,* p. 33.

50. *Nielsen Report, 1981,* p. 7.

51. A concise description of Klein's "LOP Theory" is given by Les Brown, *The New York Times Encyclopedia of Television* (New York: Times Books/Quadrangle, 1977), p. 228. For an example of how Klein applies the theory himself, see Paul Klein, "Why You Watch, What You Watch, When You Watch," *TV Guide,* 24 July 1971, pp. 6–10.

52. Chagall, "Reading the Viewer's Mind," p. 48.

53. See John G. Cawelti, *Adventure, Mystery, and Romance* (Chi-

cago: University of Chicago Press, 1976), esp. chap. 1, "The Study of Literary Formulas," pp. 5–36.

54. When I worked at NBC Television corporate headquarters in New York during 1976–77, I was shocked to learn of the kind of mail and telephone calls received by the Audience Response Department from soap opera viewers. Fans would ask for automobile directions to mythical soap opera towns. Letters were often addressed to characters, not actors, and these letters routinely offered advice concerning "decisions" the character was facing in the story line. Soap opera villains have been physically assaulted on the streets of New York and Los Angeles. For a catalog of some of these bizarre events, see David Johnson, "The Real and the Unreal," *Daytimers,* Nov. 1981, p. 17. For a more comprehensive analysis of art/life confusion among Americans, see George Gerbner and Lawrence Gross, "The Scary World of TV's Heavy Viewer," *Psychology Today,* Apr. 1976, p. 74.

55. Susan Sontag, *Against Interpretation* (New York: Delta, 1966), p. 7.

56. Herbert Gans, *Popular Culture and High Culture* (New York: Basic Books, 1975), p. 65.

57. Paul Buhle and Daniel Czitrom, Editorial, *Cultural Correspondence* 4 (1977): 1.

58. Macdonald, "Theory of Mass Culture," p. 59.

59. Ibid.

60. As cited by Macdonald, ibid., pp. 59–60.

61. Whitman, *Democratic Vistas,* p. 25.

62. Ibid., p. 23.

Chapter 2: The Situation Comedy of Paul Henning

1. Russel Nye, *The Unembarrassed Muse: The Popular Arts in America* (New York: Dial Press, 1970), p. 412.

2. As cited in Sherman Paul, *Repossessing and Renewing* (Baton Rouge: Louisiana State University Press, 1976), p. ii.

3. Norback and Norback, *TV Guide Almanac,* p. 570.

4. As cited in Grant Webster, *Republic of Letters* (Baltimore: Johns Hopkins University Press, 1976), p. 3.

5. For a discussion of the circumstances surrounding the defection of a number of major NBC Radio stars to CBS Television in 1948, see Erik Barnouw, *The Golden Web: A History of Broadcasting in the United States, 1933–53* (New York: Oxford University Press, 1968), pp. 242–45.

6. Biographical data on Paul Henning were gathered from two

sources: *CBS Television Network Press Information,* 19 Sept. 1962; and *The 1981 International Television Almanac,* ed. Richard Gertner (New York: Quigley Publishing Company, 1981), pp. 116–17.

7. Royal Tyler, *The Contrast* (New York: Dunlap Society, 1887), p. 78 (act 4, scene 1).

8. Thomas Bangs Thorp, "The Big Bear of Arkansas," in *Native American Humor,* ed. Walter Blair (San Francisco: Chandler Publishing Company, 1960), p. 338 (italics in original).

9. *CBS Television Network Press Information,* 19 Sept. 1962.

10. Ibid., 2 Oct. 1968.

11. Ibid.

12. As cited in Constance Rourke, *American Humor* (New York: Harcourt, Brace and Company, 1931), p. 216.

13. The ties between the Jed Clampett character and the Lincoln legend are perhaps obvious. A hardworking, log-splitting, rigorously honest "common sense" democrat, Jed, like Lincoln, rises from a backwoods log cabin to a great mansion in the city. What is perhaps less known is Buddy Ebsen's obsession with Lincoln. In 1966 Ebsen authored and produced a stage play, *The Champagne Generation,* in which he starred in the role of Lincoln.

14. *CBS Television Network Press Information,* 13 Sept. 1962.

15. Thorstein Veblen, *The Theory of the Leisure Class* (1899; rpt., New York: New American Library/Mentor, 1953), esp. chap. 3, "Conspicuous Leisure."

16. Waldo Frank, *The Re-discovery of America* (New York: Charles Scribner's Sons, 1929), p. 110.

17. *CBS Television Network Press Information,* 19 Sept. 1962.

18. Erik Barnouw, *Tube of Plenty: The Evolution of American Television* (New York: Oxford University Press, 1975), p. 307.

19. *CBS Television Network Press Information,* 2 Oct. 1968.

20. Nye, *Unembarrassed Muse,* p. 412.

21. In recognition of the likelihood that my description of the CBS decision might provoke some argument, I cite the description of the move by Sterling and Kitross: "CBS dropped rural programs in the 1970's because they appealed to too old an audience to attract advertisers" (*Stay Tuned,* pp. 402–3).

Chapter 3: The Comedy of Public Safety

1. Cawelti, *Adventure, Mystery, and Romance,* p. 51.

2. John G. Cawelti, *The Six-Gun Mystique* (Bowling Green, Ohio: Bowling Green University Press, 1970).

3. Warshow, *Immediate Experience.*

4. Chagall, "Reading the Viewer's Mind," p. 49.

5. Cawelti, *Adventure, Mystery, and Romance,* p. 152.

6. Barnouw, *Tube of Plenty,* p. 131.

7. Ibid.

8. Brooks and Marsh, *Complete Directory,* p. 603.

9. Ibid., p. 275.

10. Ibid.

11. Ibid.

12. Ibid., p. 802.

13. *Dragnet* might have continued winning Emmies, but the category of "Best Mystery, Action, or Adventure Program" was revised in 1955 to include such a broad range of shows that the Webb series was beaten by Walt Disney's *Disneyland* that year.

14. Brooks and Marsh, *Complete Directory,* p. 217.

15. For a glimpse of just how important a power Webb had become in television, see "The Office that Jack (Webb) Built," *TV Guide,* 2 Feb. 1957, pp. 20–21.

16. McNeil, *Total Television,* p. 207.

17. See Horace Newcomb, *TV: The Most Popular Art* (Garden City, N.Y.: Anchor/Doubleday, 1974), pp. 91–94.

18. Barnouw, *Tube of Plenty,* p. 129.

19. Dan Jenkins, "Jack Webb Revisited," *TV Guide,* 10 Jan. 1959, p. 11.

20. "Jack Webb's Blues," *TV Guide,* 23 July 1955, p. 5.

21. "Actors Try Director's Chair for Size," *TV Guide,* 31 May 1958, p. 28.

22. Jeffrey S. Miller, "Watching the Detectives: The Development of the Modern Television Detective Hero" (unpubl. ms.), p. 5.

23. Christopher Wicking and Tise Vahimagi, *The American Vein: Directors and Directions in Television* (New York: E. P. Dutton and Company, 1979), p. 63.

24. Brooks and Marsh, *Complete Directory,* p. 673.

25. McNeil, *Total Television,* p. 629.

26. Bob Schneider, "Spelling's Salvation Armies," *Cultural Correspondence,* no. 4 (1977), p. 27.

27. Ibid.

28. Cathy Schwichtenberg, "A Patriarchal Voice in Heaven," *Jumpcut,* nos. 24/25 (1981), p. 13.

29. Wicking and Vahimagi, *American Vein,* p. 54.

30. Ibid.

31. Brooks and Marsh, *Complete Directory,* p. 320.

32. For a discussion of the anti-TV-violence movement and its

effects on network programming, see Sterling and Kitross, *Stay Tuned,* esp. pp. 461–63.

33. McNeil, *Total Television,* p. 185.

34. John Gabree, "Can *Hill Street Blues* Keep Dodging the Nielsen Bullets?" *TV Guide,* 31 Oct. 1981, p. 28.

35. Michel Benamou offers this definition of postmodernism in "Presence and Play," in *Performance in Postmodern Culture,* ed. Benamou and Caramello, p. 6.

36. Gabree, "Can *Hill Street Blues* Keep Dodging?" pp. 29–30 (emphasis added).

Chapter 4: Gleason's Push

1. Barnouw, *Tube of Plenty,* p. 129.

2. Jim Bishop, *The Golden Ham: A Candid Biography of Jackie Gleason* (New York: Simon and Schuster, 1956), pp. 219–20.

3. Ibid., p. 53.

4. Ibid.

5. Ibid., p. 83.

6. Ibid., p. 176.

7. Ibid., p. 195.

8. Brooks and Marsh, *Complete Directory,* p. 432.

9. Ibid., pp. 137–38.

10. Bishop, *Golden Ham,* p. 199.

11. Ibid., pp. 196–97.

12. "One's Self I sing, a simple separate person, / Yet utter the word Democratic, the word En-Masse." This is Whitman's first "Inscription" in *Leaves of Grass* (1871); Walt Whitman, *Leaves of Grass,* ed. Sculley Bradley and Harold W. Blodgett (rpt., New York: W. W. Norton and Company, 1973), p. 1.

13. Bishop, *Golden Ham,* p. 217.

14. Gleason, as quoted by Bishop, ibid.

15. Brooks and Marsh, *Complete Directory,* p. 138.

16. Bishop, *Golden Ham,* p. 235.

17. Ibid., p. 263.

18. Richard Gehman, "The Great One" (second of three parts), *TV Guide,* 20 Oct. 1962, p. 11.

19. McNeil, *Total Television,* p. 356.

20. Al Stump, "It Was Chaos, Crazy!—The *Honeymooners* Reminisce," *TV Guide,* 24 Jan. 1976, pp. 13–14.

21. As cited in Sterling and Kitross, *Stay Tuned,* p. 532.

22. Brooks and Marsh, *Complete Directory,* p. 371.

23. Gilbert Seldes, *The Public Arts* (New York: Simon and Schuster, 1956), p. 161.

24. Bishop, *Golden Ham,* p. 141.

25. Bosley Crowther, review of *Gigot, New York Times,* 28 Sept. 1962, p. 26, col. 1.

26. Ibid.

27. A. H. Weiler, review of *Requiem for a Heavyweight, New York Times,* 17 Oct. 1962, p. 35, col. 1.

28. Steven H. Scheuer, ed., *Movies on TV,* 9th ed. (New York: Bantam Books, 1981), p. 519.

29. Gehman, "The Great One," 20 Oct. 1962, p. 11.

30. Bishop, *Golden Ham,* p. 141.

31. Brooks and Marsh, *Complete Directory,* p. 848.

32. Maxene Fabe, *TV Game Shows!* (Garden City, N.Y.: Dolphin/Doubleday, 1979), p. 292.

33. Gehman, "The Great One," 20 Oct. 1962, p. 13.

34. Les Brown, *Televi$ion: The Business behind the Box* (New York: Harcourt, Brace, Jovanovich, 1971), p. 209. The words "hip" and "relevant" are my own.

35. Robert Musel, "Jackie Gleason's Plea: Why Pay to Keep Me off the Air?" *TV Guide,* 12 Dec. 1970, pp. 37–38.

36. Robert K. Doan, "Something New in Talk Shows: Jackie Gleason" (The Doan Report), *TV Guide,* 5 Sept. 1970, p. A-1.

37. Robert K. Doan, "Gleason Signs Long NBC Pact, May Get Series" (The Doan Report), *TV Guide,* 22 Sept. 1973, p. A-1.

38. Lawrence Van Gelder, review of *Smokey and the Bandit, New York Times,* 20 May 1977, sec. 3, p. 8, col. 5.

39. Hal Himmelstein, "Horace Newcomb: Guru of the Academic Critics," in *On the Small Screen: New Approaches in Television and Video Criticism* (New York: Praeger Publishers, 1981), pp. 87–113. Interestingly, Gleason's name does not appear in Himmelstein's index, either. Praeger Publishers is a division of CBS, Inc.

40. Nye, *Unembarrassed Muse,* p. 412.

41. F. Scott Fitzgerald, *The Great Gatsby* (New York: Charles Scribner's Sons, 1925), p. 182.

42. Ibid., title page.

Chapter 5: Self-Reflexive at Last

1. In Cowley, *Whitman's "Leaves of Grass,"* p. 5.

2. Ibid., Introduction, p. xix.

3. Edgar Allan Poe, "The Philosophy of Composition," reprinted

in *American Literature,* ed. Richard Poirier and William L. Vance (Boston: Little, Brown and Company, 1970), 1: 659.

4. Poe's cynicism toward writing, a mirror reversal of Whitman's idealism, is well expressed in his story, "How to Write a Blackwood Article," in which the editor informs the writer that "the soul of the whole business" is "the filling up" of the page with phony erudition meant to impress a paying readership. A darker vision of Poe's horror and fear of the emerging "mass man" can be found in his painful story, "The Man of the Crowd."

5. Walt Whitman, "Edgar Poe's Significance," in *Specimen Days* (1882); reprinted in *The Portable Whitman,* ed. Mark Van Doren (New York: Penguin Books, 1977), p. 584.

6. As cited in *The Oxford Companion to American Literature,* 4th ed. (1978), s.v. "Poe, Edgar Allan."

7. Sterling and Kitross, *Stay Tuned,* p. 107.

8. Brooks and Marsh, *Complete Directory,* p. 670.

9. McNeil, *Total Television,* p. 715.

10. Ibid., p. 778.

11. Brooks and Marsh, *Complete Directory,* p. 277.

12. In Cowley, *Whitman's "Leaves of Grass,"* p. 5.

13. Enzensberger, *Consciousness Industry,* p. 7.

14. Edgar Allan Poe, "On the Heresy of the Didactic," in *The Poetic Principle* (1850), reprinted in Poirier and Vance, *American Literature,* 1: 668.

15. Ibid., p. 669.

16. While many noncommercial radio stations have adopted "all-Classical" formats, others offer eclectic broadcast agendas that include various types of music as well as informational dramatic programming. The radio stations licensed to the Pacifica Foundation in Berkeley, Los Angeles, New York, Houston, and Washington, D.C., are notable in this respect.

17. J. Hoberman, "Medium Cool Yule," *Village Voice,* 29 Dec. 1976, p. 129.

18. *Nielsen Report, 1981,* p. 9.

19. Ibid.

20. Ernest van den Haag, "Of Happiness and of Despair We Have No Measure," in Rosenberg and White, *Mass Culture,* p. 504.

21. All information on viewership levels and specific program ratings in this section is taken from "Fast Weekly Household Audience Report, Week of December 12–18," *Nielsen National TV Ratings* (New York: A. C. Nielsen Company, 1977).

22. Brooks and Marsh, *Complete Directory,* p. 112.

23. Ibid.

24. Ibid., p. 770.

25. As cited in Jack Paar (with John Reddy), *I Kid You Not* (Boston: Little, Brown and Company, 1959), p. 224.

26. Ibid., Introduction, p. xv.

27. Kenneth Tynan, *Show People: Profiles in Entertainment* (New York: Berkley Books, 1981), p. 112.

28. Ibid.

29. Ibid., p. 111.

30. Ibid.

31. *Performer Q, 1977* (Port Washington, N.Y.: Performer Q Company, 1977).

32. Marc Eliot, *American Television: The Official Art of the Artificial* (Garden City, N.Y.: Anchor/Doubleday, 1981), p. 31.

33. *Nielsen Report, 1981,* p. 3.

34. James Hillman, *The Dream and the Underworld* (New York: Harper and Row, 1979), p. 64.

35. Kenneth Burke, *Attitudes toward History* (New York: New Republic, 1937), vol. 2. On pp. 201–2, Burke defines "perspective by incongruity" as follows: "A method for verbal 'atom cracking.' That is, a word belongs by custom to a certain category—and by rational planning you wrench it loose and metaphorically apply it to a different category."

36. It is worth noting that in his depictions of Serling, Burns, and Hitchcock, Aykroyd has played the major on-camera narrators of American television history.

37. Ben Fong-Torres, "Live . . . from Los Angeles, It's *Fridays,*" *Rolling Stone,* 15 May 1980, p. 37.

38. Martin Esslin, *The Age of Television* (San Francisco: W. H. Freeman and Company, 1982), p. 1.

39. Richard T. Jameson, "Satire Comes to Video," *Film Comment,* no. 17 (1981), p. 76.

40. Ibid.

41. James Wolcott, "Jeepers, Creepers—Where'd You Get That Hair?" *Village Voice,* 11 Aug. 1981, p. 48.

42. Jameson, "Satire Comes to Video," pp. 76–77.

43. James Wolcott, "Mayberry, the Town that Time Forgot," *Village Voice,* 22 July 1981, p. 53.

44. Christopher Connelly, "Two Nerds from Canada," *Rolling Stone* 4 (1982): 23.

45. Wolcott, "Mayberry, the Town that Time Forgot," p. 53.

46. Whitman, "A Backward Glance on My Road," in *Democratic Vistas and Other Papers,* p. 99.

Bibliography

"Actors Try Director's Chair for Size." *TV Guide,* 31 May 1958, pp. 28–29.

Adorno, T. W. *The Jargon of Authenticity.* Translated by Knut Tarnowski and Frederic Will. Evanston, Ill.: Northwestern University Press, 1973.

Allen, Fred. *Treadmill to Oblivion.* Boston: Little, Brown and Company, 1954.

Allen, Steve. *The Funny Men.* New York: Simon and Schuster, 1956.

Anders, Gunther. "The Phantom World of TV." *Dissent* 3 (1956): 14–24. Reprinted in *Mass Culture: The Popular Arts in America,* edited by Bernard Rosenberg and David Manning White, pp. 358–67. New York: Free Press, 1957.

Andrews, Bart. *Lucy and Ricky and Fred and Ethel: The Story of "I Love Lucy."* New York: Fawcett Popular Library, 1977.

———. *The TV Addict's Handbook.* New York: E. P. Dutton and Company, 1978.

Barnouw, Erik. *The Golden Web: A History of Broadcasting in the United States, 1933–53.* New York: Oxford University Press, 1968.

———. *The Image Empire: A History of Broadcasting in the United States from 1953.* New York: Oxford University Press, 1970.

———. *Tube of Plenty: The Evolution of American Television.* New York: Oxford University Press, 1975.

Barthes, Roland. *Mythologies.* Translated by Annette Lavers. New York: Hill and Wang, 1972.

Bellow, Saul. *Herzog.* New York: Viking Press, 1964.

Benamou, Michel, and Charles Caramello, eds. *Performance in Postmodern Culture.* Madison, Wisc.: Coda Press, 1977.

Benjamin, Walter. *Illuminations.* Edited by Hannah Arendt. New York: Schocken Books, 1969.

Benton, Lewis R., ed. *The Beverly Hillbillies Book of Country Humor.* New York: Dell, 1964.

Bernstein, Basil. *Class, Codes, and Control: Theoretical Studies Towards a Sociology of Language.* New York: Schocken Books, 1975.

Bernstein, Cheryl. "Performance as News: Notes on an Intermedia Guerrilla Art Group." In *Performance in Postmodern Culture,* edited by Michel Benamou and Charles Caramello, pp. 79–83. Madison, Wisc.: Coda Press, 1977.

Bishop, Jim. *The Golden Ham: A Candid Biography of Jackie Gleason.* New York: Simon and Schuster, 1956.

Blackmur, R. P. "A Burden for Critics." In *Lectures in Criticism,* edited by Elliot Coleman, pp. 187–209. New York: Harper and Brothers, 1949.

Blair, Walter, ed. *Native American Humor.* San Francisco: Chandler Publishing Company, 1960.

Brooks, Tim, and Earle Marsh. *The Complete Directory to Prime Time Network TV Shows, 1946–Present.* Rev. ed. New York: Ballantine Books, 1981.

Brown, Les. *The New York Times Encyclopedia of Television.* New York: Times Books/Quadrangle, 1977.

———. *Televi$ion: The Business behind the Box.* New York: Harcourt, Brace, Jovanovich, 1971.

Buhle, Paul, and Daniel Czitrom. Editorial. *Cultural Correspondence* 4 (1977): 1.

Burke, Kenneth. "Perspective by Incongruity." In *Attitudes toward History,* 2: 201–8. New York: New Republic, 1937.

Cain, James M. *The Postman Always Rings Twice.* 1934. Reprint. New York: Vintage Books, 1978.

Cantor, Muriel G. *The Hollywood TV Producer: His Work and His Audience.* New York: Basic Books, 1972.

Caughey, John L. "Artificial Social Relations in America." *American Quarterly* 30 (1978): 70–89.

Cawelti, John G. *Adventure, Mystery, and Romance.* Chicago: University of Chicago Press, 1976.

———. *The Six-Gun Mystique.* Bowling Green, Ohio: Bowling Green University Press, 1970.

———. "The Concept of Formula in the Study of Popular Literature." *Journal of Popular Culture,* no. 3 (1969), pp. 381–90.

Chagall, David. "Reading the Viewer's Mind." *TV Guide,* 7 Nov. 1981, pp. 48–52.

Cogley, John. *Report on Blacklisting II: Radio-Television.* New York: Fund for the Republic, 1956. Reprint. New York: Arno Press, 1971.

Cole, Barry G., ed. *Television Today: Readings from TV Guide.* New York: Oxford University Press, 1981.

Columbia Broadcasting System. "CBS Press Information," pertaining to Paul Henning. New York: CBS, 1962–68.

Connelly, Christopher. "Two Nerds from Canada." *Rolling Stone* 4 (1982): 22–23.

Cowley, Malcolm. Introduction to *Walt Whitman's "Leaves of Grass": The First (1855) Edition.* New York: Penguin Books, 1976.

Crosby, John. *Out of the Blue: A Book about Radio and Television.* New York: Simon and Schuster, 1952.

Crowther, Bosley. Review of *Gigot,* directed by Gene Kelly. *New York Times,* 28 Sept. 1962, p. 26, col. 1.

Czitrom, Daniel. *Media and the American Mind: From Morse to Mc-Luhan.* Chapel Hill: University of North Carolina Press, 1982.

Davis, Jessica Milner. *Farce.* London: Methuen and Company, 1978.

Doan, Richard K. "Jackie Gleason Won't Do Any More 'Honeymooners' " (The Doan Report). *TV Guide,* 6 Jan. 1968, p. A-1.

———. "Something New in Talk Shows: Jackie Gleason" (The Doan Report). *TV Guide,* 5 Sept. 1970, p. A-1.

———. "Gleason Signs Long NBC Pact, May Get Series" (The Doan Report). *TV Guide,* 22 Sept. 1973, p. A-1.

Efron, Edith. "Jackie Gleason, Thinker." *TV Guide,* 6 Feb. 1965, pp. 15–18.

Eliot, Marc. *American Television: The Official Art of the Artificial.* Garden City, N.Y.: Anchor/Doubleday, 1981.

Enzensberger, Hans Magnus. *The Consciousness Industry.* New York: Seabury Press, 1974.

Ephron, Nora. *And Now . . . Here's Johnny.* New York: Avon, 1968.

Esslin, Martin. *The Age of Television.* San Francisco: W. H. Freeman and Company, 1982.

Fabe, Maxene. *TV Game Shows! A Behind-the-Screen Look at the Stars! the Prizes! the Hosts! & the Scandals!* Garden City, N.Y.: Dolphin/Doubleday, 1979.

"Fast Weekly Household Audiences Report, Week of December 12–18." In *Nielsen National TV Ratings.* New York: A. C. Nielsen Company, 1977.

181

Faulkner, William. *Absalom, Absalom!* New York: Random House, 1936.

Fiedler, Leslie. *Love and Death in the American Novel.* Briarcliff Manor, N.Y.: Stein and Day, 1975.

———. "The Middle against Both Ends." *Encounter,* no. 5 (1955). Reprinted in Rosenberg and White, *Mass Culture,* pp. 537–44.

Fiske, John, and John Hartley. *Reading Television.* London: Methuen, 1978.

Fitzgerald, F. Scott. *The Great Gatsby.* New York: Charles Scribner's Sons, 1925.

Fong-Torres, Ben. "Live ... from Los Angeles, It's *Fridays.*" *Rolling Stone,* 15 May 1980, pp. 37–38.

Frank, Waldo. *The Re-discovery of America.* New York: Charles Scribner's Sons, 1929.

———. "Seriousness and Dada." *1924* 3 (1924).

Friendly, Fred W. *Due to Circumstances beyond Our Control.* New York: Random House, 1967.

Frye, Northrop. *Anatomy of Criticism: Four Essays.* Princeton, N.J.: Princeton University Press, 1957.

Gabree, John, "Can *Hill Street Blues* Keep Dodging the Nielsen Bullet?" *TV Guide,* 31 Oct. 1981, pp. 27–32.

Gans, Herbert. *Popular Culture and High Culture.* New York: Basic Books, 1975.

Gehman, Richard. "Dave Garroway: Portrait of a Tormented Man." *TV Guide,* 15 July 1961, pp. 12–15; 22 July 1961, pp. 24–27.

———. "The Great One." *TV Guide,* 13 Oct. 1962, pp. 16–19; 20 Oct. 1962, pp. 10–13; 27 Oct. 1962, pp. 22–25.

Gerbner, George, and Lawrence Gross. "The Scary World of TV's Heavy Viewer." *Psychology Today,* Apr. 1976.

Gertner, Richard, ed. *The 1981 International Television Almanac.* New York: Quigley Publishing Company, 1981.

Ginsberg, Allen. *Howl and Other Poems.* San Francisco: City Lights Books, 1956.

Gladden, Jack. "Archie Bunker Meets Mr. Spoopendyke: Nineteenth Century Prototypes for Domestic Situation Comedy." *Journal of Popular Culture* 10, no. 1 (1976): 167–80.

Glazychev, V. L. "The Problem of 'Mass Culture.'" *Soviet Sociology* 10 (1971): 64–80.

Glut, Donald F., and Jim Harmon. *The Great Television Heroes.* New York: Doubleday, 1975.

Green, Abel, and Joe Laurie, Jr. *Show Biz: From Vaude to Video.* New York: Henry Holt and Company, 1951.

Greenberg, Clement. "Avant-Garde and Kitsch." In *The Partisan Reader,* pp. 378–89. New York: Dial Press, 1946. Reprinted in Rosenberg and White, *Mass Culture,* pp. 98–107.

Greenberg, Roberta A., and William B. Piper. *The Writings of Jonathan Swift.* New York: W. W. Norton and Company, 1973.

Harris, Jay, ed. *TV Guide: The First Twenty-five Years.* New York: Simon and Schuster, 1978.

Hawthorne, Nathaniel. *Twice-Told Tales* [1837]. Introduction by Katherine Lee Bates. New York: Thomas Y. Crowell Company, 1902.

Herne, James A. *Shore Acres and Other Plays.* Edited by Mrs. James A. Herne. New York: Samuel French, 1929.

Hillman, James. *The Dream and the Underworld.* New York: Harper and Row, 1979.

Himmelstein, Hal. *On the Small Screen: New Approaches in Television and Video Criticism.* New York: Praeger Publishers, 1981.

Hoberman, J. "Medium Cool Yule." *Village Voice,* 29 Dec. 1976, p. 129.

Hofstadter, Richard. *Social Darwinism in American Thought.* Philadelphia: University of Pennsylvania Press, 1944.

Huizinga, Johann. *Homo Ludens: A Study of the Play Element in Culture.* Boston: Beacon Press, 1955.

"Jack Webb's Blues." *TV Guide,* 23 July 1955, pp. 4–6.

Jameson, Richard T. "Satire Comes to Video." *Film Comment,* no. 17 (1981), pp. 76–77.

Jenkins, Dan. "Jack Webb Revisited." *TV Guide,* 10 Jan. 1959, pp. 11–12.

Johnson, David. "The Real and the Unreal." *Daytimers,* Nov. 1981, p. 17.

Kelly, Richard. *The Andy Griffith Show.* Winston-Salem, N.C.: John F. Blair, 1981.

Klein, Paul. "Why You Watch, What You Watch, When You Watch." *TV Guide.* 24 July 1971, pp. 6–10.

Macdonald, Dwight. *Against the American Grain.* New York: Random House, 1962.

———. "A Theory of Mass Culture." *Diogenes,* no. 3 (1953), pp. 1–17. Reprinted in Rosenberg and White, *Mass Culture,* pp. 59–73.

MacKenzie, Robert. Review of *SCTV Comedy Network. TV Guide,* 31 Oct. 1981, p. 1.

Magny, Claude-Edmonde. *The Age of the American Novel: The Film Aesthetic of Fiction between the Two Wars.* Translated by Eleanor Hochman. New York: Frederick Ungar, 1972.

183

Mailer, Norman. *An American Dream.* New York: Dial Press, 1965.

Mander, Jerry. *Four Arguments for the Elimination of Television.* New York: Morrow Quill Paperbacks, 1978.

Marcuse, Herbert. *One-Dimensional Man.* Boston: Beacon Press, 1964.

Marill, Alvin H. *Movies Made for Television.* New York: Da Capo Press, 1981.

Marx, Arthur. *Red Skelton: An Unauthorized Biography.* New York: E. P. Dutton and Company, 1979.

Matthiessen, F. O. *American Renaissance: Art and Expression in the Age of Emerson and Whitman.* New York: Oxford University Press, 1941.

McCrohan, Donna. *The Honeymooners' Companion: The Kramdens and the Nortons Revisited.* New York: Workman Publishing, 1978.

McLuhan, Marshall. *The Gutenberg Galaxy: The Making of Typographic Man.* Toronto: University of Toronto Press, 1962.

———. *Understanding Media: The Extensions of Man.* New York: McGraw-Hill, 1964.

McNeil, Alex. *Total Television: A Comprehensive Guide to Programming from 1948 to 1980.* New York: Penguin Books, 1980.

Meine, Franklin J. *Tall Tales of the Southwest: An Anthology of Southern and Southwestern Humor.* New York: Alfred A. Knopf, 1930.

Meyer, Martin. *About Television.* New York: Harper and Row, 1972.

Miller, Jeffrey S. "Watching the Detectives: The Development of the Modern Television Detective Hero." Unpublished ms.

Mostel, Kate, and Madeline Gilford. *170 Years of Show Business.* New York: Random House, 1978.

Musel, Robert. "Jackie Gleason's Plea: Why Pay to Keep Me off the Air?" *TV Guide,* 12 Dec. 1970, pp. 36–40.

Newcomb, Horace. *TV: The Most Popular Art.* Garden City, N.Y.: Anchor/Doubleday, 1974.

———, ed. *Television: The Critical View.* 2nd ed. New York: Oxford University Press, 1979.

Nielsen Report on Television, 1981. New York: A. C. Nielsen Company, 1981.

Norback, Craig T., and Peter Norback, eds. *TV Guide Almanac.* New York: Ballantine Books, 1980.

Nye, Russel. *The Unembarrassed Muse: The Popular Arts in America.* New York: Dial Press, 1970.

"The Office that Jack (Webb) Built." *TV Guide.* 2 Feb. 1957, pp. 20–21.

Ortega y Gasset, José. "The Coming of the Masses." In *The Revolt of the Masses,* pp. 11–19. New York: W. W. Norton and Company,

1932. Reprinted in Rosenberg and White, *Mass Culture,* pp. 41–45.

The Oxford Companion to American Literature. 4th ed. (1978). S.v. "Poe, Edgar Allan."

Paar, Jack (with John Reddy). *I Kid You Not.* Boston: Little, Brown and Company, 1959.

Paul, Sherman. *Repossessing and Renewing.* Baton Rouge: Louisiana State University Press, 1976.

Poe, Edgar Allan. "The Philosophy of Composition." 1846. Reprinted in *American Literature,* ed. Richard Poirier and William L. Vance, 1: 658–67. Boston: Little, Brown and Company, 1970.

———. "On the Heresy of the Didactic." In *The Poetic Principle.* 1850. Reprinted in *American Literature,* ed. Richard Poirier and William L. Vance, 1: 667–69. Boston: Little, Brown and Company, 1970.

The Random House College Dictionary. 1975 ed. S.v. "entertain."

Riesman, David. *The Lonely Crowd.* New Haven: Yale University Press, 1950.

Rosenbaum, Ron. "Saturday Night Dead." *Rolling Stone,* 19 Feb. 1981, p. 8.

Rosenberg, Bernard, and David Manning White, eds. *Mass Culture: The Popular Arts in America.* New York: Free Press, 1957.

Rosenthal, Raymond, ed. *McLuhan: Pro and Con.* Baltimore: Penguin/Pelican, 1969.

Rourke, Constance. *American Humor.* New York: Harcourt, Brace and Company, 1931.

Sarris, Andrew. *The American Cinema: Directors and Directions 1929–68.* New York: E. P. Dutton and Company, 1968.

Scheur, Stephen H., ed. *Movies on TV, 1982–83.* New York: Bantam Books, 1981.

Schneider, Bob. "Spelling's Salvation Armies." *Cultural Correspondence,* no. 4 (1977), pp. 27–31.

Schneider, Bob, and Art Spiegelman. *Whole Grains: A Book of Quotations.* New York: Douglas Links, 1973.

Schwichtenberg, Cathy. "A Patriarchal Voice in Heaven." *Jumpcut,* nos. 24/25 (1981), pp. 13–16.

See, Carolyn. "This Man Knows What America Wants to Watch." *Panorama,* June 1980, pp. 74–77.

Seldes, Gilbert. *The Great Audience.* New York: Viking Press, 1951.

———. *The New Mass Media: Challenges to a Free Society.* Washington, D.C.: Public Affairs Press, 1968.

———. *The Public Arts.* New York: Simon and Schuster, 1956.

185

———. Review of *The Beverly Hillbillies. TV Guide,* 1 Oct. 1962.

Sennett, Ted. *Your Show of Shows.* New York: Collier Books, 1977.

Shayon, Robert Lewis. *The Crowd-Catchers: Introducing Television.* New York: Saturday Review Press, 1973.

Shils, Edward. "Daydreams and Nightmares: Reflections on the Criticism of Mass Culture." *Sewanee Review* 65 (1957): 568–608.

Sklar, Robert. *Movie-made America: A Cultural History.* New York: Vintage Books, 1975.

Sontag, Susan. *Against Interpretation.* New York: Delta, 1966.

Sterling, Christopher H., and John M. Kitross. *Stay Tuned: A Concise History of American Broadcasting.* Belmont, Calif.: Wadsworth Publishing Company, 1978.

Stump, Al. "It Was Chaos, Crazy!—The *Honeymooners* Reminisce." *TV Guide,* 24 Jan. 1976, pp. 13–14.

Tashjian, Dickran. *Skyscraper Primitives.* Middletown, Conn.: Wesleyan University Press, 1975.

Terrace, Vincent. *The Complete Encyclopedia of Television Programs, 1947–1976.* 2 vols. South Brunswick, N.J.: Barnes, 1976.

Thorpe, Thomas Bangs. "The Big Bear of Arkansas." 1841. Reprinted in Blair, *Native American Humor,* pp. 337–48.

Tonnies, Ferdinand. *Gemeinschaft und Gesellschaft.* 1887. Reprinted as *Community and Association,* translated by Charles P. Loomis. London: Routledge and Kegan Paul, 1955.

TV Guide (weekly, 1953–).

Twain, Mark. "The Dandy Frightening the Squatter." 1854. Reprinted in Meine, *Tall Tales of the Southwest,* pp. 445–48.

Tyler, Royall. *The Contrast.* Publications of the Dunlap Society, no. 1. New York: Dunlap Society, 1887.

Tynan, Kenneth. *Show People: Profiles in Entertainment.* New York: Berkley Books, 1981.

van den Haag, Ernest. "Of Happiness and of Despair We Have No Measure." In Rosenberg and White, *Mass Culture,* pp. 504–36.

Van Doren, Mark, ed. *The Portable Whitman.* New York: Penguin Books, 1977.

Van Gelder, Lawrence. Review of *Smokey and the Bandit,* directed by Hal Needham. *New York Times,* 20 May 1977, sec. 3, p. 8, col. 5.

Variety (weekly, 1905–).

Veblen, Thorstein. *The Theory of the Leisure Class.* 1899. Reprint. New York: New American Library/Mentor, 1953.

Warshow, Robert. *The Immediate Experience.* Garden City, N.Y.: Doubleday, 1962.

Webster, Grant. *Republic of Letters*. Baltimore: Johns Hopkins University Press, 1976.

Weiler, A. H. Review of *Requiem for a Heavyweight,* directed by Ralph Nelson. *New York Times,* 17 Oct. 1962, p. 35, col. 1.

Whitman, Walt. *Democratic Vistas and Other Papers*. London: Walter Scott, 1888.

———. *Leaves of Grass*. 1871. Reprint. Edited by Sculley Bradley and Harold W. Blodgett. New York: W. W. Norton and Company, 1973.

Wicking, Christopher, and Tise Vahimagi. *The American Vein: Directors and Directions in Television*. New York: E. P. Dutton and Company, 1979.

Wilk, Max. *The Golden Age of Television: Notes from the Survivors*. New York: Delacorte Press, 1976.

Wilk, Stan. "Coming of Age in Sonora." *American Anthropologist* 79, no. 1 (1977): 84–91.

Williams, Aubrey, ed. *Poetry and Prose of Alexander Pope*. Boston: Riverside/Houghton Mifflin, 1969.

Williams, William Carlos. *In the American Grain*. Introduction by Horace Gregory. New York: New Directions, 1956.

Wolcott, James. "Chicks in Their Underwear?" *Village Voice,* 3 June 1981, p. 56.

———. "Mayberry, the Town that Time Forgot." *Village Voice,* 22 July 1981, p. 53.

———. "Jeepers, Creepers—Where'd You Get That Hair?" *Village Voice,* 11 Aug. 1981, p. 48.

———. "The Crane-shot that Captured Christmas." *Village Voice,* 5 Jan. 1982, p. 51.

Glossary ★

The glossary includes definitions and clarifications of several terms used in the text that may be unfamiliar, or whose usages may be unfamiliar, to some readers. Most entries are terms commonly used in the American mass communications industry; these are marked with a single asterisk (*). Others are terms I have found it necessary to invent to describe certain television and cultural phenomena; these are marked with two asterisks (**). Still others are critical terms that have been used in particular ways in relation to television; these are marked with three asterisks (***).

AOR.   Literally, "album-oriented rock." A series of FCC rule changes, initiated in 1964 and implemented over the following decade, required that FM stations cease duplicating AM broadcasts and offer programs of their own. Many station owners who held joint AM-FM licenses fulfilled the requirement by programming music from rock and roll albums on their FM outlets, as opposed to the long-standing practice of programming AM outlets with Top 40 45-rpm singles.

Comedy-variety show.   A presentational television series featuring various types of show business "acts," including stand-up comedy, sketch comedy, music, magic, trained animals, and so on. The show is hosted by a comedian, singer, or comedian/singer.

***Cosmology.*   The peculiar form of the narrative television series may result in scores or even hundreds of hours of teletext devoted to the same characters, setting, and narrative line. The sum of a series' many details, built up over the course of its production run, is its *cosmology*. Often, the peculiar details of one series are used to create another, known as a spin-off. Thus an auteur may extend a cosmology across two or more series (e.g., MTM Company's *Mary Tyler Moore Show, Rhoda,* and *Phyllis*).

*Crossover. A term used to describe an episode of one series that uses one or more characters from another series and in which these characters maintain their established identities (e.g., Jed Clampett of *The Beverly Hillbillies* visits Hooterville in an episode of *Green Acres*). Crossover episodes are often used by studios to introduce new programs (e.g., Spelling-Goldberg Productions introduced *S.W.A.T.* by placing the *S.W.A.T.* characters on an episode of *The Rookies*). This allows researchers to test public reaction to the new characters before going into production of a new series.

*Demographics. Literally, "a picture of people." This term is used as the name of a social science that purports to describe the audience for a particular cultural item (i.e., a TV show) in terms of salient marketing characteristics such as age, sex, income level, education level, religion, race, and so on.

*Desk-and-sofa show. A TV programming format that synthesizes the talk show and the comedy-variety show. "Acts," such as stand-up comedians or singers, may be presented and sketches may be performed, but the body of the show consists of interviews with personalities, politicians, and experts in various fields. The term derives from the show's archetypal stage set. Some long-running desk-and-sofa shows are *The Tonight Show, The Merv Griffin Show,* and *The Mike Douglas Show.*

*Downstream/upstream. Terms used to describe the character of a communications system. Network television is a downstream system; the image flows in one direction—from the transmitter to the viewer. Cable-TV technology, however, is capable of creating upstream systems, in which viewers may instantaneously respond to a downstream transmission. For example, Warner Brothers' Qube system, currently in use in Columbus, Ohio, allows viewers to "vote" on questions posed on a TV show or to purchase goods offered on the screen by pushing a button. Upstream television is also known as an *interactive system*.

***Entropy curve. Since a series will play until its ratings no longer justify the desired price for commercial time, the life of any series may be plotted on an *entropy curve* (or bell-shaped curve). Time is the only variable. The decay of a series' popularity is considered

inevitable. The networks attempt to slow this decay by conducting tests on popular series to discover what viewers like most and least about them. This information is then "passed on" to the production company; script changes, such as the downgrading or upgrading of a particular character or episode type, are often the result. These tests are known as Series Maintenance Studies.

F-score. Every six months a study is done by an independent company to test a personality's familiarity to the public. If, for example, 86 percent of the test group can identify a picture of Alan Alda, he has an *F-score* of 86. Those in the test group who make the correct identification are then asked a series of questions about the personality. If the personality is a favorite, he or she is then given a *Q* point. If half of the 86 percent who have correctly identified Alan Alda "agree" with a statement such as "I would make a special effort to watch a show on which Alan Alda appears," then he would have a *Q-score* of 50. *F* is familiarity; *Q* is love. *F-scores* and *Q-scores* are used extensively in casting and salary decisions in the TV industry.

191

****Gemeinschaft/Gesellschaft.* I use these terms as they were defined by the German sociologist Ferdinand Tönnies in his 1887 study, *Gemeinschaft und Gesellschaft. Gemeinschaft* (literally, "community") refers to an organic community in which social relations and constraints are defined by uncodified traditions. *Gesellschaft* (literally, "corporate association") refers to a postindustrial community in which social relations and constraints are defined by written laws.

Happy talk. A format for news presentation that first appeared on local television in the early 1970s; it features light chatter and even jokes among the anchorpeople and reporters instead of the traditional straight-faced segues.

HUT. Literally, "household using TV." This is an industry term for any household that contains a working television set. The A. C. Nielsen Company projects that over 98 percent of American homes are *HUTs.*

****Lifestyle.* A term that came into widespread use in America in the 1960s as a catch-all noun to describe the way various people live (e.g., "alternative lifestyle," "hippie lifestyle," "gay lifestyle"). However, it gradually became an important signifier of individuality in American advertising rhetoric ("We have products to fit your lifestyle"). This usage emphasized a connotation of superior discretion and taste on the part of the consumer of mass-produced products. This connotation allows usage of the term as an adjective. For example, a store that sells water beds, expensive imported coffees, and sexually suggestive greeting cards may be referred to as a "Lifestyle boutique." *Three's Company* (ABC 1977–), in which a man and two women share an apartment, is a "Lifestyle sitcom."

Minicam.   A small, relatively inexpensive mobile camera unit, which is used by many local stations to originate remote pickups from around their viewing areas.

MOR.   Literally, "middle of the road." This is a radio format featuring a species of popular music that is a synthesis of Tin Pan Alley and rock and roll. *MOR* performers include Neil Diamond, Barbra Streisand, and Barry Manilow.

Premium service.   A cable-TV channel that costs a subscriber an extra fee above basic service. Time-Life's Home Box Office (HBO), which for the most part shows recent, unedited, uninterrupted Hollywood releases, is currently the most successful. The number of premium services is expected to increase as the United States continues to be wired for cable in the coming years.

Production values.   A consciousness-industry term for the quality of technical craft in a given film, TV program, audio recording, or other production. For example, most made-for-TV movies have excruciatingly familiar and maudlin plots and show little originality in their verbal and visual language; however, their smooth "textbook" editing is evidence of their high *production values.*

Q-score.   See *F-score.*

**Schlockumentary.*   The quest for "reality" in television programming led in the late seventies to a new genre. Borrowing the form of the newsmagazine (e.g., *60 Minutes*) and filling it with staged enactments of tabloid events, the *schlockumentary* strives to offer representational films as presentational reports. *Real People* (NBC, 1979–) and *That's Incredible!* (ABC, 1980–) are two notable schlockumentaries. The ancestry of the form can be traced to the frankly representational reenactments of *You Are There* (CBS, 1953–57, hosted by Walter Cronkite) and the sensationalism of *You Asked for It* (DuMont, 1950–51; ABC, 1951–59; syn., 1981–83). The *schlockumentary* has also been called *infotainment,* and *sit-life.*

**Signatory montage.* A term I use to describe the opening sequence of a representational show that is repeated each week before the narrative commences.

*Simulcast. Simultaneous transmission of a program on television and radio (usually FM stereo).

*Special effort. An important term in market testing. The multiple-choice questions posed in test questionnaires often contain a statement such as "I would make a special effort to watch . . ." or "I would make a special effort to buy . . ." If a television show or toilet bowl cleanser gets a significant *special effort* response, it is thought to have high profit potential.

193

*Strip. A show made for weekly telecast that is scheduled to be rerun on a daily basis.

*Superstation.   When a local, independent station is fed to many cable systems and thus gains a national audience, it is known as a super-station. WTBS, Atlanta, became the first *superstation* when its owner, Ted Turner, bought transponder space on the Satcom satellite in 1977 and made the station's signal available to cable systems around the country. The Christian Broadcasting Network (CBN) uses this technique, making the signal of its local Virginia Beach, Virginia, station available, free of charge, to any cable system that will take it. The *superstation* phenomenon demonstrates how technologically obsolete the network/affiliate system is becoming.

*Sustaining program.   A show that cannot generate enough advertising revenue to justify its continued transmission but is kept on the air for other reasons (public relations, culture, civic responsibility, etc.).

*Syndication. A term referring to the creation of a "syndicate" of local stations to carry a particular show. The stations may be affiliates of any or all of the networks, or they may be independent stations. Sometimes new programs are presented nationally or quasi-nationally by means of *syndication* (e.g., Norman Lear's *Mary Hartman, Mary Hartman;* the original *Superman* starring George Reeves; the gameshow, *The Joker Is Wild*). However, most syndicated shows are reruns of network series that have gone out of production. The Viacom Company is the largest independent syndicator in the American television industry.

*Target group. The traditional definition of mass culture has characterized its audience as an undifferentiated assemblage. Increasingly, however, demographic marketing research has aimed at isolating potential customers for a given product by breaking down the mass according to various features. For example, a feminine hygiene deodorant manufacturer spends its advertising dollars more efficiently by sponsoring a program that appeals to women; a sports car ad seeks an audience of unmarried people making more than $30,000 a year; sugar-coated breakfast cereals are marketed to children under the age of twelve; and so on. Any group with a potential common consumer interest is a *target group*.

194

*Upscale.   A differential term in demographic rhetoric that refers to higher income groups. For example, since the average income of HBO subscribers is well above the national mean, HBO subscribers constitute an *upscale* group. Most credit cards are thought to be marketed to *upscale* groups, and this is the reason that credit card bills come stuffed with shop-by-mail advertisements for luxury items.

*Viewer loyalty.   A term referring to a show's ability to create, build, and hold an audience that will make a special effort to watch it. For example, in 1971 ABC canceled *The Lawrence Welk Show*, principally because of the age of the program's audience. However, *The Lawrence Welk Show* commanded intense *viewer loyalty* from its audience and was able to go into national syndication successfully. *Hee-Haw* and *Saturday Night Live* are other examples of shows with strong *viewer loyalty*.

Main Index

199

200

203

Index of Television Series

Index of Films Made for Theatrical Release